Miraculous Growth and Stagnation in Post-War Japan

This volume examines different aspects of the Japanese experience in a comparative context. There is much here of relevance to contemporary developing countries anxious to initiate the experience of miraculous growth and anxious to avoid the subsequent stagnation.

Such issues of the role of government in providing the right amount of infant industry protection, the relevance of the financial system, the country's peculiar corporate structure and the role of education in a comparative context serve to illuminate the lessons and legacies of this unique experience in development.

The relationship between various dimensions of its domestic policy experience and Japan's international experience in trade promotion and foreign aid is explored and is of special interest to an international audience of academics and policymakers.

Koichi Hamada is the Tuntex Professor of Economics at Yale University, where he specializes in the Japanese Economy and International Economics. Professor Hamada has an LLB, an MA in Economics from the University of Tokyo and an MA and PhD in Economics from Yale University. In Japan, he participated in many policy committees at the Ministry of Finance, MITI, the Economic Planning Agency and other ministries and was one of the few who applied the methodology of "Law and Economics" to Japan's legal system in the 1970s. Professor Hamada was the founding President of the Japan *Law and Economics Association* in 2003.

Keijiro Otsuka received his BA in agricultural sciences, Hokkaido University in March 1971, MA in economics, Tokyo Metropolitan University in March 1974 and PhD in economics, University of Chicago in March 1979. He is currently Visiting Professor at the National Graduate Institute for Policy Studies (April 2001 to present). Currently he is associate editor of *Economic Development and Cultural Change* and president of the International Association of Agricultural Economists.

Gustav Ranis was the Henry R. Luce Director of the Yale Center for International and Area Studies from 1996 to 2004. He was a Carnegie Corporation Scholar from 2004 to 2006, Director of the Economic Growth Center at Yale from 1967 to 1975, Assistant Administrator for Program and Policy at USAID from 1965 to 1967, and Director of the Pakistan Institute of Development Economics from 1958 to 1961. He has worked in China, Colombia, Ghana, Indonesia, Mexico, and Taiwan, among others. Professor Ranis has more than 20 books and 300 articles on theoretical and policy-related issues of development to his credit.

Ken Togo is Professor of the Faculty of Economics, Musashi University, Tokyo, and Adjunct Lecturer of the Graduate School of International Cooperation Studies, Kobe University, Kobe, Japan. He received his PhD from Yale. He was also Research Fellow of Economic Planning Agency, Government of Japan (1998–1999) and Visiting Fellow of Economic Growth Center, Yale University (2003–2004). He was previously with the *Foundation for Advanced Studies in Development* (FASID), Tokyo.

Routledge studies in the modern world economy

1 **Interest Rates and Budget Deficits**
A study of the advanced economies
Kanhaya L Gupta and Bakhtiar Moazzami

2 **World Trade after the Uruguay Round**
Prospects and policy options for the twenty-first century
Edited by Harald Sander and András Inotai

3 **The Flow Analysis of Labour Markets**
Edited by Ronald Schettkat

4 **Inflation and Unemployment**
Contributions to a new macroeconomic approach
Edited by Alvaro Cencini and Mauro Baranzini

5 **Macroeconomic Dimensions of Public Finance**
Essays in honour of Vito Tanzi
Edited by Mario I. Blejer and Teresa M. Ter-Minassian

6 **Fiscal Policy and Economic Reforms**
Essays in honour of Vito Tanzi
Edited by Mario I. Blejer and Teresa M. Ter-Minassian

7 **Competition Policy in the Global Economy**
Modalities for co-operation
Edited by Leonard Waverman, William S. Comanor and Akira Goto

8 **Working in the Macro Economy**
A study of the US labor market
Martin F. J. Prachowny

9 **How Does Privatization Work?**
Edited by Anthony Bennett

10 **The Economics and Politics of International Trade**
Freedom and trade: volume II
Edited by Gary Cook

11 **The Legal and Moral Aspects of International Trade**
Freedom and trade: volume III
Edited by Asif Qureshi, Hillel Steiner and Geraint Parry

12 **Capital Markets and Corporate Governance in Japan, Germany and the United States**
Organizational response to market inefficiencies
Helmut M. Dietl

13 **Competition and Trade Policies**
Coherence or conflict
Edited by Einar Hope

14 **Rice**
The primary commodity
A. J. H. Latham

15 **Trade, Theory and Econometrics**
Essays in honour of
John S. Chipman
*Edited by James C. Moore,
Raymond Riezman, and
James R. Melvin*

16 **Who benefits from Privatisation?**
*Edited by Moazzem Hossain and
Justin Malbon*

17 **Towards a Fair Global Labour Market**
Avoiding the new slave trade
*Ozay Mehmet, Errol Mendes and
Robert Sinding*

18 **Models of Futures Markets**
Edited by Barry Goss

19 **Venture Capital Investment**
An agency analysis of UK practice
Gavin C. Reid

20 **Macroeconomic Forecasting**
A sociological appraisal
Robert Evans

21 **Multimedia and Regional Economic Restructuring**
*Edited by Hans-Joachim Braczyk,
Gerhard Fuchs and
Hans-Georg Wolf*

22 **The New Industrial Geography**
Regions, regulation and
institutions
*Edited by Trevor J. Barnes and
Meric S. Gertler*

23 **The Employment Impact of Innovation**
Evidence and policy
*Edited by Marco Vivarelli and
Mario Pianta*

24 **International Health Care Reform**
A legal, economic and political
analysis
Colleen Flood

25 **Competition Policy Analysis**
Edited by Einar Hope

26 **Culture and Enterprise**
The development, representation
and morality of business
*Don Lavoie and
Emily Chamlee-Wright*

27 **Global Financial Crises and Reforms**
Cases and caveats
B.N. Ghosh

28 **Geography of Production and Economic Integration**
Miroslav N. Jovanović

29 **Technology, Trade and Growth in OECD Countries**
Does specialisation matter?
Valentina Meliciani

30 **Post-Industrial Labour Markets**
Profiles of North America and Scandinavia
Edited by Thomas P. Boje and Bengt Furaker

31 **Capital Flows without Crisis**
Reconciling capital mobility and economic stability
Edited by Dipak Dasgupta, Marc Uzan and Dominic Wilson

32 **International Trade and National Welfare**
Murray C. Kemp

33 **Global Trading Systems at Crossroads**
A post-Seattle perspective
Dilip K. Das

34 **The Economics and Management of Technological Diversification**
Edited by John Cantwell, Alfonso Gambardella and Ove Granstrand

35 **Before and Beyond EMU**
Historical lessons and future prospects
Edited by Patrick Crowley

36 **Fiscal Decentralization**
Ehtisham Ahmad and Vito Tanzi

37 **Regionalisation of Globalised Innovation**
Locations for advanced industrial development and disparities in participation
Edited by Ulrich Hilpert

38 **Gold and the Modern World Economy**
Edited by MoonJoong Tcha

39 **Global Economic Institutions**
Willem Molle

40 **Global Governance and Financial Crises**
Edited by Meghnad Desai and Yahia Said

41 **Linking Local and Global Economies**
The ties that bind
Edited by Carlo Pietrobelli and Arni Sverrisson

42 **Tax Systems and Tax Reforms in Europe**
Edited by Luigi Bernardi and Paola Profeta

43 **Trade Liberalization and APEC**
Edited by Jiro Okamoto

44 **Fiscal Deficits in the Pacific Region**
Edited by Akira Kohsaka

45 **Financial Globalization and the Emerging Market Economies**
Dilip K. Das

46 **International Labor Mobility**
Unemployment and increasing returns to scale
Bharati Basu

47 **Good Governance in the Era of Global Neoliberalism**
Conflict and depolitization in Latin America, Eastern Europe, Asia and Africa
Edited by Jolle Demmers, Alex E. Fernández Jilberto and Barbara Hogenboom

48 **The International Trade System**
Alice Landau

49 **International Perspectives on Temporary Work and Workers**
Edited by John Burgess and Julia Connell

50 **Working Time and Workers' Preferences in Industrialized Countries**
Finding the balance
Edited by Jon C. Messenger

51 **Tax Systems and Tax Reforms in New EU Members**
Edited by Luigi Bernardi, Mark Chandler and Luca Gandullia

52 **Globalization and the Nation State**
The impact of the IMF and the World Bank
Edited by Gustav Ranis, James Vreeland and Stephen Kosak

53 **Macroeconomic Policies and Poverty Reduction**
Edited by Ashoka Mody and Catherine Pattillo

54 **Regional Monetary Policy**
Carlos J. Rodríguez-Fuentez

55 **Trade and Migration in the Modern World**
Carl Mosk

56 **Globalisation and the Labour Market**
Trade, technology and less-skilled workers in Europe and the United States
Edited by Robert Anderton, Paul Brenton and John Whalley

57 **Financial Crises**
Socio-economic causes and institutional context
Brenda Spotton Visano

58 **Globalization and Self Determination**
Is the nation-state under siege?
Edited by David R. Cameron, Gustav Ranis and Annalisa Zinn

59 **Developing Countries and the Doha Development Round of the WTO**
Edited by Pitou van Dijck and Gerrit Faber

60 **Immigrant Enterprise in Europe and the USA**
Prodromos Panayiotopoulos

61 **Solving the Riddle of Globalization and Development**
Edited by Manuel Agosín, David Bloom, George Chapelier and Jagdish Saigal

62 **Foreign Direct Investment and the World Economy**
Ashoka Mody

63 **The World Economy**
A global analysis
Horst Siebert

64 **Production Organizations in Japanese Economic Development**
Edited by Tetsuji Okazaki

65 **The Economics of Language**
International analyses
Edited by Barry R. Chiswick and Paul W. Miller

66 **Street Entrepreneurs**
People, place and politics in local and global perspective
Edited by John Cross and Alfonso Morales

67 **Global Challenges and Local Responses**
The East Asian experience
Edited by Jang-Sup Shin

68 **Globalization and Regional Integration**
The origins, development and impact of the single European aviation market
Alan Dobson

69 **Russia Moves into the Global Economy: Breaking Out**
John M. Letiche

70 **The European Economy in an American Mirror**
Barry Eichengreen, Michael Landesmann and Dieter Stiefel

71 **Working Time Around the World**
Trends in working hours, laws, and policies in a global comparative perspective
Jon C. Messenger, Sangheon Lee and Deidre McCann

72 **International Water Treaties**
Negotiation and cooperation along transboundary rivers
Shlomi Dinar

73 **Economic Integration in the Americas**
Edited by Joseph A. McKinney and H. Stephen Gardner

74 **Expanding Frontiers of Global Trade Rules**
The political economy dynamics of the international trading system
Nitya Nanda

75 **The Macroeconomics of Global Imbalances**
European and Asian perspectives
Edited by Marc Uzan

76 **China and Asia**
Economic and financial interactions
Edited by Yin-Wong Cheung and Kar-Yiu Wong

77 **Regional Inequality in China**
Trends, explanations and policy responses
Edited by Shenggen Fan, Ravi Kanbur and Xiaobo Zhang

78 **Governing Rapid Growth in China**
Equity and institutions
Edited by Ravi Kanbur and Xiaobo Zhang

79 **The Indonesian Labour Market**
Shafiq Dhanani, Iyanatul Islam and Anis Chowdhury

80 **Cost–Benefit Analysis in Multi-level Government in Europe and the USA**
The case of EU cohesion policy and of US federal investment policies
Alessandro Ferrara

81 **The Economic Geography of Air Transportation**
Space, time, and the freedom of the sky
John Bowen

82 **Cartelization, Antitrust and Globalization in the US and Europe**
Mark LeClair

83 **The Political Economy of Integration**
Jeffrey Cason

84 **Critical Issues in Air Transport Economics and Business**
Rosario Macario and Eddy Van de Voorde

85 **Financial Liberalisation and Economic Performance**
Luiz Fernando de Paula

86 **A General Theory of Institutional Change**
Shiping Tang

87 **The Dynamics of Asian Financial Integration**
Edited by Michael Devereux, Philip Lane, Park Cyn-young and Wei Shang-jin

88 **Innovative Fiscal Policy and Economic Development in Transition Economies**
Aleksandr Gevorkyan

89 **Foreign Direct Investments in Asia**
Edited by Chalongphob Sussangkarn, Yung Chul Park and Sung Jin Kang

90 **Time Zones, Communications Networks, and International Trade**
Toru Kikuchi

91 **Miraculous Growth and Stagnation in Post-War Japan**
Edited by Koichi Hamada, Keijiro Otsuka, Gustav Ranis, and Ken Togo

Miraculous Growth and Stagnation in Post-War Japan

Edited by Koichi Hamada,
Keijiro Otsuka, Gustav Ranis, and
Ken Togo

LONDON AND NEW YORK

First published 2011
by Routledge
2 Park Square, Milton Park, Abingdon, Oxon OX14 4RN

Simultaneously published in the USA and Canada
by Routledge
711 Third Avenue, New York, NY 10017

Routledge is an imprint of the Taylor & Francis Group, an informa business

First issued in paperback 2013

© 2011 Koichi Hamada, Keijiro Otsuka, Gustav Ranis and Ken Togo

British Library Cataloguing in Publication Data
A catalogue record for this book is available from the British Library

Library of Congress Cataloging in Publication Data
Miraculous growth and stagnation in post-war Japan / edited by Koichi
Hamada ... [et al.].
    p. cm. – (Routledge studies in the modern world economy ; . 91)
    Includes bibliographical references and index.
    1. Japan–Economic conditions–1945– 2. Japan–Economic policy–1945–
    3. Economic history–1945– I. Hamada, Koichi, 1936–
    HC462.9.M5212 2011
    330.952–dc22
                                            2010043069

ISBN: 978-0-415-61518-1 (hbk)
ISBN: 978-0-203-81879-4 (ebk)
ISBN: 978-0-415-70292-8 (pbk)

Typeset in Times
by Wearset Ltd, Boldon, Tyne and Wear

To Professor Yujiro Hayami, a seminal contributor to Development Economics (with our best wishes for his full recovery)

Contents

List of figures		xv
List of tables		xvii
Notes on contributors		xviii
Preface		xx
Acknowledgments		xxi

1 Introduction: post-war Japanese economic development in a global perspective 1
KOICHI HAMADA, KEIJIRO OTSUKA, GUSTAV RANIS, AND KEN TOGO

2 Infant industry protection policy reconsidered: the case of the automobile industry in Japan 9
KEN TOGO

3 Cluster-based industrial development: applicability of Japanese experiences to contemporary developing countries 25
KEIJIRO OTSUKA AND TETSUSHI SONOBE

4 Financial systems and economic development: the case in Japan 40
YASUHIRO ARIKAWA

5 What will become of the Japanese corporation? 54
KATSUHITO IWAI

6 Dismissal regulation in Japan 74
RYO KAMBAYASHI

7 **Conditions of corporate progress as seen through post-war
   Japanese business history**   91
   KŌNOSUKE ODAKA

8 **The role of education in the economic catch-up: comparative
   growth experiences from Japan, Korea, Taiwan, and the
   United States**   112
   YUJIRO HAYAMI AND YOSHIHISA GODO

9 **The "Yoshida Doctrine" in the post-Cold War world:
   'preemptive' minimalist strategy in a multipolar world**   135
   KOICHI HAMADA AND SEIKO MIMAKI

10 **The new model of foreign aid drawn from the experiences of
   Japan and the United States**   166
   GUSTAV RANIS, STEPHEN KOSACK, AND KEN TOGO

11 **Lessons from Japan's post-war development experience**   193
   KOICHI HAMADA, KEIJIRO OTSUKA, GUSTAV RANIS,
   AND KEN TOGO

   Index   209

Figures

1.1	Changes in real per capita income among developed countries	3
1.2	Changes in real per capita income among East Asian countries	4
2.1	Four wheel vehicle supply in Japan, 1916–1939	17
2.2	Real capital stock	20
2.3	Profit/sales	21
3.1a	Development of the motorcycle industry in Japan, 1945–1965 (a) changes in the number of motorcycle enterprises	34
3.1b	Development of the motorcycle industry in Japan, 1945–1965 (b) improvement of quality index of motorcycle engines	35
4.1	The change of cash holdings from 1958 to 1998	46
5.1	Single ownership structure of a classical firm	58
5.2	Two-tier ownership structure of a business corporation	58
5.3	A "nominalistic" corporation	60
5.4	A holding corporation and a pyramidal system of ownership and control	61
5.5	A (hypothetical) self-owning corporation	62
5.6	Mutually holding corporations	63
5.7	Cross-shareholdings among 12 corporations	63
7.1	Relationship between "lines" and "staffs" in automobile factories	97
7.2	The "Lego method" and the "co-working method"	105
8.1	Changes in the female/male ratio in average schooling, Taiwan, Korea, Japan, and the USA	115
8.2	Changes in combination of average schooling and the female/male ratio in average schooling, Taiwan, Korea, Japan, and the USA	116
8.3	Comparison of per capita GDP among Korea, Japan Taiwan, and USA	118
8.4	Labor input per GDP versus physical capital per GDP	118
8.5	Japan/USA ratios in average schooling a, per capita GDP and physical capital–labor ratio	119
8.6	Japan/USA ratios in average schooling by levels of education	121
8.7	Enrollment of vocational education in Japan	123

8.8   Average schooling of vocational education in Japan   124
8.9   Korea/USA ratios in average schooling, per capita GDP and
       physical capital–labor ratio   125
8.10   Korea/USA ratios in average schooling by levels of education   126
8.11   Taiwan/USA ratios in average schooling a, per capita GDP and
       physical capital–labor ratio   127
8.12   Taiwan/USA ratios in average schooling by levels of education   128
9.1   Japan's net ODA and its share of total development assistance
       committee   139
9.2   Country performance in selected burdensharing and force
       improvement areas   141
9.3   Relative expenditures in the NATO countries plus Russia   144
9.4   Strategic substitutes   145
9.5   Strategic complements   147
9.6   Reaction curves and preemptive arms reduction   149
9.7   Relative military expenditures in Asia   150
9.8   East Asia's military expenditure 1989–2007   150
9.9a   World military expenditure and US military expenditure
       1988–2007   152
9.9b   Correlation between world total military expenditure (minus
       the US) and US military expenditure   152
9.10a Correlation between East Asian total military expenditure
       (minus China) and Chinese military expenditure   153
9.10b East Asia's military expenditure on the supposition of arms
       race between China and Japan   153
9.11   Military expenditure as a share of government spending   156
9.12   Magnified picture around the Nash equilibrium   162
10.1   Net disbursement of ODA: US and Japan   167
10.2   Breakdown of US aid commitments by sector   168
10.3   Breakdown of Japanese aid commitments by sector   169
10.4   Breakdown of US bilateral aid into grant and non-grant   170
10.5   Breakdown of Japanese bilateral aid into grant and non-grant   171
10.6   Net grants by NGOs to developing countries   179
10.7   Total capital flows   183
11.1   Balance sheets of major central banks   203
11.2   Real exchange rates   203
11.3   Industrial production   204

Tables

3.1	A list of case studies in Asia and Africa and basic characteristics	27
3.2	An endogenous model of cluster-based industrial development	30
3.3	Proportions of enterprise managers by former occupation and formal schooling in Bingo, Japan	33
3.4	Proportions of direct transactions and sale revenue by location in Bingo, Japan	33
4.1	Financial constraint and bank–firm relationship	47
5.1	Important management goals	55
5.2	Executive values	56
5.3	Recent questionnaire study on corporate objectives in Japan	57
5.4	Cross-shareholdings among core 20 corporations of Sumitomo Group	65
8.1	Human capital accumulation through educational investments in the USA, Japan, Korea, and Taiwan	114
8.2	The percentage of population aged 15–39 in the total population	117
9.1	Pay-offs table of the Cold War period (strategic substitutes)	146
9.2	Pay-offs table after the Cold War	148
11.1	Academic ranking top 100 of world universities in 2008	200–201

Contributors

Yasuhiro Arikawa is currently an Associate Professor in the Graduate School of Finance, Accounting and Law at Waseda University. He received his MA in Economics from Waseda University in 1996. He has published extensively on corporate finance and corporate governance.

Yoshihisa Godo is Professor in the Faculty of Economics, Meiji Gakuin University. His research interest is empirical analysis on the interrelationship between education and economic growth. He completed his MA and PhD in Agricultural Economics from University of Kyoto in 1986 and 1994, respectively.

Koichi Hamada is a Tuntex Professor of Economics of Yale University specializing in the Japanese economy and international economics. He is regarded as one of the few scholars who first applied game theory to international policy coordination. His publications include *Political Economy of International Monetary Independence*, MIT press, 1985.

Yujiro Hayami is Founding Director of the International Development Studies Program at the National Graduate Institute for Policy Studies. He has been working extensively on agricultural development in both developed and developing countries. He completed his PhD in Agricultural Economics from Iowa State University in 1960.

Katsuhito Iwai is Visiting Professor at International Christian University, Specially Appointed Professor at Musashino University, and Emeritus Professor at the University of Tokyo. He has a BA in Economics from the University of Tokyo and a PhD in Economics from MIT. He also received an Honorary Doctorate from University of Belgrade in 2009. His research interests encompass disequilibrium dynamics, ontology of money, evolutionary economics, corporate governance, fiduciary principles, and history of social thoughts.

Ryo Kambayashi is Associate Professor in the Institute of Economic Research, Hitotsubashi University. His research field is mainly on labor studies in Japan. He obtained his MA and PhD in Economics from the University of Tokyo in 1996 and 2000.

Stephen Kosack is currently Assistant Professor of Public Policy at the Harvard University Kennedy School of Government and studies the comparative political economy of development. His work examines the causes of good governance: When does a government make policies to improve the lives of its citizens? In researching this question, he has written on aid and foreign direct investment, democracy, collective action, and education policy. He is currently finishing a book, *Predicting Good Governance: Political Organization and Education Policymaking in Taiwan, Ghana, and Brazil*. His research interests include collective action and political entrepreneurship; the incentives behind policymaking; human development, particularly education; development capital flows (such as aid and foreign investment).

Seiko Mimaki is a Research Associate in Institute of Asian Pacific Studies, Waseda University. Her research interest is historical analysis of US–Japan diplomatic, political, cultural relationships. She completed her MA in the field of International Relations from Tokyo University in 2005, and is now trying to complete her PhD thesis.

Kōnosuke Odaka is a Professor Emeritus at Hitotsubashi University and at Hosei University. His main research interest lies in empirical analyses of labor economics, economic development, and economic history of modern Japan. He has served as editor in chief of the history of trade and industrial policies of Japan for 1980–2000. He earned his BA in Economics at Keio University in 1959 and PhD in Economics at the University of California at Berkeley in 1967.

Keijiro Otsuka is a Professor of Development Economics at the National Graduate Institute for Policy Studies in Tokyo. His research interests are diverse, covering the development of industrial clusters, green revolution and poverty, and role of human capital in Asia and Africa. He completed his PhD in Economics from the University of Chicago in 1979.

Gustav Ranis is the Frank Altschul Professor Emeritus of International Economics at Yale. He was Director of the Center for International and Area Studies from 1995 to 2003, Director of the Economic Growth Center from 1967 to 1975, and Assistant Administrator for Program and Policy at USAID from 1965 to 1967. He has authored more than 20 books and 300 articles on development.

Tetsushi Sonobe is a Professorial Fellow at the Foundation for Advanced Studies on International Development and a Professor at National Graduate Institute for Policy Studies, Japan. He received a PhD in Economics from Yale University in 1992 and has conducted a number of field surveys and experiments on industrial development in Asia and Africa.

Ken Togo is Professor of the Faculty of Economics, Musashi University. His research interest is empirical analysis of industrial development and economic growth. He completed his MA in International and Development Economics and PhD in Economics from Yale University in 1990 and 1996, respectively.

Preface

During the 1960s and 1970s, Japan achieved what was called a case of "miraculous growth," famous in economic history. Ezra Vogel of Harvard coined the phrase, "Japan as Number One." Now, the dream has been broken. The performance of the Japanese economy faltered in terms of growth, technical progress and macroeconomic management. It recently became number three.

It is perhaps not surprising that the GDP of China, with its huge population, would overtake that of Japan. Needless to say, Japan need not aim to be a Germany in Europe in its size of economy, but would be happy to be a France in its quality of life. Still, the setback in Japanese development is surprising as well as intriguing. This volume asks why the Japanese system that was admired so much has become somewhat neglected recently.

In recent decades, there were indeed problems in Japan's macroeconomic policies, particularly in the management of its monetary policy. In any long-term reflection on the Japanese growth path, real (non-monetary) and structural factors must also be considered. In this monograph, we search for all the possible factors responsible for the sudden slow-down in Japan.

We also attempt to provide answers to a number of questions affecting development more generally. What aspects of Japan's development are worth recommending to developing countries as worthy of emulation? And what aspects are not at all to be recommended?

In the various chapters we investigate different aspects of Japan's development, from the factors generating growth, i.e., education, technology, protectionist or free trade policies, firm structures and institutional governance, as well as international relations. The conclusion is a little ironical: Japan initially adjusted its system admirably well to a model of development by borrowing technology from abroad. The Japanese were indeed reflecting Japan's own success in the past. However, once the Japanese economy caught up with the international technology frontier, the existing system turned into a barrier. Corporate institutions and education, among others, must now be overhauled to cope with the current challenges and make room for innovative and creative initiatives.

Acknowledgments

This project was generously supported by Hiroshi Okuda, former Chairman of the Toyota Motor Corporation. Chairman Okuda was an impressive member of the Economic and Fiscal Consulting Committee to the then prime minister of Japan. His comments were always frank as well as invigorating, constructive, and full of both global concerns and a long-run perspective. When one of the editors of this volume, Koichi Hamada, returned in 2003 to Yale from the post of the President of the Economic and Social Research Institute of Japan's Cabinet Office and visited Chairman Okuda to say "sayonara," he responded that "good philanthropy is followed by the good sale of cars."

We are really grateful to Chairman Okuda, who patiently supported this project financially as well as substantively. We also thank Toyota executives and officers, in particular Mr Sumio Ohtsuji and Mr Akihiko Nakaoka,, for their kind cooperation, while avoiding any interference with the content of our research and findings.

We held two author meetings for discussions of the theme, in the course of which we benefited from the comments of Masahiro Endo, Shin-ichi Fukuda, Takenori Inoki, Junko Kato, Hirohisa Kohama, Ryoshin Minami, Fumio Otake, Masaya Sakuragawa, Takashi Simizu, Juro Teranishi, and Toru Yanagihara.

We thank Junko Kiyuna and Ayako Matsuda for their research assistance and Kathryn Toensmeier for her patient assistance at all stages of the process. Finally, we are indebted to Carolyn M. Beaudin for the editing of the English of all of the Japanese authors.

1 Introduction

Post-war Japanese economic development in a global perspective

Koichi Hamada, Keijiro Otsuka, Gustav Ranis, and Ken Togo

1 Introduction

Some 65 years have passed since the end of World War II. It is timely to reflect upon this short but curious Japanese economic history, beginning with the extreme hunger and poverty in the late 1940s, followed by quick recovery and "miraculous" growth since the late 1950s, to the first oil shock in 1972, slow growth in the rest of the 1970s and 1980s, and finally almost complete stagnation over the last two decades. Why has the Japanese economy experienced such a unique development path? Will the Japanese economy continue to stagnate over the coming years? What must Japan do to regain its growth momentum? What lessons can other high-performing Asian economies learn from the Japanese experience? What roles should Japan play in international political and economic arenas, given its unique history of growing from a poor country to a rich country? This volume represents an attempt to provide answers to these questions.

Needless to say, providing clear-cut answers to such critical and broad issues is a formidable task for any single researcher. Thus, we organized a project on the post-war Japanese economic development experience by inviting a variety of researchers with diverse expertise on the key economic issues critical for a proper understanding of post-war Japanese economic development. We address different issues but share a common fundamental hypothesis, namely: "Japan successfully developed the economic institutions conducive to effective learning from abroad in the early post-war period but failed to construct a new economic system designed to innovate on the world technology frontier." In other words, the success in the "miraculous growth" period led to over-confidence and, hence, complacency when major reforms of economic institutions were called for. Thus, the Japanese economic system is still efficient in imitating foreign technologies but grossly inefficient in creating its own new technologies.

At the outset, we have to emphasize that no institutions are unchangeably efficient at various stages of economic development. When the economy is at a low-income stage, it is probably the best strategy to introduce, imitate, and adapt foreign technologies. Ample evidence is provided by the pre-war Japanese experience and the post reform experience in China (Otsuka *et al.* 1988; Otsuka *et al.* 1998). In order to support such a catching-up process, we have to develop institutions useful for learning from abroad. A good example is life-time employment, which is conducive to enterprise growth to the extent that the work experience is an effective means to learn and introduce ideas from abroad. Since employment is assured, a worker has a strong incentive to learn firm-specific knowledge and ideas. This was the case in Japan during the high growth period. Yet, once such a catch-up process is over, enterprises in such a high-income country as Japan must develop their own world-class technologies based on frontier scientific and technological knowledge. Thus, the long-term employment system may no longer be appropriate for such enterprises because advanced knowledge must be constantly introduced from outside the enterprises. It should also be noted that imitation and adaptation can be made by high school, vocational school, and university graduates, but major innovations, which may bring about creative destruction, can usually only be made by high talent manpower PhD holders. In other words, while strong high school, vocational school, and college systems are needed in the catch-up process, strong graduate schools are needed in the process of creating new ideas. The point we would like to emphasize here is that Japan still adheres to a life-time employment system primarily for university graduates, when Japan actually needs far more competent scientists, engineers and management specialists who have completed high quality graduate training.[1]

While leaving the tasks of validating the basic hypothesis to each of the chapters that follow, we would like to present in the rest of this introductory chapter a simple comparison of growth paths of per capita GDP from 1950 to the present among developed countries and high-performing East Asian countries in order to develop a proper global perspective on the development experience of the postwar Japanese economy.

2   A comparison of development experiences

It was Gerschenkron (1962) who first pointed out the utmost importance of technology import for the development of less developed economies. By now this view has been widely accepted by development economists and other experts. Indeed, the Japanese development since the Meiji era provides a vivid example of rapid economic development based on technology imports (e.g., Ohkawa and Rosovsky 1973; Otsuka *et al.* 1988). In their textbook on development economics, Hayami and Godo (2005) argue that successful technology transfer from developed to less developed economies is the key to the successful development of the latter. It must be emphasized here that the technology import or technology transfer refers not only to the introduction of new "technology" but also to the transfer of management knowledge and institutions, such as the financial systems, educational systems and management institutions, as well as the employment system, that make it possible to introduce new technologies. This is why this book includes several chapters which address the issues of the relationship between institutions and development.

If technology import is the key to growth, the faster the economic growth, the larger the technology gap between developed and developing countries. Although it is difficult to measure that technology gap, it is reasonable to assume that it can be roughly measured by the gap in per capita GDP. Figure 1.1 shows changes in PPP-adjusted real per capita GDP in the United States, United Kingdom, France, and Japan in the period 1950–2005, based on the Penn World Tables (see Penn World Table website).

Several important observations can be made. First, when per capita income in Japan was substantially lower than in the advanced western nations, particularly over 1960–1973, its growth rate was high. But when it came close to that of Europe, the growth rate slowed down considerably. Such growth patterns can be seen as the result of catch-up growth based on the importation of foreign technologies.

Second, since Japan caught up with the United Kingdom and France, or even surpassed the latter around 1990, the economy has really stagnated in contrast to the slow but steady growth of the United Kingdom and France. Qualitatively the same observation can be made based on the comparison of Japan with Germany and Italy. Thus, it is no exaggeration to argue that the Japanese economy, alone among developed economies, has suffered from a long-lasting "disease." In this connection it is worth emphasizing that, although the UK economy had been stagnant for nearly a decade prior to the early 1980s, its rate of growth has increased significantly since then. Most likely the "British disease" was cured by the Thatcher reforms, which aimed to liberalize the economic system.

Third, and most importantly, although Japan caught up with the United States to some extent during its high growth period, per capita income in the United States has remained remarkably higher than in the other three countries, and the income gap between the United States and Japan has been widening in recent

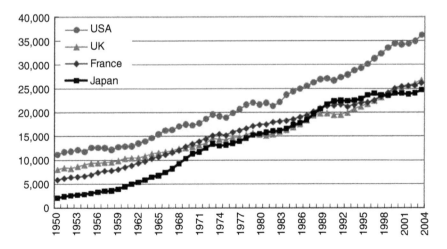

Figure1.1 Changes in real per capita income among developed countries.

years. Most of the contributors to this volume have the experience of living both in Japan and the United States. All of us agree that the Japanese are in general harder-working, better educated, and more cooperative than Americans, which, we believe, are valuable traits in modern production systems and service activities. We also fully agree that major differences lie in the development of frontier industries in the United States based on the frontier knowledge of both the natural and social sciences which are supported by strong graduate schools. While it is true that the current world economic crisis was triggered by the inappropriate application of excessive financial engineering, the fact remains that the United States succeeded in developing frontier industries including IT and bio. The quality of graduate training in the United States is outstanding, far exceeding the level in Japanese universities. Most, if not all, of the internationally prominent Japanese economists have been trained in the graduate schools of the United States. Furthermore, in the United States, many CEOs of private corporations, top government officials, and leading politicians have obtained their graduate degrees, unlike in Japan where few such leaders have been trained in graduate school. In short, the United States overwhelms Japan in the accumulation of the highest quality human capital.

It is also instructive to compare the Japanese experience with those of the four Asian Tigers and China (see Figure 1.2). There is no question that not only Japan but also Singapore, Hong Kong, Taiwan, and Korea, as well as China, have grown successfully based on technology imports (World Bank 1993). The question is whether, like Japan, they grow rapidly only when a sizable income gap exists or, unlike Japan, they continue to grow even when it doesn't.

It is striking to observe from Figure 1.2 that PPP-adjusted per capita income is higher in Hong Kong and Singapore than in Japan. Like Japan, these are resource-scarce economies and their size is small. Their economies are less

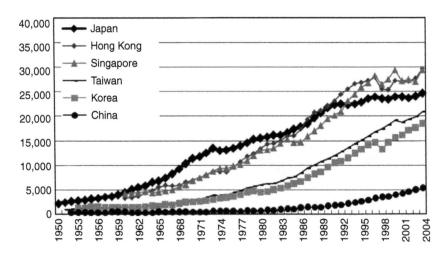

Figure 1.2 Changes in real per capita income among East Asian countries.

regulated than Japan's, however. These economies began their high economic growth roughly ten years later than Japan. Interestingly, their growth rates slowed down considerably after they had caught up with Japan in terms of per capita income in the 1990s. Such growth patterns are consistent with the catch-up hypothesis based on technology imports.

Taiwan and Korea commenced their rapid growth more than ten years after Hong Kong and Singapore. These economies are still growing rapidly, as they have not caught up with the per capita income level of Japan, Hong Kong, and Singapore. It is also important to note that their high growth periods are longer, as the income gap was wider when they began growing. Based on the experience of Japan, Hong Kong, and Singapore, Taiwan and Korea will continue to grow rapidly for a short while and then stop growing as fast once they complete the catching-up process.

It is no wonder that per capita GDP in China has been growing as fast as 10 percent per year for the three decades since 1978, considering the fact that its per capita GDP was only one-fifth of the Japanese level, even as late as 2004. The four Asian Tigers and Japan also grew at the rate of 10 percent per year during their respective high growth periods. Thus, it is reasonable to expect that China will continue to grow at the rate of nearly 10 percent for the coming decade and somewhat beyond until it catches up with the other five East Asian countries.

3 Scope of the book

Having found a strong indication that, while Japan caught up quickly with the western nations, based on technology imports, its economy has since been stagnant for nearly two decades. We would like to explore the institutional factors affecting the success and failure of the economic development of the Japanese economy during the entire post-war period. We will also attempt to draw useful lessons from the Japanese experience for other high-performing Asian countries which are likely to face similar problems in the near future. Being an advanced country, Japan ought to support the development of low-income economies and contribute to the regional security of Asia. Thus, we review and assess the Japanese ODA policy and the security policy based on the so-called "Yoshida Doctrine" by which Japan endeavored to achieve economic prosperity without allocating large government budgets to the military.

Needless to say, we believe that, in principle, no governmental market interventions shall be necessary if markets work competitively. The economic policy issue arises when markets fail, i.e., it becomes *potentially* desirable that the government take corrective action in such cases. But government failures are also ubiquitous, suppressing the function of markets rather than supporting or complementing them. In Japan many people believe that economists in the United States advocate reliance on the market mechanism without any regard to possible negative consequences. This is obviously a problem. The authors of this book, like most economists, believe that government interventions are needed where markets do not work well, for efficiency, growth, and social justice reasons (e.g., Shleifer 2000). Particularly after Japan's economic crisis, an increasing number of Japanese people seem to believe that the market mechanism is harmful not only with respect to economic efficiency but also with respect to economic welfare and distributional justice. Such beliefs, however, are largely groundless.

In this book the authors ask what the major market failures are in the context of the post-war economic development of Japan. We believe that such failures arise from imperfect information and distortions in financial markets and the imperfections of the market of useful information and knowledge. It is known that rates of return to schooling are generally high primarily due to the inability of individuals to obtain the credit for investing in education. Since the quality of human capital is the key to sustainable development, such inadequate investment in human capital likely leads to slow economic development. Similarly enterprise managers may not be able to invest in profitable projects due to poor access to financial markets. Even if they invest in the creation of useful new production methods and management systems, they may not be able to reap the full benefits of the investment, due to imitation by others. Thus, social benefits may exceed private benefits and the gap between them thwarts the private incentive to invest in innovations.

Chapters 2 and 3 are concerned with the industrial policies that correct market failures. Chapter 2 addresses the issue of the infant industry protection policies as a case in which government intervention can lead to the development of industries. While this issue itself is old, the novel contribution that this chapter makes to the literature is that it sheds new light on the process by which the Japanese automobile industry has grown, beginning with the protectionist policies afforded to "infant" enterprises in the pre-war period. Chapter 3 attempts to explore the advantages of industrial clusters for industrial development in the light of the Japanese experience. Industrial clusters play a critical role in economic development, not only in the history of advanced economies, including Japan, but also in contemporary developing economies. The authors of this chapter argue that it is what may be termed multi-faceted innovations in technology, management, and organization that lead to the significant modernization of industry. Yet, due to imitation markets fail so that prudent government policies to support cluster-based industrial development can be justified.

Neither infant industries nor cluster-based industries can grow well if financial markets are not working effectively. Chapter 4 assesses the positive role played by the main bank system of Japan during the successful catch-up process before the mid-1970s but finds that this system became an obstacle to sustained growth afterwards by leading to a flawed incentive mechanism when a lending bank official hesitates to cut back unsuccessful lending because it hurts his or her reputation by revealing the failure of outstanding loans. Thus, (inherently) non-performing loans invite additional non-performing loans. This is the zombie loan syndrome that allegedly has prolonged Japan's financial troubles. As the economy approaches the world frontier in technology, investment risks are bound to increase and, hence, it is preferable to share such risks through stock and corporate bond markets rather than relying on the risk absorption capacity of a small number of main banks. Yet, the financial system of the Japanese economy depends on the indirect financial system based on banks even now.

Chapters 5–7 are concerned with the unique Japanese company system, labor laws, and management system. Chapter 5 begins with the question of what a "company" is and ends with the implications for what a company should be in the future. What is being emphasized is that profits can be generated only by the generation of new, differentiated technologies and products in the post-industrial capitalist era. Thus, Japanese companies must transform themselves to be organizations most conducive for differentiated firm-specific innovations. In order to establish such organizations, company employees who devote themselves to the benefit of companies are needed. Such employees are those who are willing to invest in the acquisition of firm-specific knowledge. By undertaking the case study of employee dismissals in the courts, Chapter 6 explores the process by which highly secure and often life-long employment systems have been developed in Japan, which induces employees to invest in firm-specific human capital. In order to generate profits, not only effective organizations and productive workers but also efficient managers and management systems are indispensable. Chapter 7 makes a unique attempt to inquire into the thrust of the Japanese management system by conducting interviews with leaders of management in large corporations through interviews, called oral history. It is particularly fascinating to learn how effectively the development division and the production division cooperate to designs truly innovative and workable new systems in Japanese factories.

Chapter 8 attempts to shed light on the role of schooling in the catch-up process of Japanese economic development. A striking finding is that while the average schooling level of the Japanese has been nearing that of the United States in the more than 100 years of the catch-up process, the gap has widened at the graduate level. Quantitatively the proportion of young people who study in graduate school is much higher in the United States. Moreover, the quality of the US graduate training programs is undoubtedly superior. It is therefore no wonder that Japan has never completed the catch-up with the United States.

While the chapters detailed above dealt with the domestic issues, Japan also faces serious external problems, e.g., security and international cooperation. Using a game-theoretic approach, Chapter 9 assesses the consequences of the so-called Yoshida Doctrine and the Ikeda Doctrine, both of which focus on the promotion of economic development without incurring the cost of armaments. It is demonstrated that such doctrines might have worked during the Cold War period, but that this no longer the case in the post-Cold War period. Chapter 10 reviews the Japanese ODA policies critically, in the hope that Japan will make larger contributions to the development of low-income countries in the future. Indeed Japan should have much to offer to such countries, given its own unique development experience from a low-income to a high-income country over a short period of time and also its successful transfer of technological and managerial knowledge to high-performing countries in Asia. It is pointed out that what is missing is theorizing about the valuable past experience of Japan and disseminating it to organizations and people interested in development issues.

We conclude this book with proposals for reforming industrial policies, financial systems, and schooling systems. Japan has been woefully inactive in the development of frontier industries due partly to the lack of efficient financial systems which are capable of supporting such development and due partly to the lack of international level human resources. In other words, Japan has failed to develop institutions conducive to the development of frontier industries. This is likely to be the result of successful economic catch-up which led to the preservation of institutions and organizations conducive to imitation. Taking advantage of the Japanese company systems with their unique cooperative company culture, Japan must design a long-term strategy to develop knowledge-intensive frontier industries. By reflecting on why the Japanese economy was able to accomplish the task of high growth in the past, this book will suggest how Japan can learn from history to design necessary strategies for the future under different circumstances. It will hopefully suggest to other developing nations what they can learn from the experience of Japan's initially successful and later defective development strategy.

Note

1 We consider that this slow growth process was aggravated by the conservative monetary policy after the turn of the century that induced deflation, yen appreciation and recession. Governor Masaru Hayami dared to recover the positive nominal interest, that is, a high real interest rate, during the recession and deflation. A similar policy seems to be repeated in the past few years as well. Mismanagement of macroeconomic, particularly monetary policy shaved the path of GDP growth even further from the full employment path. Since this book concentrates on the long run, real and structural side of the economy, we will abstract from the effects of a possibly inappropriate monetary policy.

References

Gerschenkron, A. (1962) *Economic Backwardness in Historical Perspective*, Cambridge, MA: Harvard University Press.
Hayami, Y. and Godo, Y. (2005) *Development Economics*, Oxford: Oxford University Press.
Ohkawa, K. and Rosovsky, H. (1973) *Japanese Economic Growth*, Stanford, CA: Stanford University Press.
Otsuka, K., Liu, D., and Murakami, N. (1998) *Industrial Reform in China: Past Performance and Future Prospect*, Oxford: Clarendon Press.
Otsuka, K., Saxonhouse, G., and Ranis, G. (1988) *Comparative Technology Choice in Development: The Japanese and Indian Cotton Textile Industries*, London: Macmillan Press.
Penn World Table website (2009). Online, available at: http://pwt.econ.upenn.edu. Downloaded 1 April 2010.
Shleifer, A. (2000) "The Age of Milton Friedman," *Journal of Economic Literature* 47(1): 123–35.
World Bank (1993) *East Asian Miracle*, Oxford: Oxford University Press.

2 Infant industry protection policy reconsidered

The case of the automobile industry in Japan

*Ken Togo**

1 Introduction

Infant industry policy is a rarely heard term in advanced economies where most industries are mature. The term has also been forgotten – or intentionally shunned – by academics. The fact that many developing countries that adopted infant industry policies after World War II failed to develop their own industries led many people to think that an infant industry policy was not effective. The 1980s debt crisis in Latin America, where most countries had aggressive infant industry policies in place, strengthened the impression that an infant industry policy is harmful to growth. During the 1990s, mainstream economists concluded that an infant industry policy was undesirable.

The most influential textbook on international economics, by Krugman and Obstfeld, states the argument against infant industry policy as follows:

> In practice it is difficult to evaluate which industries really warrant special treatment, and there are risks that a policy intended to promote development will end up being captured by special interests. There are many stories of infant industries that have never grown up and remain dependent on protection.
>
> (Krugman and Obstfeld 2003, p. 258)

Although it may be difficult to identify potential industries, examples of successful infant industries do exist. Moreover, it may be possible to avoid capture by special interests through various schemes.

Infant industry policy is defined as policy that "assists an industry in its early stages of development." It includes not only protective tools, such as tariffs and import restrictions, but also promotion tools, such as subsidies and government procurement. Infant industry policy is a subset of industry policy, defined here as policy that has some effects on industry. Import substitution policy is policy that protects domestic production that competes with imported goods. If the infant industry is an industry that produces goods that are substitutes for imported goods, the policy is an import substitution policy.

Japan has long been famous for its industrial policy. In *MITI and the Japanese Miracle*, Johnson (1982) suggests that Japanese economic development was planned and achieved by the Ministry of International Trade and Industry (MITI). Japanese scholars regarded Japan's industrial policy very favorably during the 1980s (see Komiya *et al.* 1988).

During the long recession in Japan following the bursting of the bubble in 1989, the assertion was made that traditional market intervention in Japan was a cause of recession and that Japan needed to minimize such intervention and move farther toward market-oriented development. In their book *Sangyo Seisaku no Gokai* (Misunderstanding of Industrial Policy), Miwa and Ramseyer deny that industrial policy contributed to Japanese economic development:

> This book concludes that industrial policy did not work even before the 1970s, which was considered the golden age of industrial policy. Strictly speaking, the policy known as industrial policy did not have any substance. Effective industrial policy was neither planned nor implemented. In truth, there was not any effective industrial policy.[1]
>
> (Miwa and Ramseyer 2002, p. vii)

Developing countries were forced to liberalize their economies in the 1980s and the 1990s, under the structural adjustment programs of the World Bank and the International Monetary Fund (IMF). Under the World Bank's Structural Adjustment Lending (SAL) and the IMF's Structural Adjustment Facility (SAF), developing countries received aid on the condition that they adopt the laissez-faire policy known as the "Washington Consensus." Reductions in or elimination of tariffs and subsidies are examples of the "conditionalities" imposed by the multilateral institutions.

These conditions brought hardship to developing countries; adhering to the conditions meant that countries could not adopt infant industry policies if they received SALs or SAFs. The transition from the General Agreement on Tariffs and Trade (GATT) to the World Trade Organization (WTO) in 1995 forced developing countries to open their markets further.

The stagnation, in the 1990s, of Latin American and African countries that had implemented many structural adjustment programs left some doubt regarding the effectiveness of these liberalization policies. Even in the United States, some economists, such as Dani Rodrik of Harvard University, started to reevaluate industrial policy (Rodrik 2007).

In sum, the effectiveness of infant industry policy remains on open question. Today, during the world recession originated by the US subprime loan crisis, arguments against market mechanisms are being posited. The superiority of a market economy to a centrally planned economy is obvious when one looks at the collapse of the Soviet Union or the rapid growth of the Chinese economy after its economic liberalization. At the same time, the stagnation of Latin American and African countries after receiving SALs and SAFs suggests that liberalization alone does not lead to development.

This chapter reviews the arguments for and against infant industry policy and presents the case study of the Japanese automobile industry before 1945. We understand that the current internationally-competitive industry survived in the early days with assistance from the government, and we investigate what kind of infant industry policy is effective under which kinds of environment, irrespective of ideology. The chapter yields valuable insights for both developing and developed countries.

2 The case for infant industry policy

There is a long history of infant industry policy. England exported wool and imported wool textiles in the fourteenth century. It adopted an import-substitution policy by imposing tariffs on wool textiles and recruiting textile craftsmen from abroad. When Indian cotton textiles flooded the English market in the seventeenth century, England imposed high tariffs on Indian textiles. It adopted a free trade policy only after 1846, by which time the country's domestic industries had achieved international competitiveness.

The United States also adopted an infant industry policy. US tariffs on manufactured goods were 40–50 percent – the highest in the developed world – between 1820 and 1945 (Bairoch 1993). The United States adopted free trade only after World War II, by which time it too had achieved international competitiveness.

Chang (2003) shows that all but two developed countries adopted an infant industry policy. The two exceptions – the Netherlands and Switzerland – did not need such policies because they were already in the technological frontier.

Friedrich List is known as an advocate of infant industry policy. It is said that he changed his opinion – from support of free trade to support of infant industry policy – after reviewing the history of US industrial policy (Chang 2007). The first US secretary of the treasury, Alexander Hamilton, submitted the "Report on Manufactures" to Congress in 1791. In it, he argued for the need to promote domestic industries. This suggests that "infant industry policy" originated in the United States. Both leading advocates of free trade – the United Kingdom and the United States – implemented infant industry policy when their economies were in the early stages of development.

Theoretical support

The theory behind infant industry policy is based on international trade and economic growth theories. In international trade theory, the Ricardian model is the most powerful argument for free trade. The essence of the model is as follows: the world is composed of two countries, country A and country B, and there are only two goods, bananas and computers. If country A has a comparative advantage in producing bananas, it can increase its welfare by specializing in the production of bananas and exporting them in return for imported computers. This is true even if the productivity of country A is lower than that of country B in both goods. This model recommends that all countries open their domestic markets and specialize in the production of goods in which they have comparative advantages.

According to Ricardo, as long as country A has a comparative advantage in growing bananas, it will produce only bananas forever. "Economic development" means that a country climbs the ladder of products, from low-tech (bananas) to high-tech (computer) goods. If the speed of technological progress in the production of computers is greater than that of bananas (which certainly seems to be the case), income inequality between country A and country B will continuously widen.

If country A wants to produce computers under free trade, it is necessary for it to increase its relative productivity in computers. Country A cannot increase its productivity in computers, however, if it does not produce computers at all. It, therefore, cannot increase its productivity in computers under free trade.[2]

Growth theory can provide an argument against free trade. In the 1980s, new growth theories emerged. Until then, neoclassical growth theory, of which the Solow model is a mainstay, was the dominant theory in economics. Neoclassical growth theory assumes diminishing returns of two factors of production, capital and labor. The growth rates of developing countries that have a low capital–labor ratio will be higher than those of developed countries. The model implies that increases in the capital–labor ratio through capital accumulation will make growth rates decrease until they eventually reach zero. This implication, known as the convergence hypothesis, was statistically tested using cross-country economic data. The studies concluded that convergence does not exist (e.g., De Long 1988). Some developing countries experience low growth, and some developed countries experience steady growth. The neoclassical growth theory cannot explain this phenomenon. New growth theories, which posited externalities and economies of scale as theoretical reasons for steady growth, emerged.

For example, the model of Hausmann and Rodrik (2003) describes market failure in the presence of externalities. Entrepreneurs find manufactured goods to sell by trial and error. Once they discover this information, it spills over to other entrepreneurs, who can see the products in the market. As other manufacturers start to produce the same goods, the revenues of the pioneer manufacturer fall, but the costs of trial and error they incurred remain large. As a result, only a small number of entrepreneurs will choose to search for manufactured goods to produce. This will decrease the growth rate of the economy. The government, however, can increase the number of pioneer entrepreneurs by providing support to them, such as production subsidies. This will promote the growth rate of the economy.

The presence of economies of scale also supports the case for infant industry policy. If an industry enjoys economies of scale – which means that the average production costs decrease with the volume of production – the government can promote the productivity of the industry by erecting import barriers and/or providing production subsidies. Field work by Otsuka and Sonobe, (2010) shows that productivity increases in some industries after a certain volume of production.

Market failure occurs when the market mechanism alone cannot achieve the optimal resource allocation. The presence of market failure – in the form of externalities or economies of scale – warrants market intervention by the government and the adoption of an infant industry policy.

Empirical support

There are two kinds of empirical studies: case studies on individual industries, and cross-sectional studies. In case studies, there are two approaches – with and without statistical analysis. The number of studies without statistical analysis is much larger than the number with statistical analysis.

Two case studies that use statistical analysis are Irwin (2000) and Ohashi (2005). Irwin (2000) investigates the US tin industry in the 1890s. His conclusion is that, although the tariff accelerated the industry's development by about ten years, welfare calculations suggest that protection does not pass the cost–benefit test. Irwin's sample, however, was small (45 observations), casting doubt on the robustness of his conclusion.

Ohashi (2005) explores the Japanese steel industry in the 1950s and 1960s to evaluate the effectiveness of export subsidies on stimulating steel production. He estimates a partial equilibrium model of the industry, paying particular attention to both dynamic scale economies (learning by doing) and learning from spillovers across firms. Ohashi finds a significant learning rate (above 20 percent) but little evidence of intra-industry knowledge spillover. It seems likely that the Japanese practice of lifetime employment reduces the effect of intra-industry knowledge spillover because labor turnover is one of the most important mechanisms through which knowledge spillovers occur. Ohashi's simulation results indicate that the Japanese subsidy policy had only a negligible impact on industrial growth. However, these subsidies covered the losses associated with high production costs early on and provided the industry with time to increase its competitiveness through learning by doing.

These statistical investigations suffer from problems, such as the small number of observations and the fact that their results may reflect special circumstances. Case studies are vulnerable to criticism on the grounds that their results apply only to the particular industry, country, or period studied. Analysis of a cross-sectional data set can avoid such criticism.

Beason and Weinstein (1996) and Lawrence and Weinstein (2001) are good examples of cross-sectional analyses of the effect of industry policy. Weinstein and co-authors investigate the effect of industrial policy – such as loans from the Development Bank of Japan, tariffs, and subsidies for production – on the growth rates of sectoral total factor productivity in Japan. Their results suggest that there is no statistical evidence of positive effects of industrial policy.

However, Stiglitz and Charlton point out that cross-sectional analysis of total factor productivity has a serious problem. They argue that "to the extent that industrial policies in one sector led to improved productivity in other sector (so-called 'spillover effects'), the benefits of these policies would not be entirely captured by sectoral total factor productivity" (Stiglitz and Charlton 2005, p. 17).

There are problems with both case studies and cross-sectional analysis, neither of which finds concrete evidence of the effectiveness of industrial policy. Because statistical analysis is difficult for ordinary people (and sometimes professionals, too) to understand, the results of such studies are often accepted as correct. This is very dangerous. In economics, new statistical findings often con-tradict older statistical findings.

When economists discuss industrial policy, the same question is always asked, "How can the government select the industries that will grow to be com-petitive in the international market?" This problem is known as the "picking winners" problem. As Krugman and Obstfeld (2003) note, many industries that enjoyed government help did not grow. Neoclassical economists argue that gov-ernment failure is a more serious problem than market failure. The argument is also made that the government should assist all industries equally as it has no way of selecting the good ones (see Ranis 2003).

Some economists have re-evaluated industrial policy in countries including the United States. Rodrik argues that the principal-agent model, in which the government is the principal and the private sector the agent, should not be used to evaluate industrial policy. He suggests that the model for analyzing industrial policy should not be one in which the government unilaterally decides which industries to support but rather one in which the government and the private sector cooperate to find where the most significant bottlenecks are and design the most effective interventions through a deliberation council or other economic institution (Rodrik 2007). Using this approach, it seems possible to pick winners.

Infant industrial policy can be justified on theoretical grounds, but there is no robust empirical evidence to support it. As a result, policy is determined by polit-ical influence.

Infant industry policy and political influence

The East Asian Miracle, published by the World Bank in 1993, was the result of research funded by Japan's Ministry of Finance. The ministry was angry at the World Bank's claim that Japan's provision of directed credit was distorting the financial system in Asia. According to Wade (2004, p. xviii), the ministry paid 1.2 million dollars (US) to cover non-staff costs of research on East Asian devel-opment, in order to convince the World Bank that East Asian development was the result of government intervention as the ministry believed. This very ambi-tious book investigates the policies of East Asian countries and analyzes their effectiveness. Its conclusions are mixed. It finds evidence in support of export promotion policies – but not industrial policies to support specific sectors.

These findings did not influence the provision of SALs, which were popular at the World Bank at the time. Developing countries received loans under the condition that they adopt liberalization policies.

3 Infant industrial policy and the Japanese automobile industry

Japanese industrial policy regarding the automobile industry is often cited as a representative example of failure (e.g., Irwin 2005, p. 180). The case repeatedly cited is that of Honda. In 1961, the Ministry of International Trade and Industry

(MITI) attempted to persuade Honda, which manufactured only motorcycles at that time, not to enter into the automobile market because the market was over-saturated. Honda flatly rebuffed the recommendation. When we consider Honda's international competitiveness in today's market, MITI's strategy was clearly misguided.

Can judgment be passed on the effectiveness of MITI's industrial policy on the Japanese automobile industry solely on the case of Honda? There were many other MITI policies such as tariffs and subsidized loans that helped to guide the industry as a whole. Itoh (1988) argued that the high tariff placed on foreign automobiles until around 1970 helped the development of the Japanese automobile industry. This increased the profit ratio (profit/sales) of the automobile industry to a level that was higher than other manufacturing industries and attracted new entrants into the industry such as Honda. The existing manufacturers, however, invested profits to improve productivity instead of fighting with new entrants by reducing the sales price. Existing firms adopted this strategy since the government had announced a fixed schedule of the future liberalization of trade.

Itoh (1988) also pointed out the effectiveness of subsidized loans due to two factors. First, the Law on Temporary Measures for Promoting the Machinery Industries (Machine Industry Law) of 1956 effectively targeted the automotive parts industry as one of 17 industries for promotion.[3] Second, the Development Bank of Japan, a governmental bank, extended subsidized loans to automotive parts manufacturers. Of the total lending by the Development Bank of Japan to designated machine industries under the law, 32.1 percent went to the automotive parts industry during 1961–1965 and 54.2 percent went to that sector during 1966–1974 (Mutoh 1988). The development of the automotive parts industry facilitated entrance of new firms into the automobile industry. This reinforced competition among assemblers and increased the productivity of the automobile industry. Itoh (1988) concludes that the industrial policy applied to the Japanese automobile industry in the post-war period was effective.

From the above, we understand that the justifiability of industrial policy of the Japanese automobile industry remains an open question. In particular, there are very few studies on the policy regarding the Japanese automobile industry in the pre-war period. From the point of the infant industry argument, the pre-war period is more important because Japan nurtured the automobile industry from zero and achieved import-substitution of trucks and small cars before World War II.

The dawn of the Japanese automobile industry

In 1897, a European-made, steam-driven car was the first car imported into Japan (Odagiri and Goto 1993). Examples of the earliest Japanese car include the Yamaba steam car (1904) and the Takuri-go with gasoline engine (1907). Many pioneers disappeared after producing one or two prototypes (Nakamura 1957, p. 12). Until 1911, there were only 43 cars produced domestically. On the other hand, the number of imports in the same period was over 600 (Toyota Motor 1958, p. 17).

The government soon realized the importance of the automobile after World War I. The army arsenal began its study on automobiles in 1907, and the Military Automobile Subsidizing Law (Gunyo Jidosha Hojo Hou) was enacted in 1918. This law was not regarded highly because production of automobiles did not increase much in this period. Nakamura explains the reason for the failure was that the subsidy was applicable only for cars weighing more than one and half tons, but the price and quality of foreign cars were much better in this class of cars (Nakamura 1957, p. 18).

The Great Kanto Earthquake of 1923 is considered a milestone in automobile utilization in Japan. At that time, train service was disrupted and cars were urgently needed to transport people and goods. The number of vehicles in Japan was 15,731 in 1923 and jumped to 24,333 in 1924.

Since mass-produced US made cars were affordable, many cars were imported. Due to high sales, Ford started to assemble the Model T in Japan in 1925. In 1927, Ford established its knock-down assembly factory to produce the Model A in Yokohama and annually produced 20,000 units. GM also started its Japan-based mass production in 1927. As a result of mass production by Ford and GM, Japanese small automobile manufacturers such as Hakuyosha, Miyata Seisakujyo, and Orient Jidousha Seizou, which attempted to produce vehicles not subject to the military subsidy, disappeared from the market (Nakamura 1957, p. 28).

After a deterioration of the balance of trade partly due to the increase in the import of automotive parts, the government reinforced the promotion policies of the automobile industry. The Automobile Manufacturing Enterprise Law (Jidosha Seizou Jigyo Hou) was issued in 1936. This law included the following provisions:

1   If automobile manufacturers intended to annually produce more than 3,000 vehicles which had more than 750 cc, a government license, which was awarded only to Japanese companies, must be obtained.
2   A five-year tax exemption was awarded to licensed companies on their income, sales, and import of machinery for auto manufacturing.
3   Licensed companies had to obey the government's orders.
4   The companies with previous manufacturing experience had vested rights to produce vehicles. These vested rights were as of August 9, 1935.

Under this law, the government issued licenses to Nissan and Toyota. Tokyo Automobile Industries Co., Ltd. (later Isuzu) also obtained a license later. All three companies were subject to a military subsidy. This law also restricted annual production by Ford and GM to 12,360 units and 9,470 units respectively. The tariff rate on fully assembled cars was also raised to 70 percent.

After the China/Japan Incident of 1937, the army procured trucks from Japanese manufacturers and accounted for 60 percent of domestic production in the

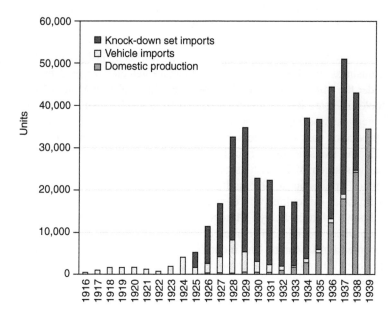

Figure 2.1 Four wheel vehicle supply in Japan, 1916–1939 (source: Cusumano 1985, appendix A. Original sources are Japan Automobile Manufacturers Association, Nissan Jidousha Sanjyunen Shi, p. 16, Nohon Jidousha Nenkan 1947, Jerome Cohen, *Japan's Economy in War and Reconstruction*, p. 26).

period 1937–1944 (Cusumano 1985, p. 14). Substantial depreciation of the yen after the revision of the foreign exchange law, coupled with complete exchange control, forced Ford and GM to exit the Japanese automobile market by 1939. Import substitution of automobiles, mostly trucks, was achieved before World War II, although it was regulated by the government (Figure 2.1). In the process of import substitution, many entrants disappeared. Only manufacturers subject to government protection survived.

Interaction between policies and the behavior of manufacturers

In this section, the interaction between policies and the behavior of manufacturers is investigated based on their *Eigyo Houkokusyo* (annual reports).

Kwaishinsha/DAT Motors/Nissan Motors

Nissan Motors traces its origins through Kwaishinsha even though the genealogy was not exactly linear. The Kwaishinsha Automobile Factory established in Tokyo in 1911 by Masujiro Hashimoto, started as a manufacturer of Japanese automobile prototypes while importing, assembling, and repairing foreign cars. Hashimoto graduated from the governmental *Tokyo Kogyo Gakko* (today's

Tokyo Institute of Technology). As a government-sponsored overseas trainee, he went to the United States in 1902 to study the technology for manufacturing steam engines.

When he started his business, he had only seven workers. Hashimoto incorporated his business in 1918 in order to manufacture vehicles targeted for the subsidies under the Military Automobile Subsidizing Law (Nissan Motors 1965, p. 25). It took six years before his car qualified for subsidies. Since the sales price of his new car was 2,000 yen lower than the actual costs, Hashimoto specialized in producing cars subject to subsidy. Kwaishinsha, however, was liquidated in 1925 after five straight years of losses.

After the liquidation of Kwaishinsha, Hashimoto established DAT Jidosha Shokai Limited Partnership in 1925 and continued manufacturing military cars. Because of financial difficulties, the company merged with another struggling automaker, Jitsuyo Motors. Jitsuyo Motors was established in 1919 and manufactured three-wheel vehicles. The merger was completed in 1926 and the company renamed DAT Motors. The monthly production yield of DAT Motors in 1928 was about 20 units and the company received subsidies on the cars and trucks it produced.

However, the army shifted its policy in 1929 and reduced the amount of subsidy per vehicle but increased the number of vehicles to be subsidized. As automakers' production capacities increased, subsidies could not be obtained for all the vehicles produced. Although DAT Motors met the subsidy quota of 92 vehicles in 1931, it had an excess capacity to produce vehicles and decided to manufacture mini cars. The government issued a ministerial ordinance in 1930 that a driver's license was not needed to drive a car with an engine of less than 500 cc. That ordinance and a lower tax per vehicle pushed DAT Motors to manufacture mini cars.

Tobata Casting which manufactured auto parts for Ford and GM purchased DAT Motors in June 1931, and by August, DAT Motors marketed the mini car. The car sold for 1,150 yen. Since the price of the British Austin Seven in Japan at that time was 1,600 yen, DAT's mini car was competitively priced. The mini car was named Datsun from 1932 (Nissan Motors 1965, p. 28). Yoshisuke Aikawa, the chairman of Tobata Casting, obtained the production rights for Datsun in August 1933 in order to manufacture Datsun and auto parts for Ford and GM. Aikawa established Jidosha Seizo in December 1933 and renamed it Nissan Motors in May 1934.

Nissan Motors actively employed foreign technicians. Nissan acquired production lines from chassis to body to mass-produce Datsun. The first Datsun emerged from this production line in April 1935. The volume of Datsun produced was 202 units in 1933, 1,170 units in 1934, and 3,800 units in 1935. Nissan was the first Japanese auto manufacturer to establish a mass production system in Japan. Datsuns were also exported to Australia in the same year.

In 1936, Nissan entered into a technical alliance with Graham–Paige, an ailing American automaker, and acquired their production line to produce a larger vehicle called "Nissan." In 1937, the production capacity of Nissan reached 8,535 units (Nissan Motors 1965, p. 45). Since the procurements of trucks by the army increased substantially, Nissan had to stop producing the passenger cars of Datsun at the end of 1938 and Nissan in January 1939.

Toyota

The origin of Toyota Motors can be traced back to the Toyoda Automatic Loom Works established by Sakichi Toyoda in 1926. While Sakichi himself had plans to manufacture automobiles, he was unable to; his son, Kiichiro, eventually realized this plan. Toyoda Automatic Loom Works sold the patent rights for the automatic loom to the Platt Brothers of Great Britain for 100,000 pounds, equivalent to one million yen at that time and spent the entire sum experimenting with motor vehicles.

In 1933, the Automobile Department was established within Toyoda Automatic Loom Works. In 1934, Kiichiro recruited Takatoshi Kan who had experience with manufacturing automobiles at another company. Mr. Kan was dispatched to the United States to purchase machines and visit factories and universities to study the automobile industry. He also studied manufacturing methods at Ford and Chrysler factories (Toyota Motor 1958, p. 35).

Toyota manufactured machine tools and established a steel factory on its own because of the scarcity and low quality of machine tool manufactures and specialty steel factories in Japan. Although Kiichiro wanted to manufacture passenger cars from the beginning, they initially manufactured trucks because they lacked press technology for passenger cars. In 1935, they marketed G1 trucks. The G1 took two years and several million yen to produce. Since the sales price of the truck was set 200 yen cheaper than Ford trucks, Toyota ran a deficit. Kiichiro stated that the Automobile Manufacturing Enterprise Law (1936) was of benefit to their business (Toyota Motor 1958, p. 26), one example of industrial policy in operation.

In 1936, a large assembly plant in Kariya was opened. This plant had three 50-meter conveyors to enable mass production. Two lines were for trucks. Eventually, the Toyoda AA, a passenger car with a 3,389 cc engine, was marketed in 1936. It was used mainly by taxi companies and the government. In 1937, the Automobile Department was split off to establish Toyota Motor which employed 1,100 (Toyota Motor 1958, p. 68).

After the China/Japan Incident in 1937, the army ordered a large volume of trucks. This was a tremendous boost to Toyota's business. In 1937, Toyota produced 4,013 units (cars and trucks). With the completion of the Koromo plant in 1938, production jumped to 11,981 units in 1939 (Toyota Motor 1958, p. 71).

Analysis of capital stock and profitability

Figure 2.2 represents the real capital stock of the auto industry between 1918 and 1940. It was calculated by adding the nominal values of machinery, utensils, and tools in annual reports of each company. This figure was then deflated by

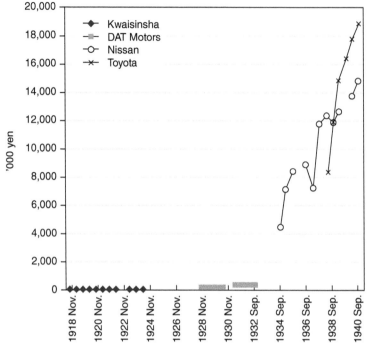

Figure 2.2 Real capital stock (base year = 1934–1936) (sources: author's calculation based on each company's Eigyou Houkokusyo (annual reports) and Ohkawa *et al.* 1967).

the price index of machinery calculated by Ohkawa *et al.* (1967). Figure 2.2 tells us that the capital formation of Kwaishinsha and DAT Motors stagnated while Nissan and Toyota increased their capital substantially.

In 1934, Nissan started mass production of the compact car "Datsun." Nissan increased production capacity by purchasing the production line from Graham–Paige in 1936 and started production of the standard size car "Nissan." This capacity expansion indicates that Nissan realized the importance of mass production in the automobile industry and gained technical knowledge to achieve mass production.

Toyota also realized the importance of mass production and established a large plant from the outset. The Automobile Manufacturing Enterprise Law (1936) certainly let licensed manufacturers envisage future high profits. This was clearly a stimulus for increased investments.

Figure 2.3 shows the ratio of profit to sales. It indicates that Kwaishinsha accumulated debt since 1920 and disbanded, even though it received subsidies under the Military Automobile Subsidizing Law (1918). This indicates that subsidies were not enough to support automobile manufacturing at that time. On the other hand, DAT Motors and Nissan made profits with the same subsidies. What

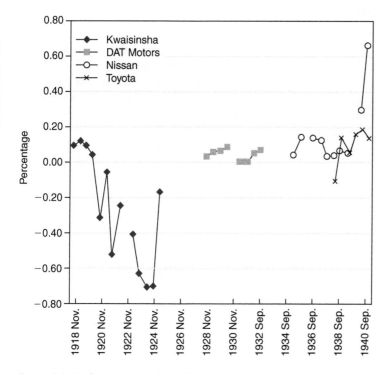

Figure 2.3 Profit/sales (sources: author's calculation based on each company's Eigyou Houkokusyo (annual reports)).

explains this difference? One explanation is that they increased productivity through accumulating experience.

In 1940, Nissan had a profit ratio as high as 66 percent. This was due to high productivity enjoying economies of scale through mass production and generous military procurement.

The above argument permits the conclusion that the above-mentioned subsidies provided a certain period for manufacturers to survive and learn in the market. This can be explained by an increase in productivity through accumulating experience. The profitability of DAT Motors and the early Nissan provided support for this argument. The manufacturers which did not receive any subsidies, such as Hakuyosha, went bankrupt. Although Kwaishinsha disbanded, DAT Motors inherited some of its technical knowledge because they were of the same lineage.

The Automobile Manufacturing Enterprise Law (1936) clearly supported Nissan and Toyota to realize the mass production of standard-sized vehicles. Kiichiro Toyoda's statement provides solid evidence. They enjoyed economies of scale and gradually replaced Ford and GM as suppliers of automobiles in Japan.

4 Conclusion

Although theoretical models show that an infant industry policy can be justified, major textbooks and empirical studies find no evidence that this is the case. Until the 1990s, Japanese scholars believed that industrial policy was effective; but recent work by Japanese researchers has not found evidence that industrial policy works. In contrast, some scholars in the United States, such as Rodrik, believe that industrial policy can spur growth.

Ideology sometimes distorts the value of economic research. The quality of research is evaluated by the editors of academic journals. One would like to believe that editors always accept or reject articles solely on the basis of their quality. The facts suggest that this is not the case. In 2005 Paul Samuelson revealed that his famous article written with Stolper was rejected by the *American Economic Review* because it would weaken the case for free trade.

Political influence also affects the application of economic knowledge. The resignation of Joseph Stiglitz as chief economist of the World Bank is said to have been an example of this influence (see, for example, Chang 2001). The ambiguous conclusion of *The East Asian Miracle* volume is another example.

The Washington Consensus clearly had negative effects on the growth of developing countries. It is too simple to think that smaller government is always better. It is also too simple to think that private companies will emerge naturally in the market. Some industries need no help from the government to start a business; others require assistance as a result of economies of scale and externalities. Researchers need to investigate what kind of infant industry policy is effective under what kinds of environment, irrespective of ideology. Such investigation would widen the spectrum of policy tools from which developing countries can choose.

The experience of the Japanese automobile industry before World War II shows that only manufacturers subject to government protection could survive. They improved profitability through accumulating knowledge and expanding production capacity under protection. Nissan and Toyota, which were licensed manufacturers of the Automobile Manufacturing Enterprise Law (1936), are now competing with Ford and GM in the international market. Japanese automobile production for 2009 was recorded as 7,934,516 units while the total value of automobiles exported was 96 billion dollars.[4] Although we cannot know how long Japanese automobile manufacturers will survive in the international market, the cost of infant industry policy in support of the Japanese automobile industry does not seem to have exceeded the benefits.

During the current global economic crisis, apprehension about increased protectionism is evident. Infant industry policy should be adopted as a tool for economic development, but should not be used to protect domestic industries in developed countries. These countries should open up their markets to developing countries' products and move on to higher-tech industries. It is irrational to produce goods with high-wage labor if the same goods can be produced by low-wage labor. High-wage labor needs to produce high value-added goods.

Notes

* This research was partly supported by Toyota and Musashi University. I thank those entities for the benefits provided.
1 This is the translation by the author.
2 Foreign direct investment (FDI) could be a way for developing countries to establish a computer industry, but how many of the world's 100 developing countries can be chosen as places to invest?
3 The final assembly industry was not chosen for promotion.
4 See the internet site of the Japan Automobile Manufacturers Association, Inc.

References

Bairoch, P. (1993) *Economics and World History: Myths and Paradoxes*, Chicago: University of Chicago Press.

Beason, R. and Weinstein, D. (1996) "Growth, Economies of Scale, and Targeting in Japan (1955–1990)," *Review of Economics and Statistics*, 78 (May), pp. 286–295.

Chang, H.-J. (ed.) (2001) *The Rebel Within: Joseph Stiglitz and the World Bank*, London: Anthem Press.

Chang, H.-J. (2003) "Kicking Away the Ladder: Infant Industry Promotion in Historical Perspective," *Oxford Development Studies*, 31 (1), pp. 21–32.

Chang, H.-J. (2007) *Bad Samaritans: Rich Nations, Poor Policies, and the Threat to the Developing World*, New York: Random House.

Cusumano, M.A. (1985) *The Japanese Automobile Industry: Technology and Management at Nissan and Toyota*, Cambridge, MA: Harvard University Press.

De Long, J.B. (1988) "Productivity Growth, Convergence, and Welfare: Comment," *American Economic Review*, 78 (5), pp. 1138–1154.

Hausmann, R. and Rodrik, D. (2003) "Economic Development as Self-discovery," *Journal of Development Economics*, 72, pp. 603–633.

Irwin, D.A. (2000) "Did Late-Nineteenth-Century US Tariffs Promote Infant Industries? Evidence from the Tinplate Industry," *Journal of Economic History*, 60 (2), pp. 335–360.

Irwin, D. (2005) *Free Trade under Fire*, second edition, Princeton, NJ: Princeton University Press.

Itoh, M. (1988) "Competition in Green House: The Result of Industrial Policy," in H. Itami, T. Kobayashi, M. Itoh, T. Kagono, and K. Sakakibara (eds.), *Competition and Innovation* (Kyosoh to Kakushin: Jidoushasangyo no Kigyo Seichou), Tokyo: Toyo Keizai Shinposha.

Japan Automobile Manufacturers Association, Inc. (no date). Online, available at: www.jama-english.jp/statistics/production_export/2009/100129.html#automobileexport_year.

Johnson, C. (1982) *MITI and the Japanese Miracle: The Growth of Industrial Policy, 1925–1975*, Stanford, CA: Stanford University Press.

Komiya, R., Okuno, M., and Suzumura, K. (1988) *Industrial Policy of Japan*, Tokyo: Academic Press.

Krugman, P.R. and Obstfeld, M. (2003) *International Economics: Theory and Policy*, sixth edition, New York: Addison-Weily.

Lawrence, R.Z. and Weinstein, D.E. (2001) "Trade and Growth: Import Led or Export Led? Evidence from Japan and Korea," in J.E. Stiglitz and S. Yusuf (eds.), *Rethinking the East Asian Miracle*, Cambridge: Oxford University Press.

Miwa, Y. and Ramseyer, M.J. (2002) *Sangyo Seisaku ron no Gokai: Kodo Seicho no Shinjutsu* (Misunderstandings about Industrial Policy: The Truth about High Growth), Tokyo: Toyo Keizai (in Japanese).

Mutoh, H. (1988) "The Automotive Industry," in R. Komiya, M. Okuno and K. Suzumura (eds.), *Industrial Policy of Japan*, Tokyo: Academic Press.

Nakamura, S. (1957) *Nihon no Jidousya Kougyou* (Japanese Automobile Industry), Tokyo: Nihon Hyouron Shinsya (in Japanese).

Nissan Motors (1965) *Nissan Jidosha Sanjyuunenshi* (Thirty Years' History of Nissan Motor), Japan: Nissan Motor Co. Ltd.

Odagiri, H. and Goto, A. (1993) "The Japanese System of Innovation: Past, Present, and Future," in R.R. Nelson (ed.), *National Innovation System*, New York: Oxford University Press.

Ohashi, H. (2005) "Learning by Doing, Export Subsidies, and Industry Growth: Japanese Steel in the 1950s and 1960s," *Journal of International Economics*, 66, pp. 297–323.

Ohkawa, K., Sinohara, M., and Umemura, M. (eds.) (1967) *Estimates of Long-Term Economic Statistics of Japan since 1868, Volume 8: Prices*, Tokyo: Toyo Keizai Shinposha.

Otsuka, K. and Sonobe, T. (2010) "Cluster-Based Industrial Development: Applicability of Japanese Experience to Contemporary Developing Countries," mimeo.

Ranis, G. (2003) "Symposium on Infant Industries: A Comment," *Oxford Development Studies*, 31 (1), pp. 33–35.

Rodrik, D. (2007) "Normalizing Industrial Policy," mimeo.

Samuelson, P.A. (2004) "Where Ricardo and Mill Rebut and Confirm Arguments of Mainstream Economists Supporting Globalization," *Journal of Economic Perspectives*, 18 (3), pp. 135–146.

Samuelson, P.A. (2005) "Response from Paul A. Samuelson," *Journal of Economic Perspectives*, 19 (3), pp. 242–244.

Stiglitz, J.E. and Charlton, A. (2005) *Fair Trade for All: How Trade Can Promote Development*, New York: Oxford University Press.

Togo, K. (2007) "Infant Industry Policy: A Case of Japanese Automobile Industry Before 1945," Musashi University Discussion Paper No. 56, February.

Togo, K. (2010) "The Dispute over Infant Industry Policy: A Brief Survey," Musashi University Discussion Paper No. 56, February.

Toyota Motor (1958) *Toyota Jidousha Nijyunenshi* (Twenty Years' History of Toyota Motor), Japan: Toyota Motor Corporation, Ltd.

Wade, R. (2004) "Introduction to the 2003 Paperback Edition: Creating Capitalism," in *Governing the Market: Economic Theory and the Role of Government in East Asian Industrialization*, Princeton, NJ: Princeton University Press.

World Bank (1993) *The East Asian Miracle: Economic Growth and Public Policy*, Washington, DC: The World Bank.

3 Cluster-based industrial development

Applicability of Japanese experiences to contemporary developing countries

Keijiro Otsuka and Tetsushi Sonobe

1 Introduction

How can low-income economies in South Asia and sub-Saharan Africa develop to be like high performing East Asian economies? In order to answer such a question, we must have a proper understanding of the development process during which East Asian economies have been growing rapidly. Thus, initially we conducted detailed comparative case studies in eight industries in Japan, Taiwan, and China (Sonobe and Otsuka 2006). Subsequently we proceeded to undertake case studies in Southeast Asia, South Asia, and sub-Saharan Africa. We focused on industrial clusters, simply because so many industries are clustered and many of them have successfully developed. Focusing on the most important common factor, we interpret the industrial cluster as "the geographical concentration or localization of enterprises producing similar and closely related products (e.g., parts and final products) in a small area."

Historically, cluster-based industrialization took place in Europe even before the Industrial Revolution, but its importance was recognized by Piore and Sabel's (1984) pioneering study on the development of industrial clusters in Northern Italy, in which flexible inter-enterprise division of labor played a critical role in producing fashionable products (see also Porter 1990). Added to this is the development of such high-tech industrial clusters as the Silicon Valley (Krugman 1991, chapter two; Saxenian 1994). It is well known that industrial clusters have played critical roles in the development of manufacturing industries in Japan (e.g., Whittaker 1997; Yamamura *et al.* 2003, 2005). In addition, it has become increasingly known that a similar development is observed in China and Vietnam (Sonobe *et al.* 2004; Ruan and Zhang 2009; Nam *et al.* 2009, 2010). Having recognized the importance of industrial clusters in the development of manufacturing industries, the Japan International Cooperation Agency supported their development in Indonesia, Thailand, and other Southeast Asian countries. Schmitz and Nadvi (1999), report that industrial clusters are ubiquitous in Latin America and South Asia. According to our own studies, industrial clusters are no less important in sub-Saharan Africa (e.g., Akoten and Otsuka 2007; Sonobe *et al.* 2010).[1]

Why are so many industries clustered? According to the pioneering study by Marshall (1920), the agglomeration economies arise from (*a*) information spillover (or imitation), (*b*) division of labor between manufacturing enterprises, and (*c*) the development of skilled labor markets within an industrial cluster. Although we do not have any objection to the existence of these advantages in a cluster, we believe that they are insufficient. We would like to argue that not only imitations but also innovations take place in industrial clusters owing to the endogenous process that induces innovations which lead to the improvement of the quality of products and the efficiency of management. In fact, we found a number of industrial clusters in Asia which have grown successfully due to innovations or to a large number of small improvements (Sonobe and Otsuka 2006; Mottaleb and Sonobe 2010).[2] The purpose of this chapter is to draw lessons for the development of poor countries from the successful development experiences of industrial clusters in Japan and other high-performing Asian countries.

The organization of this chapter is as follows. In Section 2, we briefly describe major characteristics of our study sites in Asia and sub-Saharan Africa with a special focus on the Northeast Asian cases. We summarize the similar or common patterns of successful cluster-based industrial development in terms of the "endogenous model of cluster-based industrial development" in Section 3. After briefly explaining the Japanese experience, we compare it with the current situation of a leather-shoe cluster in Ethiopia in Section 4. Finally we discuss the policy implications of this study in Section 5.

2 Study sites in Asia and Africa

In order to identify the similarities and differences in development patterns across industries in three Northeast Asian countries, we have selected cases in such a way that the same industry is compared as much as possible between two countries (see Table 3.1), i.e., the garment and motorcycle industries in Japan and China, and the machinery and printed circuit-board industries between Taiwan and China.[3] In China we selected industries whose development has been driven by private enterprises rather than state-owned enterprises since we are interested in the natural evolutionary process of industrial development governed by the free interplay of economic forces.[4]

In each case study, we spent approximately two weeks on informal interviews, primarily with the managers and owners of enterprises, to explore the ideas of a cluster's development process and then conducted formal surveys of enterprises using compact questionnaires. Through informal interviews we found that: (*a*) the cost of initiating new enterprises based on imitation becomes lower once the founding enterprise establishes new production methods through trial and error; (*b*) the cost of entry to the industry declined as the markets for inputs and output developed with an expansion of the cluster; and (*c*) finally, the cost of innovation is reduced as a variety of human resources, such as engineers, designers, and merchants, is accumulated in the cluster over time.

There are remarkable similarities in the development pattern between the garment clusters in Bingo in Hiroshima Prefecture in Japan and Jili in Zhejiang Province in China. First, they were located in rural areas but not too far from

Table 3.1 A list of case studies in Asia and Africa and basic characteristics

Region	Place	Industry	Type of leaders	Location
Northeast Asia	Bingo, Japan	Garment	Merchants	Rural
	Hamamatsu, Japan	Motorcycle	Engineers	Urban
	Taoyuan, Taiwan	Printed c. board	Engineers	Suburban
	Taichung, Taiwan	Machine tools	Engineers	Suburban
	Jili, China	Garment	Merchants	Rural
	Chongqing, China	Motorcycle	Engineers	Urban
	Jiangsu, China	Printed c. board	Merchants	Suburban
	Wenzhou, China	Low-voltage electric	Merchants	Rural
Southeast Asia	Hanoi, Vietnam	Garment	Merchants	Suburban
	Hanoi, Vietnam	Const. materials	Merchants	Suburban
	Manila, Philippines	Footwear	Merchants	Suburban
South Asia	Dhaka, Bangladesh	Garment	Merchants	Urban
	Sargoda, Pakistan	Low-voltage electric	Merchants	Urban
	Delhi, India	Garment	Merchants	Urban
Sub-Saharan Africa	Addis Ababa, Ethiopia	Leather shoe	Merchants	Urban
	Addis Ababa, Ethiopia	Garment	Unclear	Urban
	Nairobi, Kenya	Garment	Unclear	Urban
	Nairobi, Kenya	Metalwork	Engineers	Urban
	Kumasi, Ghana	Metalwork	Engineers	Urban
	D. E. Salaam, Tanzania	Garment	Unclear	Urban

large cities, Osaka in the case of Bingo and Shanghai in the case of Jili. Second, because of the poor soil and limited availability of farmland, wives and other members of farm households had to supplement their meager farm incomes by weaving *kasuri* (traditional cotton cloth) in the case of Bingo, and by producing pillowcases and other miscellaneous merchandise in the case of Jili. Third, to sell these products, local merchants emerged who travelled around various parts of the country, and thus the tradition of commerce was established in these rural towns. Fourth, it was these local merchants who introduced the current major products, that is, working clothes in Bingo and infant clothing in Jili. Like rural industrialization in other places in East Asia (Otsuka 1998, 2007), the development of the garment industry in Bingo and Jili rested on the availability of cheap unskilled labor mobilized by merchants. We call this pattern of industrial development "merchant-led."

In contrast, the development of the motorcycle industries in both Japan and China can be characterized as "engineer-led." It is technically more difficult to manufacture motorcycles than garments; hence, it is natural for engineers to take entrepreneurial initiatives in the industry. Since engineers tend to reside in urban areas and the production of motorcycles requires parts and skilled workers more readily available in urban areas, these industries tend to be urban-based. Yet, the motorcycle industry has not developed in the largest industrial cities, such as Tokyo and Shanghai, but in local cities such as Hamamatsu and Chongqing.[5] These local cities had traditions of manufacturing and relatively low wages.

The clusters of printed circuit-board (PCB) enterprises are found in the suburban areas of large cities, such as Taipei in Taiwan and Shanghai and Nanjing in China. Since this industry emits pollutants such as lead and halogen, metropolitan areas with strict environmental regulations are not suitable locations for PCB enterprises. Additionally, since large electric and electronics manufacturers have major customers located in urban areas, remote cities are not suitable either. Thus, this industry tends to be located in suburban or semi-urban areas. In the case of Taiwan, it was initiated in the late 1960s by a US–Japan joint venture located in Taoyuan, a county near Taipei. Subsequently, many workers quit the enterprise and established their own ventures in the vicinity. The development of this industry in Taiwan can be characterized as engineer-led since industry leaders were engineers or experienced workers with engineering skills. In China, however, the same industry is merchant-led because, overwhelmingly, private enterprises, the prime mover of development since the early 1990s, were established by salesmen working for PCB enterprises owned by the state or local government. While they recruited engineers from their previous workplaces, they undertook initiatives in the new business both because entrepreneurship with marketing knowledge was a very scarce factor in China and because their products were the simplest type of single-sided circuit-boards.

The machine tool industry in Taiwan was initiated in Taichung City by a Taiwanese airplane mechanic who formerly worked at a Japanese military base during World War II (Sonobe *et al.* 2003). As the industry expanded, its location gradually shifted from the central district to suburban areas of Taichung. Clearly, engineers led the development of this industry and the story of the initial phase is similar to that of the PCB industry in Taoyuan. Like the PCB industry in Jiangsu Province in China, the low-voltage electric machinery industry in Wenzhou in Zhejiang was merchant-led, beginning with the production of simple switches. Similar to the garment town in Jili, Wenzhou used to be a poor rural area with a strong tradition of commerce, in which low-quality merchandise produced by farm households was sold in large cities across the country.[6] Indeed, "made in Wenzhou" was synonymous with inferior products for Chinese consumers. The electric machinery enterprises in Wenzhou had to overcome this poor reputation in order to market their improved products when, from the late 1980s, consumers with rising income levels became increasingly fastidious about product quality. Among them, an enterprise managed by a former merchant was the first to succeed in meeting this challenge.

After completing our Northeast Asian studies, we continued to work in Vietnam, the Philippines, Bangladesh, India, Pakistan, and several sub-Saharan African countries (see Table 3.1).[7] It seems to us that clusters tend to be located in either urban or suburban areas in these countries, presumably due to the poor transportation and communication infrastructure. Like Northeast Asia, the industries are merchant-led if the products are easy to produce but difficult to sell, whereas they are engineer-led if the products are more difficult to produce, such as metalworking and the production of relatively simple machines. By and large, industrial clusters in Southeast and South Asia continue to develop in a manner similar to the Northeast Asian cases, whereas clusters in sub-Saharan Africa stopped growing due to the absence of innovations, even though there are exceptions, as will be discussed in Section 4.

3 An endogenous model of cluster-based industrial development

Despite significant differences in political regimes and stages of economic development among the three Northeast Asian countries, and in production methods and skill requirements across the selected industries, we found extremely similar processes of industrial development across the eight cases. These processes may be referred to as "An East Asian Model of Cluster-Based Industrial Development." We categorized the development processes into three distinct phases: (*a*) initiation, (*b*) quantity expansion, and (*c*) qualitative improvement (see Table 3.2 for a summary of the endogenous model of industrial development). Later, we discovered that the successful development of industrial clusters follows essentially the same pattern outside Northeast Asia, e.g., the garment cluster in Bangladesh (Mottaleb and Sonobe 2010) and the shoe cluster in Ethiopia (Sonobe *et al.* 2010), whereas unsuccessful cases are characterized by failure to enter the quality improvement phase, e.g., the garment cluster in Nairobi (Akoten and Otsuka 2007).

If the production method is simple but it is not easy to sell the products, as in the case of the garment and shoe industries, it is likely to be merchants who

Table 3.2 An endogenous model of cluster-based industrial development

Phase	Prior experience of managers	Education	Innovation, imitation, and productivity growth	Institutions
Initiation	Merchants/engineers	Low	Imitate foreign technology directly or indirectly	Internal production of parts, components, and final products
Quantity expansion	Spin-offs and entry from various fields	Mixed	Imitate imitated technology; stagnant productivity; and declining profitability	Market transactions; division of labor; and formation of industrial cluster
Quality improvement	Second-generation of founders and newcomers with new ideas	Very high	Multi-faceted innovations; exit of many enterprises; and increasing productivity	Reputation and brand names; direct sales; sub-contracts or vertical integration; and emergence of large enterprises

establish new enterprises in the early stage of industrial development. They would do so often in the suburbs of large cities or villages not too far away from large cities, taking advantage of their experience in commercial activities in other industries. If the production method is complicated, engineers tend to be the new entrepreneurs. Once they succeed in the production of new products, often after long trial and error processes, a swarm of imitators appears, as envisaged by Schumpeter (1912) in his theory of economic development.

The imitators are often spin-offs, i.e., those who have worked for the pioneering enterprises and initiated their own endeavors by imitating production methods and products. Since most enterprises produce the same (or almost the same) low-quality products using the same low-quality materials and parts, anonymous market transactions develop, which, in turn reduce the entry barriers for new firms. Indeed, new firms can easily procure all the required materials and parts, sell their products through merchants and recruit workers with desired skills from inside the cluster while investing in indispensable equipment. Because of the low income of consumers, there is a strong demand for low-quality products in the domestic markets, which represents a clear advantage for initiating new business activities in developing countries. As a matter of fact, the founders of a new industry can earn huge profits owing to the large demand for their low-quality products. This attracts the entry of new enterprises.

The active entry results in a geographical concentration of enterprises, which attracts merchants, parts suppliers, skilled workers, and engineers to the industrial cluster. In this way, the industrial cluster is expanded. Note that up to this point, productivity growth is modest or could even be negative, as imitators do not improve production efficiency even though the quantity of production registers impressive growth. Typically, enterprises at this stage are very small in size and use highly labor-intensive production methods.

The active entry sharply increases the supply of products to domestic markets, reducing output prices, hence, the profitability of producing low-quality products. This triggers new competition centered on product improvement and development. At this stage, innovative entrepreneurs begin employing a larger number of engineers and designers to improve their products, using high-quality materials, often developing long-term subcontracts with specific parts suppliers to acquire firm-specific and high-quality parts. The improvement of product quality alone, however, does not ensure high profits for innovative enterprises. In fact, the production costs are now higher than before. In order to differentiate their new high-quality products from low quality products produced by the majority of other enterprises, these entrepreneurs must establish a reputation as high-quality producers and develop their own marketing channels using marketing agents and managing retail shops in order to sell their products directly to consumers and users of their products.

If they are successful, they tend to absorb those enterprises that fail to innovate and let those that remain produce items with the same brand names as those of successful enterprises. Many enterprises which cannot catch up with the innovative ones have to exit the industry. In our observations, it is at this stage that the production efficiency of the industry as a whole visibly improves. The size of successful enterprises grows and many of them begin to export. Another important point we would like to emphasize here is that the industrial cluster sets the stage for an innovation generating quality improvement by attracting a pool of human resources useful for improving the product quality and improving the marketing efficiency of improved products. To realize a new combination of these resources, high-quality entrepreneurial ability is found to be indispensable. In other words, successful entrepreneurs at this stage are highly educated, almost without exception, unlike founders of the industry who are often uneducated but endowed with skills and ambition.

Although our empirical knowledge is insufficient to identity the phases following the quality improvement, our studies suggest that the "eruption" phase often follows. Here we have to note that the pioneering enterprises tend to be located in the center of the cluster and they tend to be more innovative, whereas late-comers are located on the periphery and are often less innovative. Indeed, there are many cases in which educated sons of pioneers succeed in the business and are successful in innovations. Then, the eruption or the relocation of successful enterprises takes place because of their demand for larger factory space, congestion in the cluster, and the expected loss due to imitation by non-innovative enterprises in the cluster. The eruption is "small" or "short-distance," if the subcontracting with parts suppliers or the transactions with merchants is important for the efficient management of innovative enterprises, or if local government sets up new industrial zones nearby. The eruption is "big" or "long-distance" if the major motivation to move is to expand the scale of production to a significant extent and to escape imitation. The eruption can be still bigger if the main purpose of the relocation is to seek cheap labor abroad. The geographic dispersion of industries due to eruption is much more important than generally assumed in the literature.

4 A few examples of cluster-based industrial development

In order to substantiate our preceding arguments, this section presents some supporting evidence. Cases are taken from the garment and motorcycle industries in Japan (Yamamura *et al.* 2003, 2005), and the leather shoe industry in Ethiopia (Sonobe *et al.* 2010).

As was mentioned earlier, in Bingo, the development of the garment industry was led by former local merchants. Their presence remained strong for many years after the industry was initiated before the war. Even as of 1968, the enterprises owned and operated by the former local merchants accounted for 41 percent of the total (see Table 3.3). The spin-offs, i.e., imitators who had earlier worked for other garment enterprises, accounted for 42–56 percent for several decades since the late 1960s. Their entry was prompted by the high entrepreneurial profits earned by their employers, that is, the former local merchants. As the new entry expanded the scale of production in the cluster, the division of labor involving a large number of small subcontractors specializing in particular

Table 3.3 Proportions of enterprise managers by former occupation and formal schooling
in Bingo, Japan, 1968–1998

Year	Number of enterprises	Former occupation (%)			Average schooling (years)		
		Local merchants	Spin-offs	Others	Local merchants	Spin-offs	Others
1968	66	40.9	42.4	16.7	10.2	11.9	9.7
1977	86	32.5	53.4	14.1	11.5	12.0	9.9
1986	89	31.4	56.1	12.5	13.1	12.1	12.0
1998	75	34.6	52.0	13.4	14.1	13.1	13.6

Source: Shin-yo Kokan Jo (1970–1998).

parts of the entire production process was further developed. This development
rested on the community mechanism of contract enforcement, like rural industrialization in other places in Asia (Hayami and Godo 2005; Otsuka 1998, 2007).
Meanwhile, the schooling levels of owner/managers increased, particularly
because many of the successful ex-merchants sent their children to universities,
who later took over their fathers' businesses. It was these educated entrepreneurs
who initiated innovations.

The former local merchants were not only the first to introduce the factory
production system to the Bingo area but also the first to deal directly with large
urban retailers such as department stores, when indirect transactions with small
retailers through local merchants were common practice. Direct transactions
with urban retailers became profitable for the former local merchants because
they began producing higher quality, differentiated products (see Table 3.4).
According to our interviews, the quality of garment products in Bingo improved
in the 1970s, even though the number of enterprises remained largely unchanged.
In general, increases in direct transactions are associated with quality improvement and attempts to establish brand names. Innovative entrepreneurs also relo-
cated their production base, first, to Kyushu where wages were somewhat lower,

Table 3.4 Proportions of direct transactions and sale revenue by location (%) in Bingo,
Japan, 1968–1998[a]

	Direct transaction ratio[a]	Revenue generated by location		
		Bingo	Kyushu	Abroad
1968	24	74	25	1
1982/1986	60	51	39	10
1996/1998	74	29	23	48

Source: authors' survey.

Note
a Proportion of direct transactions with non-local merchants, as opposed to transactions through
local merchants.

and then abroad, mainly to China, where wages were definitely lower than in Bingo. This industrial relocation is reminiscent of the product cycle proposed by Vernon (1966).

Figure 3.1a shows the changes in the number of motorcycle enterprises in Japan in the period 1946–1964. Clearly the number of enterprises increased sharply up until the early 1950s, because of the sizable entry of new enterprises. Roughly speaking, the annual growth rate of the total number of motorcycles produced was as high as 100 percent in the early 1950s. According to Figure 3.1b, the engine quality index, computed by using the formula developed by Taylor (1960), did not rise until 1953, indicating that this period corresponded to the quantity expansion phase. After the mid-1950s, however, the quality index rose steadily and a number of enterprises that used lower-quality engines exited. While the growth rate of production decreased to less than 50 percent per year, the average size of the surviving enterprises grew to approximately ten times their original size in the six-year period in the late 1950s. Genuine innovator, Soichiro Honda, the founder of the Honda Motor Co., played a key role in this quality improvement phase. Indeed, Hamamatsu City, where Honda was originally located, became the leading cluster of the industry, dominating the clusters in Tokyo and Nagoya. Honda then "erupted" to Suzuka City, far from Hamamatsu, to begin the vertically integrated mass production of high-quality products in huge factories in the new production base.

It may be surprising to learn that the shoe industry in Ethiopia, which is one of the poorest countries in sub-Saharan Africa, has been growing very rapidly. There are at least 1,000 and possibly nearly 2,000 informal small shoe workshops in downtown Addis Ababa. Out of such an informal sector, more than a few enterprises have become large, with the employment of hundreds of workers

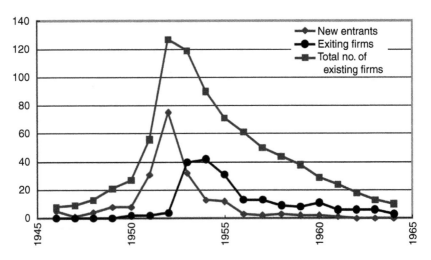

Figure 3.1a Development of the motorcycle industry in Japan, 1945–1965: changes in the number of motorcycle enterprises.

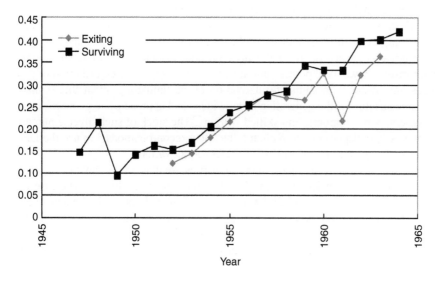

Figure 3.1b Development of the motorcycle industry in Japan, 1945–1965: improvement of quality index of motorcycle engines.

operating their new factories in industrial zones. Their owners are often the adult children of the shoe producers and merchants, well-educated and highly motivated. We believe that successful development of these enterprises in Ethiopia was due importantly to the repeated visits of Ethiopian entrepreneurs to Italy to learn designs, production methods, and marketing skills (Sonobe *et al.* 2010). As a result, they often use high-quality imported materials, establish brand names, and operate their own retail shops in downtown locations. Having overcome the so-called "China shock," which occurred due to massive imports of cheap Chinese shoes around 2000, these leading enterprises now export their products to Italy and other European countries. It is hard to distinguish this case from the many successful cases of cluster-based industrial development widely observed in Asia.

5 Implications for developing countries and the future of the Japanese economy

In our view, industrial clusters prosper by taking advantage of the geographic proximity that reduces the transaction costs between manufacturers (e.g., parts suppliers and assemblers) and between manufacturers and merchants. In other words, the cluster helps markets work by reducing the transactions costs arising from moral hazard and other opportunistic behavior. Thus, the industrial cluster is particularly important in industries in which the division of labor among enterprises is advantageous, e.g., the automobile, motorcycle, machinery, electric, and electronics industries, and industries in which marketing is the key to the success in business, such as the garment and shoe industries. Although enterprises within an industrial cluster tend to be small and subject to scale diseconomies in many developing countries, the industrial cluster as a whole may be characterized by scale advantages arising from the division and specialization of labor among enterprises. As we have pointed out above, another important contribution of the industrial cluster is to stimulate innovation by accumulating invaluable human resources useful for the generation of new ideas and approaches, e.g., merchants, designers, parts suppliers, and skilled workers. The stock of such diverse human resources is indispensable in realizing the "new recombinations," to use the language of Joseph Schumpeter (1912) to refer to innovations.

Because of these advantages, many industries are clustered in both developed and developing countries. A major defect of the industrial cluster is the ease of imitation that reduces the incentive to innovate.[8] Indeed, the social benefit of an innovation exceeds the private benefit of an innovator by the amount of benefits captured by imitators. Thus, we expect that, although the cluster is uniquely suited for innovation, the amount of innovation actually generated is expected to fall short of the social optimum.

A critical question to examine is why industrial clusters in Asia in general have developed so successfully. Like China over the last 28 years, the Japanese economy had grown at a rate of about 10 percent per year during the "miraculous growth period" from the late 1950s to the early 1970s. The growth rates of the Taiwanese economy and that of contemporary China have been no less rapid than Japan's. Besides rapid economic growth, there are more similarities than dissimilarities in the patterns of industrial development among the three countries. In our view, the successful imitation and assimilation of foreign technologies, the formation of geographically dense industrial clusters consisting of a large number of small enterprises producing similar and related products, and the advent of multi-faceted innovations leading to a great leap forward in the industrial structures, are three of the important ingredients of the East Asian model of cluster-based industrial development.

In all likelihood, learning from the successful experience of other countries is also the key to the success in low-income developing countries, even though it is extremely difficult to quantify this effect. During our surveys, we repeatedly heard that Taiwanese enterprise managers learned a great deal from the Japanese experience. Similarly, it seems obvious to us that enterprise managers in China have learned many lessons from both the Taiwanese and the Japanese experiences. While it is difficult to provide answers to the question of why Japan has been successful in the transition from the quantity expansion to the quality improvement phases in much earlier years, it seems clear that the successful development of Japanese industries became the model for industrial development in other East Asian countries.

We believe that the successful development of the shoe industry in Ethiopia was due primarily to the repeated visits of Ethiopian entrepreneurs to Italy to learn designs, production methods, and marketing skills (Sonobe *et al*. 2010). We were also told by producers of knitwear in the rural cluster of northern

Vietnam that visiting China was critically important to improving their techno-logy and management. The remarkable success of the development of the huge garment cluster in Dhaka, Bangladesh owes much to the transfer of technology and management know-how from South Korea and also, in more recent years, from China (Mottaleb and Sonobe 2010). The cases of the garment and motor-cycle industries in Japan, examined by Sonobe and Otsuka (2006), are two of the early examples of successful industrial development based on foreign technolo-gies in post-war Japan.

Roughly 20 cases of the industrial clusters we have studied so far did not differ much in the process of "quantity expansion," which led to the formation of industrial clusters consisting of small enterprises. Setting up industrial zones by the government is useful and common in East Asia. In China, marketplaces set up by the local governments played an important role in the improvement of marketing efficiency. In Taiwan and Japan, the same purpose was achieved by densely clustered wholesalers.

Multi-faceted innovations were commonly implemented with success by highly educated entrepreneurs in industrial clusters, which have led to the "quality improvement" phase. In other words, the ample supply of entrepreneur-ship leads to the introduction of improved production methods, the initiation of the use of brand names for the sake of strengthening the reputation of enter-prises, the development of new marketing channels, and the establishment of long-term subcontracting systems in East Asia.

In conclusion, we would like to propose that the Japanese government should actively support the development of industrial clusters in low-income countries based on its own experience and the similarly successful experiences of other East Asian countries. More specifically, the Japanese government should offer training programs or establish vocational schools in low-income countries in order to stimulate multi-faceted innovations based on more advanced but "neigh-boring" foreign technologies and management practices. Once multi-faceted innovations begin taking place, it makes sense to support the establishment of industrial zones and the provision of cheap credit for those innovative enterprises which can profitably utilize new space and subsidized credit.

Our arguments for the development of industrial clusters have relevance for the revitalization of the current Japanese economy, insofar as industrial clusters confer a number of advantages. We must recognize, however, that Japan needs to develop advanced industrial clusters based on the development of its own technologies, because there is no longer ample opportunity for Japan to learn much from abroad. Note that unlike the case of developing countries, such industrial clusters are of necessity scientist-led, as in Silicon Valley, and the comparative advantage of the Japanese economy *potentially* lies in scientific, knowledge-intensive industries. In order to do so, therefore, the Japanese government must invest in scientific research and the establishment of internationally competitive graduate schools which are capable of generating the next generation of entrepreneurs who can compete internationally. Unless and until such investments are made and bear fruit, the Japanese economy will continue to stagnate in years to come.

Notes

1 Recently the importance of industrial clusters in developing countries is clearly recognized by the World Bank (2008).
2 Innovation here should not be understood as a major technological change leading to "construction destruction," but rather as minor technological and managerial improvements that lead to substantial improvements in the enterprise's performance.
3 For the machinery industry, we selected the machine tool industry in Taiwan and the low-voltage electric machinery industry in China. We decided not to choose the machine tool industry in China, because it is dominated by state-owned enterprises (Murakami *et al.* 1996; Otsuka *et al.* 1998), thus precluding us from observing the evolutionary process of industrial development guided by market forces.
4 A possible exception is the motorcycle industry in Chongqing, which was dominated by state-owned enterprises in the earlier period. Since the mid-1990s, however, the accelerated growth of this industry was achieved by private as well as privatized former state-owned enterprises.
5 In the late 1940s and early 1950s in Japan, motorcycle clusters were also found in Tokyo and Nagoya, but they declined rapidly compared with Hamamatsu.
6 According to our inquiries into the development of the garment cluster in Wenzhou, its development pattern is surprisingly similar to that in Jili, even though Jili's development lagged behind Wenzhou's.
7 We failed to collect reliable data in Delhi, and, therefore, we gave up this case study. On the other hand, we have started an interesting case study in Dar es Salaam in Tanzania.
8 As is aptly pointed out by Marshall (1920), the ease of imitation or information spillover is also a main advantage of industrial clusters, once innovations are introduced.

References

Akoten, J. and Otsuka, K. (2007) "From Tailors to Mini-Manufacturers: The Role of Traders in the Transformation of Garment Enterprises in Kenya." *Journal of African Economies* 16(4), pp. 564–595.
Hayami, Y. and Godo, Y. (2005) *Development Economics: From the Poverty to the Wealth of Nations*, Oxford: Oxford University Press.
Krugman, P. (1991) *Geography and Trade*, Cambridge, MA: MIT Press.
Marshall, A. (1920) *Principles of Economics*, London: Macmillan.
Mottaleb, K.A. and Sonobe, T. (2010) "An Inquiry into the Rapid Growth of the Knitwear Industry in Bangladesh," mimeo. Tokyo: Foundation for Advanced Studies on International Development.
Murakami, N., Liu, D., and Otsuka, K. (1996) "Market Reform, Division of Labor, and Increasing Advantage of Small-Scale Enterprises: The Case of the Machine Tool Industry in China." *Journal of Comparative Economics* 23(3), pp. 256–277.
Nam, V.H., Sonobe, T., and Otsuka, K. (2009) "An Inquiry into the Transformation Process of Village-based Industrial Clusters: The Case of an Iron and Steel Cluster in Northern Vietnam." *Journal of Comparative Economics* 37(4), pp. 568–581.
Nam, V.H., Sonobe, T., and Otsuka, K. (2010) "An Inquiry into the Development Process of Village Industries: The Case of a Knitwear Cluster in Northern Vietnam." *Journal of Development Studies* 46(2), pp. 312–330.
Otsuka, K. (1998) "Rural Industrialization in East Asia." In Y. Hayami and M. Aoki (eds.), *The Institutional Foundations of East Asian Economic Development*, London: Macmillan.

Otsuka, K. (2007) "Rural Industrialization in East Asia: What Influences its Nature and Development." In S. Haggblade, P. Hazell and T. Reardon (eds.), *Transforming Rural Nonfarm Economy*, Baltimore, MD: Johns Hopkins University Press.

Otsuka, K., Liu, D., and Murakami, N. (1998) *Industrial Reform in China: Past Performance and Future Prospects*, Oxford: Clarendon Press.

Piore, M.J. and Sable, C.F. (1984) *The Second Industrial Divide: Possibility for Prosperity*, New York, NY: Basic Books.

Porter, M.E. (1990) *The Competitive Advantage of Nations*, Basingstoke: Macmillan.

Ruan, J. and Zhang, X. (2009) "Finance and Cluster-Based Industrial Development in China." *Economic Development and Cultural Change* 58(1), pp. 143–164.

Saxenian, A. (1994) *Regional Advantage: Culture and Competition in Silicon Valley and Route 128*, Cambridge, MA: Harvard University Press.

Schmitz, H. and Nadvi, K. (1999) "Clustering and Industrialization." *World Development* 27(9), pp. 1503–1514.

Schumpeter, J.A. (1912) *The Theory of Economic Development*, New York: Oxford University Press.

Sonobe, T., and Otsuka, K. (2006) *Cluster-Based Industrial Development: An East Asian Model*, Hampshire: Palgrave Macmillan.

Sonobe, T., Akoten, J., and Otsuka, K. (2010) "An Exploration into the Successful Development of the Leather Shoe Industry in Ethiopia." *Review of Development Economics* 14(1), pp. 89–105.

Sonobe, T., Hu, D., and Otsuka, K. (2004) "From Inferior to Superior Products: An Inquiry into the Wenzhou Model of Industrial Development in China." *Journal of Comparative Economics* 32(3), pp. 542–563.

Sonobe, T., Kawakami, M., and Otsuka, K. (2003) "Changing Role of Innovation and Imitation in Development: The Case of the Machine Tool Industry in Taiwan." *Economic Development and Cultural Change* 52(1), pp. 103–128.

Taylor, C.F. (1960) *The Internal Combination Engine in Theory and Practice*, New York: Technology Press of MIT and John Wiley and Sons.

Vernon, R. (1966) "International Investment and International Trade in Product Cycle." *Quarterly Journal of Economics* 80(2), pp. 197–207.

Whittaker, D.H. (1997) *Small Firms in the Japanese Economy*, Cambridge: Cambridge University Press.

World Bank (2008) *World Development Report 2009: Reshaping Economic Geography*, Washington, DC: World Bank.

Yamamura, E., Sonobe, T., and Otsuka, K. (2003) "Human Capital, Cluster Formation, and International Relocation: The Case of the Garment Industry in Japan." *Journal of Economic Geography* 3(1), pp. 37–56.

Yamamura, E., Sonobe, T., and Otsuka, K. (2005) "Time Paths in Innovation, Imitation, and Growth: The Case of the Motorcycle Industry in Postwar Japan." *Journal of Evolutionary Economics* 15(2), pp. 169–186.

4 Financial systems and economic development

The case in Japan

Yasuhiro Arikawa

1 Introduction

In this chapter, we examine the effects of the financial system on Japanese economic development after World War II. The Japanese financial system, which gives banks a more prominent role than their counterparts in other countries, has been categorized as a "bank-centered" financial system, while the financial system based on the stock or bond market, such as in the United States or United Kingdom, is categorized as a "market-based" financial system (Allen and Gale 2000).[1]

There is a huge volume of research which investigates the role of the financial system in the economic development of Japan. In the typical point of view, during the rapid growth period, the banking sector in Japan played an active role not only in supplying funds to client firms but also in being engaged in ex-ante and ex-post monitoring to discipline top management (Aoki *et al.* 1994). Banks which have a close relationship with borrowing firms, which are called "main banks," were charged with the task of supplying new money for the investment projects of clients, and, through intensive monitoring, mitigated asymmetric information problems between lenders and borrowers (Hoshi *et al.* 1991). Main banks generally did not intervene in the management of well-performing borrowers, although, in times of financial distress, they dispatched representatives to troubled clients, and on occasion took over their boards and assumed the initiative in restructuring efforts.

This bank–firm relationship in Japan was affected remarkably by the fall of asset prices in the early 1990s, which, in turn, caused the non-performing loan problem in the banking sector. The financial difficulties that beset the banks themselves put bank–firm relationships under tremendous stress. The banking crisis of the 1990s not only placed financial constraints on bank-dependent firms (Kang and Stultz 2000) but also gave banks an incentive to engage in the "evergreening" of old loans to nearly insolvent firms to improve their own balance sheets (Peek and Rosengren 2005). Along with the development of the financial crisis, the darker aspects of the bank-centered financial system overshadowed the brighter aspects observed until the 1970s or early 1980s.

The purpose of this chapter is to re-examine the cost and benefits of the bank-centered financial system in Japan after World War II. Based on Arikawa (2011), we first investigate the cash flow sensitivity for Japanese firms in the rapid growth period from the late 1960s to the mid-1970s to determine whether the stable bank–firm relationship, which is one of the characteristics of a bank-centered financial system, helps to reduce the costly cash savings of Japanese firms by mitigating their financial constraint.

We show that, in the rapid growth period (1965–1975), young firms with less reputation in the financial market were under financial constraint, while we find no evidence that large Japanese firms faced financial constraints in the 1980s. Further, in the rapid growth period, young firms with stable bank–firm relationships reduced their cash savings from their current cash flow even if they faced a financial constraint, while those without such relationships with banks saved more cash from their cash flow under severe financial constraint. In the 1980s, the stable bank–firm relationship had no influence on the cash policy of the sample firms regardless of the accessibility of the public bond market. At least, for the large Japanese firms, the stable bank–firm relationship reduced its importance in the 1980s.

Second, we discuss the cost of a bank-centered financial system. Referring to the growing literature on this topic such as Arikawa and Miyajima (2007), that focuses on whether main banks encourage corporate restructuring or discourage profitable projects that are slow to pay off, we show that a high bank dependence has encouraged corporate restructuring, while the high commitment of a stable bank–firm relationship clearly became an impediment to creative destruction in the late 1990s by reducing the credibility of the threat to the termination of loans. What is unique in the bank–firm relationships of the late 1990s is that bank lending imposed a hard budget constraint on firms, while the high main-bank commitment imposed a soft budget constraint on firms with poor performance.

This chapter is organized as follows: Section 2 explains the basic framework for understanding the financial system: arm's length and relationship finance. Section 3 examines the role of close bank–firm relations with respect to financial constraints in the high growth period. Section 4 addresses the role of close bank–firm relations in the restructuring of firms with declining profits. In Section 5, we discuss the relation between the financial system and "the lost decade" in Japan. The final section provides conclusions.

2 Arm's-length finance and relationship finance

Merton (1995) points out six core functions of a financial system:

1   A financial system provides a payment system for the exchange of goods and services.
2   A financial system provides a mechanism for the pooling of funds to undertake large-scale indivisible enterprises.
3   A financial system provides a way to transfer economic resources through time and across geographic regions and industries.
4   A financial system provides a way to manage uncertainty and control risk.
5   A financial system provides price information that helps coordinate decentralized decision-making in various sectors of the economy.

6   A financial system provides a way to deal with the asymmetric information and incentive problems when one party in a financial transaction has information that the other party does not.

Except for the first function (providing a payments system), the level of economic development in a country determines which factor among the remaining five requires priority for designing a financial system, and the difference among these priorities for each country leads to a diversity of financial systems globally.

The basic framework for comparing financial systems is found in the system of arm's-length finance compared to the system of relationship finance (Allen and Gale 2000). In arm's-length finance, the price mechanism plays a more important role compared with relationship finance, and this requires security issuing (or borrowing) firms to disclose more precise financial information in the market.

It is not guaranteed, however, that firms disclose the required information voluntarily. Grossman and Hart (1980) and Zingales (2009) show that a firm voluntarily discloses all its information if, and only *if*, three assumptions are satisfied: (*a*) investors know that firms have the information; (*b*) firms cannot lie; and (*c*) disclosure is costless. If one of these assumptions is violated, voluntary disclosure is less than complete, and there is a basis to argue in favor of mandatory disclosure.

Under relationship finance, most of the information produced by the external lender is private and the price of the security issued by the firm does not incorporate that information (Ikeo 2006). It should be noted that making a contract based on private information or transferring it to another party is difficult (Uchida 2008). If private information is easily transferred, lenders lose incentive to produce the information because of the free-rider problem. This gives the provider of financial resources greater bargaining power over financing firms in the case of relationship finance.

Furthermore, within relationship finance, investors or lenders have an incentive to make long-term commitments with firms since they pay fixed costs for information in the initial stage. This makes it possible for them to continue financing even though financing firms face financial distress temporally, and allows them to smooth the risk inter-temporally (Allen and Gale 2000).

After World War II, the bank-centered financial system with the characteristics of relationship finance, which is referred to as the "main-bank system," was adopted in Japan. Since the aggregate savings of households in Japan at that time was not enough to supply financial resources directly to firms using the security market (Ikeo 2006; Ogawa 2009), it was more efficient for the Japanese economy to concentrate individual savings on the banking sector and distribute those savings to borrowing firms. Given this mechanism, the banking sector faced systemic risk; therefore, the regulation of the interest rate and entry to the banking sector were introduced to provide enough rents to existing banks to absorb that risk.

It should be noted that the bank-centered financial system does not exclude other financial resources except bank borrowing. In Japan, the stock markets and bond markets were established before World War II, and trade credit and retained earnings have been regarded as important financial resources. Nevertheless, the high dependence on retained earnings as a financial resource does not mean that bank borrowing played a less important role in the economy. The choice between retained earnings and other financing options, including bank borrowing, are not independent of one another, and the availability of outside financing resources determines the level of retained earnings. We will discuss this problem in the next section.

While Japan and Germany are famous for their adoption of the relationship-based financial system, the medium and small sized firm lending in the United States is also regarded as an example of relationship finance (Ono 2007). In Japan, less than 10 percent of small and medium sized enterprises (SMEs), hiring more than 100 employees, receive finances from only one bank, while more than 80 percent of SMEs in the United States trade with only one bank. Furthermore, private equity such as venture capital or buyout funds engage in information production and keep monitoring the investing firm. This is also regarded as an example of relationship finance.

3 The benefits of relationship finance[2]

In this section, we examine the effects of relationship finance, or the main bank system, on the financial constraints of Japanese firms during the rapid growth period. In a world where no informational problem exists, a firm's investment decisions would not be affected by a financial decision. However, asymmetric information problems between investors and managers drive a wedge between the cost of internal and external funds. If an outside investor has less information about a firm's assets or the profitability of a project than the internal manager, they demand a premium to invest in it. Therefore, if an investment project requires more than available internal funds, a firm faces high capital costs and, consequently, the actual investment level will be below the optimal level. Given this setting, Myers and Majluf (1984) suggest that cash holdings are beneficial because they enable firms to finance the profitable investments that would have been given up due to the more costly external funds. Fazzari, Hubbard and Petersen (1988) (hereafter FHP), then propose that when firms face financing constraints, investment spending varies with the availability of internal funds, rather than just the availability of positive net present value projects.

Based on the work of FHP, Hoshi *et al.* (1991), presented empirical evidence concerning the role of the main-bank for mitigating the asymmetric information problem concerning the investment. They show that investment is less sensitive to measures of liquidity for *Keiretsu* firms than for independent firms. They use the sample covering the period 1977–1982, and claim that the close bank relationship enjoyed by group firms is likely to mitigate the information problem of Japanese firms for financing the capital expenditure.

Some studies, however, cast doubt on the strategy of using cash flow sensitivity to investment for identifying financially constrained firms from both theoretical and empirical points of view. Theoretically, Kaplan and Zingales (1997) point out that cash flow sensitivity to investment does not necessarily mean the existence of a financial constraint just by the fact that the cash flow sensitivity is positive. Empirically, Alti (2003) shows that the cross-sectional patterns reported by FHP can be consistent with a model with a financially unconstrained situation because cash flow contains information about a firm's investment opportunity.

Almeida *et al.* (2004) argue that the link between financial constraints and a firm's demand for liquidity can be used to identify whether financial constraint is one of the determinants of firm behavior. In their model, firms anticipating a financial constraint in the next period respond to those potential constraints by reserving cash in this period. However, having cash in their balance sheet is costly because higher cash savings require a reduction in current, profitable investment opportunities. Firms under financial constraint choose their optimal cash holdings to balance the profitability of future and current investment opportunities. They claim that the financially constrained firm increases its cash holdings in response to its positive cash flow. In contrast, a firm's cash policy is irrelevant in the absence of financial constraints, and a firm should display no such systematic behavior in managing liquidity. Since cash is a financial variable, it is difficult to argue that the explanatory power of cash flow over cash policy could be ascribed to its ability to forecast future investment demands.

Using this methodology, Arikawa (2011) examines the benefit of the Japanese relationship-based financial system during the rapid growth period. As Hoshi and Kashyap (2001) point out, most of the work concerning the benefit and cost of the main-bank system in Japan relates to the period from the late 1970s to the 1990s. For example, the sample period of Pinkowitz and Williamson (2001) covers 1975–1995, and that of Hoshi *et al.* (1991) is 1977–1982. On the other hand, the main-bank system emerged and matured from the early 1950s to the mid-1970s (Hoshi and Kashyap 2001). By investigating the cash flow sensitivity to cash for Japanese firms in the rapid growth period from the late 1960s to the mid-1970s and from the late 1980s to the early 1990s, we examine the following questions: (*a*) Were Japanese large firms under financial constraint or not during the rapid growth period? What about during the 1980s? (*b*) Did the close bank–firm relationship help to reduce the costly cash savings of the Japanese firms, or rather increase the cash holdings to provide rents to banks?

To confirm whether the sensitivity of cash flow to cash is larger for a firm with severe financial friction, sample firms can be separated according to a priori measures of the financial constraint following the idea of Hubbard *et al.* (1995). For an analysis of the period from the 1960s to the 1970s, the sample is separated into two groups according to whether or not a firm was listed in 1961. The second section of TSE was established in 1961, and the number of listed firms increased after this year. Using these criteria means that relatively younger firms in the high growth period are included as sample firms. It is assumed that firms which had already been listed in TSE in 1961 (hereafter old firms) had a relatively higher reputation concerning their credibility in the market, and these firms faced less serious information asymmetry problems with investors and banks during this period. On the contrary, the firms listed after 1961 (hereafter young firms) are supposed to be the firms faced with more severe financial constraints because they are not well known.

For the investigation of the cash policy in the 1980s, sample firms were separated into two groups, whether qualified to issue secured bonds or not. Because of the deregulation in the bond market, a certain number of firms which passed the qualification could issue public bonds in the 1980s. Sample firms that had no access to public bonds were regarded as financially constrained, while the firms with access to the bond market faced less serious financial constraints.

Using the above criteria, Arikawa (2011) first examined whether young firms which are assumed to be financially constrained increased their stock of cash holdings in response to the positive change in the current cash flow in the rapid growth period. In contrast, we do not anticipate a positive relationship between the current cash flow and the annual change in cash holdings for old firms. Similarly, we can check as to whether or not the cash flow sensitivity to cash is positive or not for the firm with access to the bond market in the 1980s.

Given the argument about the relationship between the firm's financial constraint and cash policy, we examine the impact of a close bank–firm relationship on the financial constraint. If the main bank which has a long-term relationship with the borrowing firm plays a significant role in mitigating the asymmetric information problems in Japanese corporate finance, we anticipate the cash flow sensitivity of cash to be lower for the firm with a stable main-bank relationship relative to the firm without such a relationship with banks. We test this hypothesis using the samples 1966–1975 and 1987–1992.

Figure 4.1 shows the time series changes of the median of the cash holdings ratio by sample firms. It is clear that the cash holdings ratio is higher from the 1950s to the mid-1970s and decreases after that. This is consistent with the results of Pinkowitz and Williamson (2001) that Japanese large banks had larger monopoly power over the client firms and were forced to save cash until the end of the 1970s because the capital market was repressed by regulation.

Arikawa (2010) examines whether the increase in the current cash flow leads to an increase in the cash stock on the balance sheet, using multivariate analysis.[3] Overall, the firms listed after 1961 (young firms) display a significantly positive sensitivity of cash to cash flow, while the firms listed before 1961 (old firms) show insignificant cash to cash flow sensitivities when we use the samples 1966–1975. The sensitivity of young firms is statistically significant at the 1 percent level, while old firms show insignificant cash to cash flow sensitivity. This supports the hypothesis that old firms faced less financial constraints, while young firms were under financial constraints during the high growth period.

When we use the sample 1987–1992, the coefficient of the cash flow for the firms with access to public bonds (unconstrained firms) shows insignificant sensitivity of cash to cash flow, while that of the firms without access to the bond market (constrained firms) also show insignificant cash to cash flow sensitivities. Even firms without access to the bond market did not face financial constraints in the 1980s. Since sample firms were relatively large and mature in this period, they had enough credibility to finance their needs from banks or private bonds.

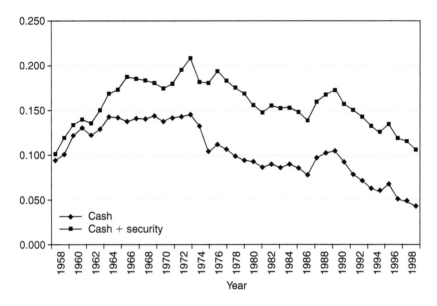

Figure 4.1 The change of cash holdings from 1958 to 1998.

The above results show that young firms with less reputation in the financial markets were under financial constraint during the rapid growth era. Then, did the close bank relationship (or main-bank) mitigate the financial constraint problem for Japanese firms? To investigate the role of the main-bank relationship for the cash policy, Arikawa (2010) constructs a dummy variable, MB, equal to one if a firm's main bank is the same as the one last year, its largest lender and also its top shareholder among banks, and others equal to zero.[4]

The summary of the results from the rapid growth period is shown in the first and second columns of Table 4.1. In the rapid growth period, young firms with less reputation in the financial market were under financial constraint. For the effect of the main-bank relationship, the coefficient of the interaction term between the MB dummy and cash flow is insignificant for old firms. This is not surprising because old firms faced less financial constraint during this period. The coefficient of the interaction term between the MB dummy and the cash flow for younger firms is, to the contrary, significantly negative during this period. Young firms with a stable bank–firm relationship reduced their cash savings from the current cash flow even if they faced a financial constraint, while those without a stable bank–firm relationship saved more cash from the cash flow during severe financial constraints. Since younger firms faced a more severe financial constraint, they tried to avoid missing profitable investment opportunities due to the lack of financial resources, by saving part of their cash flow as internal funds. A stable bank–firm relationship made it possible for these firms to reduce this unprofitable cash savings because firms could expect their stable liquidity supply from the main bank if they needed it in the future.

Table 4.1 Financial constraint and bank–firm relationship

Model	1	2	3	4
	Old Firm	Young Firm	Access	No-Access
Cash Flow	0.047	0.192**	0.050	0.637
	0.244	0.089	0.795	0.631
Cash Flow × MB	0.037	−0.228*	0.529	−0.398
	0.319	0.118	0.742	0.643
q	−0.059	0.011	−0.002	0.012
	0.039	0.013	0.031	0.025
Size	0.077*	0.014	0.294***	0.094
	0.042	0.013	0.113	0.078
R²	0.0507	0.0268	0.0563	0.0249
NOB	2,059	1,084	1,364	547

Source: Arikawa (2011).

Notes
***, ** and * denote coefficients significant at the 1, 5, and 10 percent levels, respectively.
In the results (1) and (2), we use the listed companies on the TSE from 1966 to 1975 fiscal year as the sample. In the result (3) and (4), we use the listed companies on the TSE from 1987 to 1992 fiscal year as the sample. We use the fixed-effect model. The dependent variable is the annual change-in holdings of cash to lagged total assets. Cash Flow is the ratio of the after-tax profit and depreciation(minus dividend) to lagged total asset. q is the sum of market capitalization and book alue of debt divided by book value of asset. Size is the natural log of a firm's total. MB is the dummy variable equal to 1 if the firm has the stable main bank relationship, and otherwise zero. Firms which had already listed in TSE in 1961 are defined as Old Firm, and firms which listed in TSE after 1961 are defined as Young Firm. Sample firms are defined as Access if they are qualified to issue secured bond. Sample firms are defined as No-Access if they are not qualified to issue secured bond.

The summary of results using the samples from the late 1980s to early 1990s is shown in the third and fourth columns of Table 4.1. Not surprisingly, the coefficient of the interaction term between the MB dummy and cash flow is insignificant for all specifications. This means the stable main-bank relationship did not have any influence on the cash policy of the sample firms regardless of the accessibility to the public bond market. For the large Japanese firms, the importance of the stable bank–firm relationship lost its importance in the 1980s.

4 The cost of relationship finance

In this section we discuss the cost of relationship finance, especially focusing on banks lending to severely impaired firms in the 1990s. What is unique in the main-bank system is the existence of an output level where the banks bail out borrowers in financial distress because the rents that banks can extract from borrowers exceed the total costs of rescuing them (Aoki 2001).

When this corporate governance mechanism works well, the efforts of insiders of the firm (managers or workers), increase because they have strong incentives to defend themselves against bank intervention. Hoshi *et al.* (1990) have pioneered this field by documenting that firms with close main-bank ties maintained investment levels comparable to independent firms even when the firms faced financial distress during the structural adjustment period (1978–1985). Until the 1980s, the Japanese banking system was supported by regulations for new entry, interest rates on deposits, and market financing (bond issuance). These regulations guaranteed banks the monopolistic rents that gave them the incentive to bail out distressed firms with the expectation that they would be able to impose higher interest rates in the future (Petersen and Rajan 1995).[5, 6]

Nevertheless, there exist commitment problems in this system. If the threat of termination were not credible, it would be highly plausible that borrowers adopt moral hazard behaviors with the expectation of being rescued by banks. This leads to over-investment problems for the borrowing firms.

Furthermore, in the 1990s, Japanese banks had an incentive to dress up their balance sheets by lending to insolvent borrowers. Suppose that a bank's balance sheet is deteriorating and the bank is committed to an unprofitable borrower; it may decide to supply additional lending to a borrower not based on the possibility of its future reconstruction, but to dress up a non-performing loan to meet capital requirements under the Basel Accord. This perverse incentive for banks is stronger if the bank is the main bank of the client firm because loans from the main bank are supposedly subordinated to other loans.

Peek and Rosengren (2005) find that banks increased credit to poorly performing firms between 1993 and 1999, and main banks were more likely to lend to these firms than other banks. They also show that credit misallocation was more frequent when the banks' balance sheet was weak. Peek (2009) shows that increases in main-bank loans were associated with improved firm performance subsequent to entering distress during the 1980s. However, not only did that pattern disappear during the post-bubble period, but also, increased main bank loans were associated with a deterioration in operating income during the late 1990s and early 2000s.

Arikawa and Miyajima (2007) investigated whether firms with close main-bank ties implemented necessary corporate restructuring when they faced serious performance declines. In the estimation equation, the dependent variable was the percentage change in employment. Following Kang and Shivdasani (1997), they used a dummy variable as a proxy for the necessity of corporate restructuring.[7] We define a firm as facing the need to restructure if this dummy variable equals one. The ratios of employment reduction, leverage, bank dependence and main-bank loan concentration are much larger for the firm facing the need to restructure.[8]

Then, Arikawa and Miyajima (2007) find, first, that leverage has a negative effect on employment. This implies that the firm facing a higher bankruptcy risk had an incentive to implement necessary corporate restructuring. Second, among firms facing a serious need to restructure, bank dependence was associated with rapid employment adjustment, while the high concentration of borrowing from main banks was associated with slow employment adjustment.

In relationship finance, main banks are expected to help firms avoid inefficient corporate restructuring, while fostering appropriate discipline for firms facing serious earnings declines. However, in the 1990s, main banks urged some firms to reduce employment, while allowing firms facing larger performance declines to delay necessary restructuring if their commitment to these firms was large.

5 Financial systems and financial crisis

In this section, we discuss the key connection between relationship finance or the main-bank system and "the lost decade of the Japanese economy." Combining the results of previous literature, we find first that misdirected bank lending played an important role in prolonging the Japanese macroeconomic stagnation. Caballero *et al.* (2008) investigated the widespread practice of Japanese banks continuing to lend to otherwise insolvent firms. By supporting unprofitable borrowers, called "zombie" firms, the banks allowed them to distort competition throughout the rest of the economy. The increase in the number of zombie firms was associated with falling levels of aggregate restructuring, with job creation especially depressed in the sectors with the most zombie firms. The rise in the number of zombie firms also lowered productivity at the industry level, and investment and employment growth in healthy firms also fell as the percentage of zombies in their industry rose.

Second, as the banking crisis took its toll on banks, their ability to fund their customers was impaired, restraining investment by firms that had relied heavily on their main banks for credit. When banks wanted to call in a nonperforming loan, they were likely to have to write off existing capital, which in turn pushed them up against minimum capital levels. For example, Gibson (1995), using data of the late 1990s finds that firms with the lowest rated main banks invested substantially less than firms with higher rated main banks. Ito and Sasaki (2002) show that banks with lower capital ratios tended to issue more subordinated debt and also reduce lending. This literature demonstrates credit contraction in the 1990s because the banking sector had to keep the risk-based capital ratio excessively high. Especially SMEs which depend for most of their financial resources on banks, faced significant loan contraction when the health of their main bank was impaired (Fukuda *et al.* 2007). Furthermore, commercial land prices fell by roughly 50 percent after their 1992 peak during the next ten years. This shock so impaired collateral values that the banking sector reduced its lending for firms' investment. For example, Gan, (2007) found that a 10 percent decline of land price led to the reduction of investments by 0.8 percent.

As we discussed in Section 3, the zombie lending problem is closely related to the characteristics of relationship finance. The long-term commitment between banks and borrowing firms gives an incentive to lend to otherwise insolvent firms under the name of bail-out.[9] On the other hand; a "credit crunch" happens whether a financial system is relationship based or arm's length. For example, Ivashina and Scharfstein (2008) point out that banks that were in a better position to attract deposits were likely less credit constrained and thus in a better position to lend than banks without a strong deposit base in the United States in

2008. This is consistent with the empirical results of Ito and Sasaki (2002) to the effect that bank health affected lending behavior in Japan in the 1990s.

Finally, comparing the global financial crisis of 2007 to 2009 and the financial crisis in Japan in the1990s, we find that the particular characteristic of a financial system reflects each financial crisis. In the 1990s in Japan, the bad loan problem was the key problem for the banking sector which was the originator of loans. In the 2000s, on the other hand, the original lenders rarely continued to hold the loans, instead repackaging them in a different way based on their risk, and sold them to investors all over the world. Thus, the holders of these securitized products were far from the originators, and had little incentive to look into the quality of any individual loan (Akerlof and Shiller 2009).

6 Conclusion

In this chapter, we investigated the impact of the financial system on the economic development of Japan after World War II. We discussed whether the close bank–firm relationship (or main-bank relationship) helped to mitigate the financial constraints on the large Japanese firms by investigating the cash flow sensitivity of cash. We found that young firms with a stable main-bank relationship reduced cash saving from the current cash flow even if they faced a financial constraint, while those without a main-bank relationship saved more cash from cash flow in the high growth period. The stable bank–firm relationship played a positive role for the newly listed young firms by reducing the unprofitable cash holdings in this period.

On the contrary, we found no evidence that the banking sector had any positive influence on reducing the cash holdings of the borrowing firms without access to the bond market in the late 1980s and early 1990s. In the late 1980s to early 1990s, close ties with main banks induced firms to undertake over-investment (Miyajima *et al.* 2001, 2002). Furthermore, the banking crisis of the 1990s gave banks an incentive to engage in the "evergreening" of old loans to nearly insolvent firms in order to improve their own balance sheets. Along with the achievement of enhanced Japanese economic development, the darker aspects of the main-bank system overshadowed these brighter aspects.

These empirical results indicate that the financial function and regulation required for an efficient financial system has to be adjusted in keeping with the stage of economic development.[10] In the catch-up process of economic development, it might be rational for a country to have a financial system in which a small number of banks provide financial resources, providing information production and controlling the financial risk of borrowing firms inter-temporally. That is because firms face less uncertainty in seizing investment opportunities during the catching up process, and it is not necessarily important for the household to own a variety of financial products because of the high degree of risk aversion due to insufficient financial asset accumulation. Since the banking sector faces the systemic risks of the economy in this case, the government should build a regulatory system which allows the banking sector to have enough profits to absorb the risk.[11] Nevertheless, concentrating financial resources on a small number of banks might be inefficient after the economy matures and the uncertainty of future investment opportunities increases (Allen and Gale 2000). In this situation, a decentralized financial system is required to bring about efficient risk sharing among investors with different risk preferences.

Appendix 4.1 Data used in Arikawa (2011)

We selected the sample firms by the following procedure. To include both growing firms and mature firms, we selected the sample firms based on R&D intensities in the fiscal year 1990. We picked textiles, pulp and paper, metals, iron and steel, pharmaceuticals and chemicals, general machinery, electrical machinery, transport equipment, and precision machinery.

Among these industries, we selected firms whose sales were more than 50 billion yen in the fiscal year 1990 in order to obtain sample firms that are relatively homogeneous in size. The data range from the period 1958–1998. The data on R&D were derived from the Report on the Survey of Research and Development (1990), Toyo Keizai's Tokei Geppo (Statistics Monthly), and Kaisya Shikiho (Japan Company Handbook). We collected all the financial data from Nikkei NEEDS, and stock price data from Toyo Keizai's Kabuka CD-ROM, and AMUSUS.

Notes

1 See Hoshi and Kashyap (2001) for the details of the history of the financial system in Japan.
2 This section is based on Arikawa (2011).
3 The details of the analysis are shown in Arikawa (2011).
4 A "main" bank of each firm is defined as the top bank in its trading bank list in *Kaisya Shikiho* (the Japan Company Handbook).
5 Kang and Shivdasani (1997) show that firms with close main-bank ties reduced their assets even more during the business upturn of the late 1980s, and insist on the exertion of appropriate discipline on client firms.
6 Since the number of firms which was troubled but economically viable was limited from the rapid growth period to the 1980s, main banks had enough capacity to bail out these firms.
7 This dummy variable equals one if the three-year average of operational profits over 1993–1995 of sample firms is 50 percent lower than that of 1988–1990, and otherwise zero.
8 See table 5 in Arikawa and Miyajima (2007).
9 Zombie and credit-crunch hypotheses are fundamentally complementary. If there were financial frictions then the zombie congestion would exacerbate them by lowering collateral values (even for healthy firms) (Caballero *et al.* 2008).
10 The global financial crisis after 2007 implies that the regulatory system has to be adjusted not only based on real sector development but also on the development of financial technology.
11 As Hellman *et al.* (1997) argue, governments have to construct a system which prevents rent-seeking activity on the part of incumbent banks.

References

Akerlof, G.A. and Shiller, R. (2009) *Animal Spirits: How Human Psychology Drives the Economy, and Why It Matters for Global Capitalism*, Princeton, NJ: Princeton University Press.

Almeida, H., Campello, M., and Weisbach, M.S. (2004) "The Cash Flow Sensitivity of Cash," *Journal of Finance* 59, pp. 1777–1804.

Allen, F. and Gale, D. (2000) *Comparing Financial Systems*, Cambridge, MA: MIT Press.

Alti, A. (2003) "How Sensitive is Investment to Cash Flow When Financing is Frictionless?" *Journal of Finance* 58, pp. 707–722.

Aoki, M. (2001) *Toward a Comparative Institutional Analysis*, Cambridge, MA: MIT Press.

Aoki, M., Patrick, H., and Sheard, P. (1994) "The Japanese Main Bank System: An Introductory Overview" in M. Aoki and H. Patrick (eds.), *The Japanese Main Bank System: Its Relevancy for Developing and Transforming Economies*, Oxford: Oxford University Press, pp. 1–50.

Arikawa, Y. (2011) "The Cash Flow Sensitivity of Cash and the Bank–Firm Relationship," Unpublished Paper.

Arikawa, Y. and Miyajima, H. (2005) "Relationship Banking and Debt Choice: Evidence from Japan," *Corporate Governance: An International Review* 13, pp. 408–418.

Arikawa, Y. and H. Miyajima (2007) "Relationship Banking in Post-Bubble Japan: the Coexistence of Soft- and Hard-Budget Constraints," in M. Aoki, G. Jackson, and H. Miyajima (eds.) *Corporate Governance in Japan: Institutional Change and Organizational Diversity*, Oxford: Oxford University Press, pp. 51–78.

Caballero, R., Hoshi, T., and Kashyap, A. (2008) "Zombie Lending and Depressed Restructuring in Japan," *American Economic Review* 98:5, pp. 1943–1977.

Fazzari, S.M., Hubbard, R.G., and Petersen, B.C. (1988) "Financing Constraints and Corporate Investment," *Brookings Papers on Economic Activity* 1, pp. 141–195.

Fukuda, S., Kasuya, M., and Nakajima, J. (2007) "Hijyojyokigyo no Setsubitoshi no Kettei Yoin-Kinyu Kikan no Kenzensei oyobi Kajyotousi mondai no Eikyo" (The Determinants of Investment by Non-Listed Companies: The Effect of Soundness of Financial Institutions and Overinvestment Problem.) in F. Hayashi (ed.), *Kinyu Shijyo no Kino Fuzen* (Functional Failure in Financial Market), Tokyo: Keiso Syobo, pp. 65–97.

Gan, J. (2007) "Collateral, Debt Capacity, and Corporate Investment: Evidence from a Natural Experiment," *Journal of Financial Economics* 85, pp. 709–734.

Gibson, M. (1995) "Can Bank Health Affect Investment? Evidence from Japan," *Journal of Business* 68, pp. 281–308.

Grossman, S. and Hart, O. (1980) "Disclosure Laws and Takeover Bids," *Journal of Finance* 35, pp. 323–334.

Hellmann, T., Murdock, K., and Stiglitz, J. (1997) "Financial Restraint: Toward a New Paradigm," in M. Aoki, H. Kim, and M. Okuno-Fujiwara, (eds.), *The Role of Government in East Asian Economic Development: Comparative Institutional Analysis*, Oxford: Oxford University Press, pp. 163–207.

Hoshi, T. and Kashyap, A. (2001) *Corporate Finance and Governance in Japan*, Cambridge, MA: MIT Press.

Hoshi, T., Kashyap, A., and Sharfstein, D. (1990) "The Role of Banks in Reducing the Costs of Financial Distress in Japan," *Journal of Financial Economics*, 27, pp. 67–88.

Hoshi, T., Kashyap, A., and Sharfstein, D. (1991) "The Investment, Liquidity, and Ownership: The Evidence from the Japanese Industrial Groups," *Quarterly Journal of Economics*, 106, pp. 33–60.

Hubbard, R.G., Kashyap, A., and Whited, T. (1995) "Internal Finance and Firm Investment," *Journal of Money, Credit and Banking* 27, pp. 683–701.

Ikeo, K (2006) *Kaihatsu Syugi no Bousou to Hoshin – Kinyusisutemu to Heisei Keizai* (Abuses and Self-protection of Developmentalism), Tokyo: NTT Press.

Ito, T. and Sasaki, Y. (2002) "Impacts of the Basel Capital Standard on Japanese Banks Behavior," *Journal of Japanese and International Economics* 16, pp. 372–397.

Ivashina, V. and Sharfstein, D. (2008) "Bank Lending During the Financial Crisis of 2008," Unpublished Paper, Harvard Business School.

Kaplan S. and Zingales, L. (1997) "Do Investment-Cash Flow Sensitivities Provide Useful Measures of Financing Constraints?" *Quarterly Journal of Economics* 112, pp. 159–216.

Kang, J. and Stulz, R. (2000) "Do Banking Shocks Affect Firm Performance? An Analysis of the Japanese Experience," *Journal of Business* 73, pp. 1–23.

Kang, J. and Shivdasani, A. (1997) "Corporate Restructuring During Performance Declines in Japan," *Journal of Financial Economics* 46, pp. 29–65.

Merton, R.C. (1995) "A Functional Perspective of Financial Intermediation," *Financial Management* 24, pp. 23–41.

Myers, S. and Majluf, N. (1984) "Corporate Financing and Investment Decisions When Firms Have Information that Investors Do Not Have," *Journal of Financial Economics* 13, pp. 187–221.

Miyajima, H., Arikawa, Y., and Kato, A. (2002) "Corporate Governance, Relational Banking and R&D Investment: Evidence from Japanese Large Firms in the 1980s and 1990s," *International Journal of Technology Management* 23, pp. 769–787.

Miyajima, H., Arikawa, Y., and Saito, N. (2001) "Nihon-gata Kigyōtōchi to Kajyō-tōshi: Sekyū Shock Zengo to Bubble Keizai ki no Hikaku Bunseki (Corporate Governance in Japan and Over-investment: Comparison between the Oil-shock Period and Bubble Period)," *Financial Review* 49, pp. 139–168.

Ogawa, K. (2009) *Ushinawareta Jyunen no Shinjitsu* (The Fact of Lost Decade), Tokyo: Toyokeizai Shimposya.

Ono, A. (2007) *Sinjidai no Chusho Kigyo Kinyu* (Finance of SME in the New Era)," Tokyo: Toyokeizai Shimposya.

Peek, J. and Rosengren, E. (2005) "Unnatural Selection: Perverse Incentives and the Misallocation of Credit in Japan," *American Economic Review* 95, pp. 1144–1166.

Peek, J. (2009) "The Changing Role of Main Banks in Aiding Distressed Firms in Japan," Unpublished Paper, University of Kentucky.

Petersen, M.A. and Rajan, R.G. (1995) "The Effect of Credit Market Competition on Lending Relationships," *Quarterly Journal of Economics* 110, pp. 407–443.

Pinkowitz, L. and Williamson, R. (2001) "Bank Power and Cash Holdings: Evidence from Japan," *Review of Financial Studies* 14, pp. 1059–1082.

Uchida, H. (2008) "*Rireisyonship Bankingu ha Chusho Kigyo no Bannoyaku ka* (Is Relationship Banking a Panacea for Financing of Small- and Medium-Sized Enterprises?)" in T. Watanabe and I. Uesugi (eds.) *Kensho Chusho Kigyo Kinyu: Konkyo naki tsusetsu no Jissyo Bunseki* (Verifications of SME Finance: Empirical Analysis of Unfounded Common Belief), Tokyo: Nikkei Publishing.

Zingales, L. (2009) "The Future of Securities Regulation," CEPR Discussion Paper Series, No. 7110.

5   What will become of the Japanese corporation?

Katsuhito Iwai

1 Introduction

There have been at least two conflicting views on the objectives of business corporations in a capitalistic world. On one hand is the "shareholder-oriented view" that insists that the major objective of business corporations is to maximize the returns to its shareholders, and on the other, is the "organization-oriented view" (or "employee-oriented view") that claims that the chief concern of the managers of business corporations is the survival and growth of the corporation as an organizational entity comprised of employees and other stakeholders. US business corporations tend to uphold the shareholder-oriented view and Japanese business corporations the organization-orientated view.

There is no doubt that the above dichotomy is a simplification. There is a wide disparity as well as a wide fluctuation in corporate objectives both within the United States and Japan. And yet, this is a simplification, not an oversimplification. Notwithstanding large variations within each country, we still find it a useful working hypothesis to assume that US managers are generally expected to maximize their returns to shareholders and that Japanese managers are generally expected to emphasize the survival and growth of the corporation as an organizational entity.

These expectations give rise to further thought. In spite of the wide difference in attitudes towards the objectives of business corporations, both the United States and Japan are full-fledged capitalistic economies. Not only US corporations but also Japanese corporations are organized in accordance with "corporate law" that is based firmly on the system of private property. In fact, the current Japanese corporate law can be regarded as an amalgam of German law and US law. There thus emerges a theoretical puzzle to be solved: How can the same legal framework of private property allow these seemingly contradictory systems of business corporations to co-exist in this world? One of this chapter's main theses is that it is the very legal concept of "corporation" that is responsible for the co-existence of two seemingly contradictory forms of corporate systems.

2 Varieties of corporate systems

Table 5.1 reports the results of a 1988 survey that asked managers of large business corporations in the United States, Japan, and Europe to pick the three most

Table 5.1 Important management goals

(%)	America	Japan	Europe
Sustenance and improvement of ROI	78.1	35.6	64.2
Capital gains of shareholders	63.0	2.7	10.6
Maintenance and expansion of market share	53.4	50.6	61.8
Improvement of product portfolio	28.8	11.5	26.0
Maximization of sales volume	15.1	27.9	17.9
Increase in own capital ratio	13.7	21.8	18.7
Rationalization of production and distribution systems	13.7	27.0	27.6
Reinforcement of global strategy	12.3	32.8	30.9
Expansion of new products and new operations ratio	11.0	60.8	14.6
Improvement of corporate social image	6.8	18.6	18.7
Retention of employees	1.4	3.8	6.5
Improvement of employees' benefits	0	7.7	0.8

Source: Keizai Doyu Kai, *Showa 63 nendo Kigyou Hakusho* (*1988 White Paper on Corporations*), (1988).

Note
Number of corporations responding to questionnaire: 73 in America, 724 in Japan and 123 in Europe (58 in Italy, 33 in Germany, 18 in France, and 14 in Great Britain).

important goals of their management policies. We can see from the entries in the first column that answers given by the US corporate managers were consistent with the traditional assumption in economics and law that the whole purpose of the business corporation is to maximize returns to its shareholders. They ranked ROI (the rate of return on investment) at the top (78.1 percent) and capital gains of shareholders second (63.0 percent). In stark contrast to American counterparts, the Japanese corporate managers placed capital gains of shareholders at the very bottom of their ranking (2.7 percent). It is true, that they ranked ROI third, but the points it gets are not so high (35.5 percent). Instead, they put the ratio of new products and new operations at the top (60.8 percent) and ranked market share second (50.6 percent).[1] These goals are more or less related to the survival and growth of the business corporation as an organizational entity. The answers given by European corporate managers, however, were somewhat murky due to the diversity of the countries in this category.

This study was conducted more than 20 years ago. Indeed, the 1980s was the decade of Japan. Buoyed by the 1979 publication of Ezra Vogel's *Japan as Number One*, the Japanese-style business corporation took center stage in the capitalist world, hailed as the model of the future – it was stable, egalitarian, and superproductive. With the collapse of the stock market and land market bubbles in 1991, however, the stage suddenly went dark and the Japanese economy fell into "the lost decade." In sharp contrast, the 1990s became the decade of the United States. Riding on the wave of globalization, the US economy stood at the forefront of both the IT revolution and financial liberalization, and sustained a high productivity growth throughout the decade. The shareholder-oriented model of US corporations then appeared to have established itself as "the global standard" to which all corporations in the world must converge sooner or later, and the sooner the better. In 2000, Henry Hansmann and Reinier Kraakman, two of the leading scholars on law and economics, claimed in their widely quoted article that "the basic law of corporate governance" – indeed, most of corporate law – has achieved a high degree of uniformity across "advanced capitalist countries" and "there is no longer any serious competitor to the view that corporate law should principally strive to increase long-term shareholder value."[2]

Despite such widespread belief in the universality of the shareholder-orientation model of the business corporation, and despite the rapid integration of financial markets and competitive pressure from globalized markets, all the comparative studies on corporate objectives and management practices (as far as the author is aware) suggest that there still remains, between the United States and Japan, a large difference in the way business corporations are structured and governed.[3] Table 5.2, taken from Jacoby *et al.* (2005), reports the executive values of human resource managers both in Japan and in the United States in 2001–2002, together with the values expressed by Japanese directors in 1993. There were certainly signs of movement towards shareholder-orientation in Japan from 1993 to 2001, but more important is the fact that in spite of such movement, Japanese corporate managers still emphasize the job security of their employees (for that matter the autonomy of corporate organization) far more than their US counterparts do. This is again confirmed by Table 5.3 that summarizes the results of the 2005 study by Tanaka (2006) who asked Japanese managers to scale their answers from 1 (Yes) to 7 (No) to such questions as (*a*) "Should the share value be maximized?" (*b*) "Should shareholders be the sole power holder of the corporation?" and (*c*) "Are employees mere inputs to production?" The managers were also asked: "What would have been your or your predecessor's answer ten years ago?" If we look at the column for the total, we can again discern a trend in the direction of shareholder-orientation in contemporary Japan. (The average score is 3.7 in 2005, but it was 4.5 in 1995.) Yet, the study has also shown that those managers who were relatively employee-oriented in 2005, on average expressed their belief that they had become even more so in the last ten years. (Their score is 5.1 in 2005, but was 4.9 in 1995.)

Table 5.2 Executive values: Japan (1993), Japan and the US (2001–2002)

"What is important to you in your job?" 1 = not important, 4 = most important			
	Japanese directors 1993	*Japanese human resource executives 2001*	*US human resource executives 2001–2002*
Share price	2.0	2.3	3.3
Safeguard employees' jobs	3.3	3.2	2.1

Source: Jacoby *et al.* (2005).

Table 5.3 Recent questionnaire study on corporate objectives in Japan

Should share-value be maximized?	Yes 1 ⟷ 7 No
Should shareholders be the sole power holder?	Yes 1 ⟷ 7 No
Are employees mere inputs to production?	Yes 1 ⟷ 7 No

Average score	Total	Shareholder-orientated	Intermediate	Employee-orientated
Present	3.7	2.9	3.9	5.1
	↑	↑	↑	↑
10 years ago	4.5	4.4	4.8	4.9
Frequency	231	64	110	57

Source: Kazuhiro Tanaka (2006).

3 What is a business corporation?

What is a business corporation? The simplest definition is that it is a firm that is set up as a corporation. In the first place, a business corporation is a firm. In this sense there is no difference between a "mom and pop" grocery shop around the corner and Toyota Motor Corporation. As depicted in any textbook of economics, both the grocery store and Toyota are organizational entities that supply goods to markets for profit. Of course, there is a huge difference in their size – while our grocery store around the corner is owned and run by a good-natured couple with little capital of their own, Toyota has capital of about 400 billion yen (5 billion dollars), generates sales of over 25 trillion yen (30 billion dollars), and hires more than 300,000 employees. Their differences, however, cannot be reduced solely to size; Toyota is set up as a corporation but our grocery shop is not.

Suppose you are an owner of a mom and pop grocery shop. Whenever you feel hungry, you can pick up an apple from the shelf and eat it right away. That apple is your property, and the only thing you have to worry about is the wrath of your spouse – your co-owner. As Figure 5.1 shows, a firm consists of a single ownership relationship between an owner, in the case of a single proprietorship firm, or a group of owners in the case of a partnership firm, and assets such as apples and oranges on the shelf of the grocery store. However, as soon as a firm is set up as a "corporation" and become a "business corporation," its ownership structure undergoes a fundamental change.

Suppose now that you are a shareholder of a business corporation, e.g., a big supermarket chain. You feel hungry and on your way home you enter one of the stores in the chain, grab an apple from its shelf and eat it right away. What will happen to you? You will be arrested as a thief, even if you are a shareholder! Why? It is because a corporate shareholder is not the legal owner of the corporate assets. Who, then, is the owner of those corporate assets? The corporation as a "legal person" is. Then, what is a legal person? The law treats a corporation as the subject of property rights, capable of owning real property, entering into contracts, suing and being sued, all in its own name, separate and distinct from its shareholders.[4] A corporation is, in other words, a "thing" that is treated legally

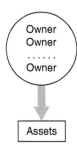

Figure 5.1 Single ownership structure of a classical firm.

as a "person." And it is the corporation as a legal person that is the owner of the corporate assets. You were arrested as a thief simply because you took the property of another "person."

Who, then, are corporate shareholders? The answer is that they are the owners of the corporation. Corporate shareholders are literally the holders of a corporate share – a bundle of rights that includes the right to vote on issues affecting the corporation as a whole, the right to share in the residual assets when the corporation is liquidated, and the right to receive dividends the corporation generates. These three rights in fact correspond to the three basic rights of property ownership – *ius utendi* (the exclusive right to use one's property), *ius abutendi* (the exclusive right to alienate one's property), and *ius fruendi* (the exclusive right to enjoy the whole fruits from the use and from the alienation of her property).[5] Holding these rights against the corporation can thus be regarded as owning the corporation as a "thing," i.e., as an object of property rights. A corporate shareholder is thus an owner of a share or a fraction of the corporation as a "thing," separate and distinct from the underlying corporate assets. Indeed, we can buy and sell a corporate share freely just as any other "thing," and in the case of a publicly-held corporation, a centralized market, called the stock market, is organized for daily transactions of its shares.

This observation leads us to the most crucial characteristic of the business corporation. In contrast to a single ownership firm or a partnership firm, an

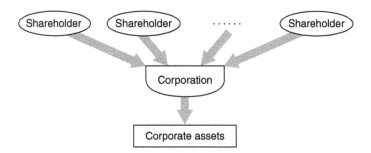

Figure 5.2 Two-tier ownership structure of a business corporation.

incorporated firm, or what we have called a business corporation, is composed of not one but *two* ownership relations: the shareholders own the corporation, and the corporation in turn owns the corporate assets, as is shown in Figure 5.2. Indeed, in this two-tier ownership structure there is a division of labor between the person-side and the thing-side of the corporation. In regard to things (corporate assets), a corporation acts legally as a person, as a subject of property rights; and in regard to persons (shareholders), a corporation is acted upon legally as a thing, as an object of property rights.

4 The corporate personality controversy and the comparative corporate system

For many centuries, legal scholars and legal philosophers have debated heatedly as to what constitutes the "essence" of the corporation. This is called the "corporate personality controversy" – one of the most celebrated controversies in legal theory and legal philosophy. In this age-old controversy, two competing legal theories have emerged advancing opposing answers – "corporate nominalism" and "corporate realism." Corporate nominalism asserts that the corporation is a contractual association of individuals, whose legal personality is no more than an abbreviated way of writing their names together. Corporate realism, in opposition, claims that the corporation is a full-fledged entity whose legal personality is no more than an external expression of its real personality in society. (And both claim to have superseded the "fiction theory" or the "concession theory" – the traditional doctrine since the twelfth century, which maintained that the corporation is a separate and distinct social entity but that its legal personality is a mere fiction conceded by the state or created by law.)[6]

The corporate personality controversy is not something of the past. The rivalry between corporate nominalism and corporate realism has continued until the present. On one hand, the contractual theory of the firm, whether it is an agency-theory version or a transactions costs economics version, is a direct descendent of corporate nominalism.[7] On the other hand, the evolutionary theory of the firm, variously known as the resource-base view or the core-competence view or the organizational capability model, can be interpreted as a modern representative of corporate realism.[8] The former regards "private corporations" as "simply legal fictions which serve as a nexus for a set of contracting relationships among individuals" (Jensen and Meckling 1976, p. 310). The latter posits corporate firms as "organizations that know how to do things,... while individual members come and go" (Winter 1988, p. 136). The corporate personality controversy is far from a relic of the past.

It is not hard to see that the age-old controversy between corporate nominalism and corporate realism and the more recent rivalry between the contractual theory of the firm and the evolutionary theory of the firm more or less correspond to the difference between the US corporate system and the Japanese corporate system.

What I would like to do now is to "end" this long-standing controversy between corporate nominalism and corporate realism once and for all. It is, however, not by declaring victory for one side or the other. It is rather by declaring victory for both sides by elucidating two legal mechanisms through which the legal concept of the corporation is capable of generating two seemingly contradictory corporate structures – one approximating corporate nominalism and the other approximating corporate realism.

If we only look at the upper tier of the two-tier ownership structure depicted in Figure 5.2, the corporation appears as something owned and controlled by shareholders, and we draw near to the position of corporate nominalists and that of US corporate system. If, on the other hand, we look only at the lower tier, the corporation appears as a person owning and managing corporate assets, and we draw near to the position of corporate realists and that of the Japanese corporate system.

We can go further. What I am going to demonstrate is that there are even ways to eliminate both personality and "thingness" from the corporation, thereby turning it into a mere "thing" or a full "person," respectively.

5 How to make a "nominalistic" corporation

The way to eliminate the personality from a corporation is simple and well-known; it is to have someone own more than 50 percent of its shares. That someone then acquires absolute control over the corporation. The corporation is deprived of its subjectivity and turned into a mere object of property rights. Legally speaking, the corporation is still the sole owner of the corporate assets, but in practice it is the dominant shareholder who can exercise ultimate control over these assets. We are certainly in the world of the corporate nominalists here.

This is of course common sense, but I now argue that the so-called corporate raiders are daily putting this legal mechanism into practice in the real economy.

That a business corporation consists of a two-tier ownership relationship implies that it contains two kinds of "things" – the corporate assets and the corporation itself. This fact immediately implies that there are also two kinds of

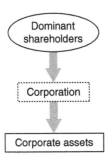

Figure 5.3 A "nominalistic" corporation.

values residing in a business corporation. They are, respectively, the value of corporate assets and the value of the corporation as a thing. The former can be defined as the present discounted value of the future profit stream that would accrue from the most efficient use of these assets. This can also be called the "fundamental" value of the corporation. The latter can be identified as the total share price of the corporation in the stock market. The business of corporate raiders is to exploit the potential difference between these two values by buying corporations whose stock market values are lower than the fundamental value of the underlying assets. In the process, they become dominant shareholders and turn the target corporation into a purely "nominalistic" corporation.

Corporate raiders thus help to realize the idea of corporate nominalism in this world. It is claimed that even if they are not raiding corporations on a daily basis, the mere perception that they may at any time enter the scene works as an effective threat to incumbent managers, steering them away from management policies that may fail to realize the corporate assets' fundamental value. If this is the case, the stock market is said to function as the "market for corporate control."[9]

6 How to make a "realistic" corporation (1)

We know that as a legal person a corporation can own things and that as a legal thing a corporation can be owned by persons. This at once suggests that a corporation as a person can, in principle, own another corporation as a thing. In fact, since the state of New Jersey in the United States legalized "holding" corporations in 1889, corporations all over the world have been buying and holding the shares of other corporations. A holding corporation is a corporation that is created solely for the purpose of owning other corporations, as is shown in Figure 5.4. It acts as a person in regard to the corporations it owns.

The holding corporation has paved the way to an important organizational innovation – the pyramidal system of ownership and control. At the top is a group of capitalists or a Zaibatsu family that owns a corporation as a thing, but

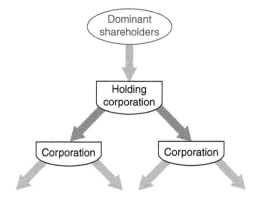

Figure 5.4 A holding corporation and a pyramidal system of ownership and control.

that corporation can also, as a legal person, own another corporation as a thing, which again as a legal person can own another corporation as a thing, and so on. Such ownership hierarchy can extend ad infinitum. This is not the whole picture because you do not have to own all the shares to control a publicly-held corporation. As long as minority shares are sufficiently diffused among passive investors in the stock market, only a share slightly greater than *50 percent* is sufficient for control. This implies that one unit of capital can in principle control almost two units of capital, if each half buys a bare majority of the shares of a corporation with a capital close to one unit. It then follows that, as more and more layers are added to the ownership hierarchy, a group of capitalists at the top can multiply the controlling power of their capital by the order close to 2^n, where n is the number of hierarchical layers beneath.[10] One can regard the pre-war Japanese Zaibatsu and present-day Italian family empires and Korean Chaebols as typical examples of this pyramidal system of ownership and control.

7 How to make a "realistic" corporation (2)

Nevertheless, a holding corporation still falls short of shedding its "thingness" entirely because it has its own dominant shareholders watching over it. One can, however, go a step further at least in theory. A corporation as a person can own itself as a thing. Indeed, nothing prevents us from imagining a corporation that becomes its own controlling shareholder by holding a majority block of its own shares under its own name, as is shown in Figure 5.5. If this were possible, that corporation would be free from any control by real human beings (natural persons) and become a self-determining subject. It would thus acquire a full personality in the province of law.

One might dismiss all this as idle speculation. Some countries prohibit a corporation from repurchasing its outstanding shares. And, in many other countries that allow share repurchases, the repurchased shares usually lose their voting rights in shareholders' meetings. In the real economy, therefore, it appears impossible for the corporation to become its own owner.

There is, however, an important leeway. Imagine a situation where two corporations, A and B, hold a majority of each other's shares. Corporation A as a person owns corporation B as a thing, and corporation B as a person in turn owns corporation A as a thing. As is shown in Figure 5.6, even though each corporation does not own itself directly, it does indirectly through the intermediacy

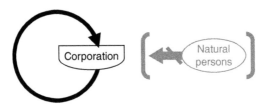

Figure 5.5 A (hypothetical) self-owning corporation.

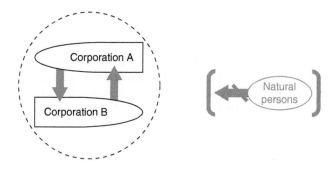

Figure 5.6 Mutually holding corporations.

of the other corporation. One might still object to the practical possibility of this leeway by pointing out that some countries impose legal limits on the extent of cross-shareholdings between corporations.

Yet, it is possible to circumvent even these limits. Suppose that 12 corporations get together and that each holds 5 percent of each of the other's shares. Then, simple arithmetic $((12 - 1) \times 5\% = 55\%)$ tells us that a majority block of each corporation's shares could be effectively sealed off from real human-beings without violating legal restrictions on cross-shareholding in any of advanced capitalistic countries. These 12 corporations would indeed become their own owners at least as a group, as is depicted in Figure 5.7. It is therefore practically impossible to prevent corporations from becoming their own owners, if they so wish. We have now reached the paradigm of corporate realism – through extensive cross-shareholding, corporations can eliminate their "thingness" and become self-determining subjects in the system of law.

Figure 5.7 is not a mere doodle of an armchair theorist. One can see how such a doodle was "realized" in Table 5.4. It is well-known that one of the

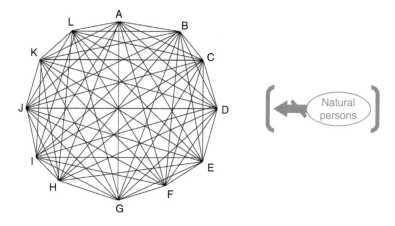

Figure 5.7 Cross-shareholdings among 12 corporations.

distinguished features of the post-World War II Japanese economy was the extensive cross-shareholding among large corporations. Table 5.4 summarizes cross-shareholding among 20 corporations of the Sumitomo group in 1993. Indeed, Japan used to have six major corporate groups (Mitsubishi, Mitsui, Sumitomo, Daiichi-Kan-Gin, Fuji, and Sanwa), each of which was clustered around a main bank, extended over the whole industry, and connected through mutual holdings of shares and mutual exchanges of directors. The percentage of cross-shareholdings reached as high as 32.9 percent of the total shareholdings of publicly-held corporations in 1990.

8 Traditions and corporate systems

I now believe I have succeeded in "ending" the age-old controversy on the essence of the corporations in corporate nominalism and in corporate realism. There should also be a clearer understanding about the more recent rivalry concerning the nature of the firm according to contractual theory and the nature of the firm with respect to evolutionary/resource-base/core-competence/organizational capability theory. It is indeed the very legal concept of the corporation that is capable of eliminating either personality or thingness from the person-cum-thing corporation, thereby turning it into a mere "thing" or a full "person," respectively. I also believe I have provided a resolution to the real-life opposition between the shareholder-oriented US corporate system and the organization-oriented Japanese corporate system. The US and the Japanese systems are but two extreme forms of the genus "corporation." Each society can choose any position along an extensive spectrum that runs from a purely "nominalistic" structure to a purely "realistic" structure, on the basis of or at least under the influence of, economic efficiency, political interests, ideological forces, cultural traditions, historical evolution and other extra-legal factors. My contention is that in the long history of their capitalistic development, the US economy and the Japanese economy have both chosen from this long legal menu, the position close to the "nominalistic" end as their dominant corporate structure, respectively.

It appears, however, that traditional Japanese-style management has completed its historical mission. The stock market and property market bubbles burst in the late 1980s. The financial markets were belatedly but rapidly liberalized in the 1990s. And the wave of globalization began to expose Japanese corporations to mega-competition in the world markets. All these movements have weakened the traditional ties between major banks and industrial corporations and loosened the tight network of corporate cross-shareholdings. In fact, the percentage of cross-shareholdings declined to 12.0 percent in 2006, and the six major corporate groups are now consolidated into three (Mitsubishi–Tokyo–UFJ, Mitsui-Sumitomo, and Mizuho).

Do these facts mean that the long-run tide of the Japanese corporate system is flowing in the "nominalistic" direction? Is there a "convergence" towards the US corporate system?

Table 5.4 Cross-shareholdings among core 20 corporations of Sumitomo Group, 1993

Holder % \ Issuer	S. Bank	S. Trus Bank	S. Life	S. Mar Ins.	S. Corp	S. Coal Mini	S. Cons	S. Fore	S. Che	S. Bake	Jap Glas	S. Cem	S. Meta	S. Meta Mini	S. Ligh Meta	S. Elect	S. Heav Ind.	NEC	S. Real Esta	S. Stor	Total
S. Bank	–	2.8	6.1	1.8	1.7	0.0	0.0	0.1	1.1	0.2	1.1	0.2	1.3	0.4	–	0.9	0.2	1.1	0.1	0.2	19.3
S. Trust Bank	3.3	–	4.2	1.5	2.5	0.0	0.0	0.2	1.2	0.5	1.4	0.5	2.3	1.2	0.0	1.7	0.4	2.8	–	1.5	25.3
S. Life	–	–	–	–	–	–	–	–	–	–	–	–	–	–	–	–	–	–	–	–	–
S. Marine Ins.	4.4	6.3	4.6	–	2.3	0.1	0.1	0.1	1.2	0.3	1.2	0.3	1.0	1.0	–	0.9	0.6	1.8	0.1	0.8	27.1
S. Corporation	4.8	5.8	5.1	2.9	–	0.1	0.0	0.3	1.6	0.3	1.0	0.4	2.7	1.7	–	1.0	0.8	3.7	0.1	0.4	32.8
S.Coal Mining	4.8	4.0	2.5	2.4	3.4	–	0.8	–	2.5	–	0.4	1.0	4.9	2.1	–	–	1.7	4.2	0.1	0.2	34.8
S.Construct'	4.4	2.9	5.8	1.4	–	3.1	–	0.6	1.1	–	0.6	2.3	–	3.3	–	1.0	–	–	0.4	0.2	27.0
S. Forestry	4.3	7.0	7.2	–	2.6	0.1	0.4	–	–	0.4	0.4	0.3	–	7.3	–	0.3	0.2	1.4	–	–	31.1
S. Chemical	4.7	5.3	8.9	1.4	1.3	0.0	0.1	0.1	–	0.1	–	0.3	–	0.2	–	0.3	0.2	0.5	0.0	0.1	23.9
S. Bakelite	4.8	7.1	5.9	1.3	2.1	–	0.3	0.4	21.6	–	0.3	0.5	0.9	–	–	0.3	–	1.3	0.4	0.1	48.2
Japan Glass	5.0	6.8	5.5	2.3	1.6	–	0.1	0.1	1.2	0.5	–	0.8	–	0.3	–	–	0.6	–	0.5	0.2	25.6
S. Cement	4.6	5.4	8.5	1.0	2.3	1.9	0.6	0.4	1.1	0.4	0.8	–	1.0	1.1	–	0.3	2.2	0.8	0.2	–	32.8
S. Metals	4.0	6.2	5.5	–	1.6	0.1	0.0	–	–	0.1	0.1	0.1	–	0.5	–	0.3	0.2	0.6	0.0	0.1	19.2
S.Metal Min'g	4.6	10.0	4.8	1.5	2.5	0.1	0.2	0.3	–	–	0.3	0.7	0.8	–	–	1.0	0.3	2.4	0.1	0.1	29.6
S.Light Metals	4.7	5.8	4.0	1.4	4.0	–	–	–	1.3	–	–	0.4	23.3	0.9	–	0.8	0.6	0.8	–	0.2	48.2
S. Electrics	3.8	5.4	7.0	–	0.8	0.0	0.0	–	–	–	0.5	0.1	–	0.8	–	–	0.1	2.4	–	0.1	20.6
S. Heavy Ind.	4.6	6.4	7.8	2.5	3.0	0.1	0.1	0.1	–	–	0.2	1.3	–	0.7	–	0.7	–	–	–	0.3	27.9
NEC	5.0	4.8	6.8	2.6	2.2	0.0	0.0	–	0.4	0.1	0.5	0.1	0.7	1.0	–	2.2	0.1	–	0.0	0.2	26.4
S. Real Estate	3.4	5.1	2.3	1.6	0.5	0.0	0.2	–	0.4	0.2	0.7	0.1	0.5	0.3	–	0.5	–	0.7	–	0.5	17.2
S. Storage	4.7	6.7	8.4	5.4	2.4	–	0.3	–	1.5	0.1	0.8	–	2.2	–	–	0.9	0.9	3.9	0.3	–	38.5

Sources: Toyo Keizai, *Kigyo Keiretsu Soran '95 (Survey on Corporate Groups, '95)*, (Toyo Keizai Shinpo Sha, 1995).

Note

"0.0" means a very small percentage, and "–" means no holding.

The answer is "no!" Indeed, I am also discerning another tide that is moving strongly in the opposite direction. It is a tide brought about by the transition of the advanced capitalistic economies from the stage of "industrial" capitalism to the stage of "post-industrial" capitalism.

9 Two sources of inefficiency in corporate organizations

In order to explain this, we must re-examine the nominalism/realism dichotomy of corporate forms from the standpoint of economic efficiency, leaving the consideration of cultural, political, and ideological factors to another time. We have learned from the recent literature in economics of imperfect information that two of the most important sources of inefficiency in economic organizations are "moral hazard problems" and "hold-up problems" – both related to the management of human capital, especially knowledge-orientated human capital, endowed in organizations.[11]

First, the moral hazard problem refers to the inefficiency caused by the separation of control and ownership in corporate organizations. Insiders of an organization, such as workers, engineers, researchers, and managers, may take advantage of the shareholders' weak monitoring of their performances and covertly pursue their private interests at the expense of those of shareholders. For instance, managers may accumulate perks, researchers may seek academic reputation, engineers may indulge in creating experimental designs, and workers may simply be lazy.

The hold-up problem, on the other hand, is concerned with another kind of inefficiency. For a corporate organization to survive and grow, its workers, engineers, researchers and managers have to develop skills, know-how, technologies, communication-networks, visions, leadership, etc. that are specialized for the organization. In economics, they are called "organization-specific human capital." These employees, however, are in a vulnerable position because the organization-specific human capital has, by definition, little value outside of the organization. Once these employees have invested their time and effort in organization-specific human capital, their vulnerable position may be taken advantage of by shareholders who are seeking only short-term returns. For instance, a corporate raider may buy out their corporation and then slash the funds for research and development in order to increase the dividend payout. For fear of such potential exploitation, these employees are reluctant to commit themselves to organization-specific human capital even if the accumulation would enhance the economic value of the corporation in the long-run. This is called the hold-up problem, and the so-called incomplete contract theory in economics explains this situation in detail.

I now maintain that there is a real trade-off between the two kinds of economic inefficiency – the one caused by moral hazard problems and the other due to hold-up problems, and that the choice of the legal form of corporation – whether it is nominalistic or realistic – depends very much on this trade-off.

It is evident that the nominalistic form of corporation has an advantage over the realistic form with respect to the moral hazard problem. It allows the shareholders to monitor the performance of managers and other core employees or it allows the stock market to pressure the managers to maximize returns to shareholders.[12] In contrast, the realistic corporation has an advantage over the nominalistic corporation with respect to the hold-up problem. The realistic corporation can by its very nature shield corporate decisions from the pressures of often short-sighted shareholders, thereby protecting the organization-specific human capital from their hold-ups. It encourages those workers, engineers, researchers, and managers to commit themselves to investing in organization-specific human capital. The claim can then be made that the realistic corporation, with its long-term commitment to the survival and growth of its organization, can function as a de facto owner of organization-specific human capital.

10 Transition from industrial capitalism to post-industrial capitalism

Let us now come back to what was referred to earlier – the transition of capitalism from the industrial stage to the post-industrial stage. By the transition to post-industrial capitalism we mean a recent shift in the major source of profits, from economies of scale and scope of large factory systems, to skills, know-how, technologies, communication networks, visions, and leadership of workers, engineers, researchers, and managers. What is critical to the long-run competitiveness of business corporations is no longer physical capital, but human capital, especially knowledge-based human capital. There is a growing body of literature suggesting that the capital values of human capital and other "intangibles" have shown a phenomenal rise in recent years in the United States and other advanced capitalist economies.[13]

I maintain that it is the exhaustion of the "industrial reserve army" – the surplus population deposited in rural areas and supported by communal networks – that is the ultimate cause of this massive phase-transition of capitalistic systems from "industrial" to "post-industrial."[14] The consequent rise in real wages of industrial workers relative to their marginal productivity has reduced the profit margins of the existing production facilities and distribution networks so that capitalist enterprises are able to reap profits only by undertaking what Schumpeter (1950) called "innovations." By innovations Schumpeter designated a broad range of events which includes

> The introduction of new commodities…, the technological change in the production of commodities already in use, the opening-up of new markets or of new sources of supply, Taylorization of work, improved handling of material, the setting-up of new business organizations … – in short, any "doing things differently" in the realm of economic life.

Obviously, in order to do things differently, capitalist enterprises need the ideas, know-how, coordinating skills, forecasting capabilities, strategic prowess, strong leadership, etc. of real human beings.

11 Inalienability of human capital and the increasing importance of organization-specific human capital

We understand that knowledge-based human capital now occupies the central place in post-industrial capitalism. Does this mean, however, that any knowledge or any information can be the source of profits for business corporations? Even if one has a brilliant idea, if that idea can be accessed easily by others, or if that idea can be imitated easily by others, it has no or little economic value.

In the age of post-industrial capitalism only the differences matter! That is, only the knowledge that is within an organization and cannot be easily transferred to outside of the organization can generate positive profits for business corporations. This is precisely what is meant when we refer to organization-specific human capital.

What does this mean to our nominalism/realism dichotomy of corporate form?

The single most important characteristic of human capital is its inalienability. Money can buy factories, machines, offices, land, and other physical capital. Physical capital is alienable. Money, however, cannot directly buy ideas, know-how, skills, human-networks, visions, and other human capital, because they all entail some form of knowledge stored inside human brains or gray cells. All money can do is to provide a variety of incentives that would encourage the workers, engineers, researchers, and managers to invest their time and efforts on human capital that is specific to the organizations in which they are working.

In the era of traditional industrial capitalism where the large factory system was the major source of profits, it was the shareholders who had the upper-hand in the balance of power within a business corporation because they were the ultimate suppliers of money that could buy factories and other productive facilities. Of course, a large force of workers has to be hired in order to operate factory systems, but their role within a corporate organization remains subordinate to physical capital, and hence subordinate to the shareholders.

In contrast, in this new era of post-industrial capitalism, the physical capital has surrendered its central position to the knowledge-based human capital that money can no longer buy and hence control directly. The balance of power within a business corporation is clearly tilting away from suppliers of money towards suppliers of knowledge-based human capital, especially to those who contribute to organization-specific human capital, that is, from shareholders to workers, engineers, researchers, and managers who have made a long-term commitment to the corporation.

Thus, we have seen that there are two fundamental sources of inefficiency in corporate organizations – moral hazard problems and hold-up problems, and there is a trade-off between them.

The nominalistic corporate system is able to solve or at least mitigate the moral hazard problem, but only at the expense of the hold-up problem. Nominalistic corporations are thus better adapted to the stage of industrial capitalism, because its major source of profits is physical capital over which shareholders have direct control, whereas human capital is only a helping factor to run the physical capital efficiently.

On the other hand, the realistic corporate system has a comparative advantage in minimizing the hold-up problem, but of course at the expense of moral hazard problems. To the extent that organization-specific human capital plays a central role in a corporation's capability of generating profits, we expect many business corporations to adopt realistic forms in this new era of post-industrial capitalism.

12 The future of the Japanese corporate system

Global capitalism is now on a slow road to recovery from a global depression on a scale not seen since the Great Depression of 1930s. Since the onset of the twenty-first century, the US economy has undergone a series of crises that have increasingly shaken the confidence in its corporate model – the collapse of the IT-boom-turned-IT-bubble in 2001, the Enron and other big corporate scandals during 2001–2002, and the subprime loan crisis that began in 2007 and ended up being what the former FED chairman Alan Greenspan called the "once in a hundred years" financial crisis. The shock triggered by the spectacular collapse of Lehman Brothers, the fourth largest US securities corporation, on September 15, 2008 not only spread across the entire world instantaneously through tightly-knit international networks of financial markets, but also led to a sharp downturn in the real economy through extensive international trades of goods and services. As an almost reflexive reaction to the swiftness, breadth, and depth of the crisis, we have seen a sudden revival of large scale fiscal and monetary stimuli and a concerted effort to implement tighter financial regulations among advanced capitalist countries: initiatives which only a few years ago would have been summarily dismissed as harmful to the smooth working of the market system's "invisible hand." The lessons of the Great Depression have not been completely forgotten, and global capitalism will in all likelihood be saved from the catastrophe of the dimension of 1930s. Yet, the fact that the epicenter of this global economic crisis is the US economy, above all, its financial sector has severely undermined the shareholder-orientated view of the corporate system – a view that had been championed as the "global standard."

It is now widely agreed that one of the underlying causes of the speculative bubbles whose collapse led to the US subprime loan crisis is the "excess liquidity" in the global financial markets. This is indeed the inevitable consequence of the transition of capitalism from the stage of "industrial" to the stage of "post-industrial" that has shifted the major source of profits for business corporations from physical capital that money can buy to human capital that money cannot buy. In this sense, this "once in a hundred years" financial crisis has marked the dramatic beginning of post-industrial capitalism that will bring about the eclipse of the nominalistic/shareholder-orientated model of corporate system.

Does this not suggest the revival of the Japanese-style corporate system?

On the basis of the two-tier nature of corporate structure, a theoretical possibility has been illustrated that a corporation can free itself from the control of outside shareholders and become purely realistic without violating any of the basic framework of corporate law. Indeed, the post-war Japanese corporate system not only demonstrated historically that such realistic corporate systems actually inhabited the capitalist world but also displayed empirically that they are even capable of outperforming the nominalistic corporate system for a considerable period of time. If there is indeed a tendency in the age of post-industrial capitalism for the leading corporate model to shift from the nominalistic to the realistic form, does this not suggest that the Japanese-style corporate system with its emphasis on the autonomy of organization will make a swift comeback in the future?

The answer is not as simple as the question might imply. It is true that extensive cross-shareholding has enabled the Japanese-style corporate system to minimize the influence of short-sighted shareholders, thereby providing employees, engineers, researchers, and managers with an organizational environment that is congenial to their in-house accumulation of skills and knowledge. Yet, in the era of industrial capitalism, even in its "late stage" where capital-intensive industries became dominant, the major source of profits was the scale and scope of economies of production facilities and distribution networks. The organization-specific human capital was subordinate to physical capital in that their contribution to corporate profits was only to coordinate the flow of inputs and outputs and maintain the efficient rate of capacity utilization. In contrast, in the era of post-industrial capitalism the large scale factory system takes a back seat and in its place the human organization itself, capable of doing things differently, plays the central role as the major source of profits. Even though both late-industrial capitalism and post-industrial capitalism require organization-specific human capital, the former requires the specificity to productive facilities and distributional networks fixed in factories and the latter the specificity to the human organization itself in each corporation. Needless to say, it is not an easy task to transform the skills and knowledge of workers, engineers, researchers, and managers from those specific to productive facilities and distributional networks fixed in corporate factories to those specific to the very human organization in which they are working.

My message for the future of Japanese corporate system is therefore a seemingly contradictory one: it does not have to change but it does have to change.

The Japanese corporate system does *not* have to change, because its history of distancing itself from the ideology of shareholder sovereignty may work as an advantage in the new era of post-industrial capitalism, in contradiction to the orthodox view in economics and law.

The Japanese corporate system *does* have to change, because its destiny in the new era of post-industrial capitalism hinges not on the designing of a corporate organization that assists the efficient use of the scale and scope of economies of physical capital but on the cultivation of the corporate organization itself that is able to inspire its employees, engineers and managers to generate different ways of doing things from others. The Japanese corporate system is poised and well-positioned for the future; we can only wait to see what unfolds.

Notes

1 One puzzle in this result is that "Retention of Employees" and "Improvement of Employees' Benefits" earned low scores even among Japanese managers. This is perhaps due to the fact that unless the corporation as a business organization would survive and grow it is not possible to secure the job of and improve the benefits of employees. Note also that the more recent questionnaire study by Jacoby *et al.* (2005) has shown a high mark for the job security in Japanese corporations.

2 Hansmann and Kraakman (2000).

3 See, for instance, Yoshimori (1998), Jacoby *et al.* (2005), Tanaka (2006), Itami (2006), Japan Management Association (2009).

4 Section 3.02 of the American Bar Association's *Revised Model Business Corporation Act (RMBCA)* states that:

> Unless its articles of incorporation provide otherwise, every corporation ... has the same power as an individual to do things necessary or convenient to carry out its business and affairs, including without limitation power: (1) to sue and be sued, complain and defend in its corporate name;... (4) to purchase, receive, lease, or otherwise acquire, and own, hold, improve, use, and otherwise deal with, real or personal property, or any legal or equitable interest in property, wherever located; (5) to sell, convey, mortgage, pledge, lease, exchange, and otherwise dispose of all or any part of its property.

5 Other rights are rights to inspect the records and books, rights to sue the directors and officers against their wrongful acts on the corporation, rights to share in the proceeds recovered when the corporation liquidates its assets, etc.

6 There is a huge body of writings on this controversy. Some of the best-known works available in English are Machen (1911), Maitland (1900), Dewey (1926), Radin (1932), Hart (1954), Hessen, (1979), Dan-Cohen (1986), Teubner (1988). For a comprehensive review of various theories of corporate personality before 1930, see Hallis (1930). In Iwai (1999) I have given an extensive discussion on this controversy. See also Iwai (2002).

7 See, for instance, Coase (1937), Alchian and Demsetz (1972), Jensen and Meckling (1976), Easterbrook and Fischel (1991), and Williamson (1985), Grossman and Hart (1986), Hart (1995).

8 See, for instance, Penrose (1959), Nelson and Winter (1982), Teece (1982), Werner-felt (1984), Prahalad and Hamel (1990), and Chandler (1990).

9 For the notion of the market for corporate control, see Manne (1965).

10 Moreover, if this hierarchical structure is combined with cross-shareholdings at each hierarchical layer, the capitalist family at the top can further enhance the leverage of their own capital.

11 The classic work that applies the moral hazard model to the theory of firm is Jensen and Meckling (1976). For the hold-up problem, see, for instance, Hart (1995).

12 The traditional corporate governance theory, reviewed, for instance, by Shleifer (1997), has been mostly concentrated on this problem.

13 See, for instance, Hall (2000), Blair and Wallman (2001), and Corrado *et al.* (2005).

14 In fact, what I am maintaining is that the industrial capitalism is a form of capitalism that presupposes the dualistic structure *à la* Arthur Lewis (1954). Kindleberger (1967) applied Lewis's dual structure model to the explanation of the post-war European economies' "miraculous" growth. He also suggested that the same explanation might also be applied to the British industrial revolution in the eighteenth century as well as to the US catching-up process to the British economy in the late nineteenth century. Ranis (2004) and Hayami and Godo (2005, chapters 3–5) are the recent and insightful reviews on the relevance of the Lewis model. Note that all that is necessary for industrial capitalism to work as profit-generating mechanism is the persistence of wage difference between the industrialized urban sector and the traditional rural area.

References

Alchian, A. and Demsetz, H. (1972) "Production, Information Costs, and Economic Organization," *American Economic Review* 62, 777–795.

Blair, M. and Wallman, S. (2001) *Unseen Wealth*, Washington, DC: Brookings Institute Press.

Chandler, A. (1990) *Scale and Scope: The Dynamics of Industrial Capitalism*, Cambridge: Belknap Press.

Coase, R. (1937) "The Nature of the Firm," *Economica N.S.* 4, 386–405.

Corrado, C., Haltinger, J., and Sichel, D. (eds.) (2005), *Measuring Capital in the New Economy*, Chicago: University of Chicago Press.

Dan-Cohen, M. (1986) *Rights, Persons, and Organizations*, Berkeley, CA: University of California Press.

Dewey, J. (1926) "The Historical Background of Corporate Legal Personality," *Yale Law Journal* 35, 655–673.

Easterbrook, F. and Fischel, D. (1991) *The Economic Structure of Corporate Law*, Cambridge, MA: Harvard University Press.

Grossman, S.J. and Hart, O.D. (1986) "The Costs and Benefits of Ownership: A Theory of Vertical and Lateral Integration," *Journal of Political Economy* 94 (4), 691–719.

Hall, R. (2000) "E-Capital: The Link between the Stock Market and the Labor Market in the 1990s," *Brookings Papers on Economic Activity*, 2, 73–118.

Hallis, F. (1930) *Corporate Personality: A Study of Jurisprudence*, Oxford: Oxford University Press.

Hansmann, H. and Kraakman, R. (2000) "The End of History for Corporate Law," *Georgetown Law Journal*, 89, 439.

Hart, H.L.A. (1954) "Definition and Theory in Jurisprudence," *Law Quarterly Review*, 70, 37–60.

Hart, O. (1995) *Firms, Contracts and Financial Structure*, Oxford: Oxford University Press.

Hart, O. (2005) "Incomplete Contracts and Public Ownership: Remarks, and an Application to Public–Private Partnerships," in D. Grimsey and M.K. Lewis (eds.) *The Economics of Public Private Partnerships*, Cheltenham: Edward Elgar Publishing.

Hayami, Y. and Godo, Y. (2005) *Development Economics: From the Poverty to the Wealth of Nations*, Oxford: Oxford University Press.

Itami, H. (eds.) (2006) *Corporate Profitability in Japan and US*, Tokyo: Yuhikaku (in Japanese).

Iwai, K. (1999) "Persons, Things and Corporations: The Corporate Personality Controversy and Comparative Corporate Governance," *American Journal of Comparative Law* 47, 583–632.

Iwai, K. (2002) "The Nature of the Business Corporation – Its Legal Structure and Economic Functions," *Japanese Economic Review*, 53 (3), 243–273.

Jacoby, S., Nason, H., and Saguchi, K. (2005) "The Role of the Senior HR Executive in Japan and the United States: Employment Relations, Corporate Governance, and Values," *Industrial Relations: A Journal of Economy and Society* 41 (2), 207–241.

Japan Management Association (2009), News Release on "The 12th Survey on Newly Appointed Executives." Online, available at: www.jma.or.jp/news/release_detail.html?id=53 (in Japanese).

Jensen, M. and Meckling, W. (1976) "The Theory of Firm: Managerial Behavior, Agency Costs and Ownership Structure," *Journal of Financial Economics*, 3, 305–360.

Kindleberger, C.P. (1967) *Europe's Postwar Growth: The Role of Labor Supply*, Cambridge, MA: Harvard University Press.

Lewis, W.A. (1954) "Economic Development with Unlimited Supplies of Labor," *Manchester School of Economic and Social Studies*, 22, 139–191.

Machen, Jr., A. (1911) "Corporate Personality," *Harvard Law Review* 24, 253, 347–365.

Maitland, F.M. (1900) "Translator's Introduction," to Otto Gierke, *Political Theories of the Middle Age*, Cambridge: Cambridge University Press.

Manne, H. (1965) "Mergers and the Market for Corporate Control," *Journal of Political Economy* 73, 110–120.

Minami, R. (1973) *The Turning Point in Economic Development: Japan's Experience*, Tokyo: Kinokuniya.

Nelson, R. and Winter, S. (1982) *An Evolutionary Theory of Economic Change*, Cambridge, MA: Harvard University Press.

Penrose, E. (1959) *The Theory of the Growth of the Firm*, Oxford: Oxford University Press.

Prahalad, C.K. and Hamel, G. (1990), "The Core Competence of the Corporation," *Harvard Business Review* 68, 79–91.

Radin, M. (1932) "The Endless Problem of Corporate Personality," *Columbia Law Review* 32, 643–667.

Ranis, G. (2004) "Arthur Lewis' Contribution to Development Thinking and Policy," *Manchester School*, 72 (6), 712–723.

Shleifer, A. (1997) "A Survey of Corporate Governance," *Journal of Finance* 52, 737–783.

Schumpeter, J.A. (1950) *Capitalism, Socialism and Democracy*, third edition, New York: Rand McNally.

Tanaka, K. (2006) "Shareholders Sovereignty vs. Employees Supremacy: Dilemma of Publicly-held Corporations in Japan," RIETI Discussion Paper Series 06-J-035, Tokyo: RIETI (in Japanese).

Teece, D.J. (1982) "Towards an Economic Theory of the Multi-Product Firm," *Journal of Economic Behavior and Organization* 3, 39–63.

Teubner, G. (1988) "Enterprise Corporatism: New Industrial Policy and the 'Essence' of the Legal Person," *American Journal of Comparative Law* 36, 130–155.

Vogel, Ezra (1979) *Japan as Number One: Lessons for America*, Cambridge: Harvard University Press.

Wernerfelt, B. (1984) "A Resource-Base View of the Firm," *Strategic Management Journal* 5, 171–180.

Williamson, O. (1985) *The Economic Institutions of Capitalism*, Glencoe: Free Press.

Winter, S. (1988) "On Coase, Competence, and the Corporation," *Journal of Law, Economics, and Organization* 4, 163–184.

Yoshimori, M (1998) "Whose Company Is It? The Concept of the Corporation in Japan, the United States and Europe," *Yokohama Keiei Kenkyu*, 19 (1), 42–54.

6 Dismissal regulation in Japan[1]

Ryo Kambayashi

1 Legal systems, economic growth, and human capital investment

Do legal systems affect economic growth? Intuition suggests that indeed better approaches are likely to result in higher growth, yet, there are plenty of historical examples which seem to present evidence to the contrary. For example, the divergence between Japan and China during the twentieth century shows that legal systems certainly changed the course of economic development. On the other hand, the economic convergence during the latter half of the twentieth century between the United Kingdom, (West) Germany, and France, with their different legal traditions, suggests that legal approaches did not matter much for the achievement of economic growth.

A typical perspective on this issue is provided by the economic historians Douglass North and Richard Thomas (North and Thomas 1976). Conducting a qualitative examination of economic growth in pre-modern Europe, they argue that the key for economic development is legal systems, that is, the extent to which checks are imposed on the arbitrary exercise of power. As an example, they chose the case of Spain and Portugal. During the sixteenth century, the two countries flourished and led the world into the Age of Discovery. Their economic development, however, slowed during the seventeenth century and they were eventually left behind by Britain in the eighteenth century. Although Spain and Portugal were able to gain tremendous wealth from trade and from their colonies, they never became leading international powers again. According to high school textbooks, the turning point was the defeat of the Spanish Armada in 1588 at the hands of Francis Drake. North and Thomas, however, argue that it was the artisans in the wool industry that were responsible for the turn in fortunes. The wool industry was the most innovative industry of the day, but, North and Thomas argue, the unconstrained exercise of power by the rulers – including the collection of arbitrary taxes and the confiscation of private assets – led to an exodus of artisans from the Iberian Peninsula to England, where, following the revolution of 1688, Parliament imposed constraints on the Crown. Political rulers were prevented from the arbitrary exercise of power. Legal systems, to protect private ownership, provided incentives for investment in the industry and laid the foundation for the Industrial Revolution. Thus, explaining why the Industrial Revolution occurred at this particular time, in the eighteenth century, and in this particular place, England. North and Thomas provide a clear illustration of how legal arrangements affected the incentive for investment which resulted in different trajectories of economic development.

All developed countries today have in place legal systems that provide protection for private property and a legal basis for financial and physical transactions. It is not only investment in physical assets that is important for economic development. As has been widely pointed out, another important source of economic growth is human capital accumulation, such as through experience, formal education, and vocational training. Thus, if we were to extend North and Thomas's argument concerning pre-modern Europe to industrialized societies today, one could argue that the legal protection of human capital also plays a crucial role in economic growth.

Of course, in the case of investment by workers in their own human capital, "confiscation" of such human capital would require physical constraints on workers and amount to slavery. When it comes to investment by one person in the human capital of another, however, a more realistic, economic problem arises since the realized value of such investment will depend on the effort of the person in whom the investment is made; the latter can "confiscate" or "free-ride" on the investment of the former. Without mechanisms to safeguard the investor's return on investment in human capital, it is unlikely that sufficient investment in human capital will be forthcoming. This is especially the case at early stages of development, when, due to poverty, workers have few resources to invest in human capital accumulation. It is important to establish mechanisms to ensure that those in a society with surplus funds shoulder the costs of human capital accumulation of others.

2 The role of legal systems in the labor market

The preceding considerations suggest that legal systems have a role to play in providing the necessary incentives for human capital formation. Finding the appropriate legal arrangements so that such an investment in human capital is forthcoming is anything but straightforward. The use of direct coercion in this context is clearly in conflict with fundamental rights; someone who has invested in the human capital of another can neither force that person to perform a particular job assignment nor confiscate a portion of that person's salary simply because of the investment in that person's human capital. The investor does not have ownership of that human capital. One theoretical possibility, instead of such direct coercion, would be to use indirect coercion through a loan contract where the recipient of the human capital investment borrows the funds from the investor. Investments and loan contracts, however, are generally different legal arrangements in terms of implementation, risk allocation, etc. For example, a loan contract has to fix, ex ante, the future return and the borrower faces various uncertainties. Moreover, with a loan contract, the borrower can use the funds for purposes other than investing them in his human capital. For these reasons, Becker (1993) proposed the simple rule that to achieve efficient investment in human capital, workers themselves should bear the cost of investment in general human capital which is useful anywhere in the economy, while employers should bear the cost of investment in specific human capital which is beneficial only in a specific environment such as a particular firm or industry.

Becker's classic argument, however, cannot be applied to joint investment in human capital. A widespread example of such joint investment is on-the-job training (OJT) where employers bear costs in terms of lower productivity during training, while employees make an effort to achieve higher productivity. Typically, the size and share of the costs borne by the two parties is anything but clear and, should the employee leave the company (or be dismissed), it would be very difficult to determine how the employer should be compensated for the investment which is being lost. Therefore, in the case of joint investment in human capital, it is difficult to find efficient contractual arrangements between employers and employees. The simple extension of civil or commercial law to labor market transactions does not provide a framework that safeguards the benefits of human capital investment. This is one of the reasons that labor law, as an independent legal field separate from civil and commercial law, has developed since the beginning of the twentieth century.

The purpose of this chapter is to take a closer look at the role of legal arrangements and their impact on human capital accumulation using the Japanese case of "dismissal regulation" as an example. Dismissal can be seen as a unilateral breach of contract by the employer, and dismissal practices affect workers' incentives regarding the amount of effort they devote to OJT, which in turn affect the efficiency with which the labor market operates. The Japanese case offers an instructive example because joint investment in human capital through OJT plays a particularly important role. The rise in competitiveness of Japan's manufacturing industries since the 1960s is closely associated with the sharing of production information across occupations, and investment in specific human capital through OJT. Human resource practices have also fostered a deep commitment of workers to their company. For instance, the so-called "Quality Control Circles" were formed through the voluntary participation of workers after their regular working hours. Such "Quality Control Circles" provided workers with the opportunity to share productivity-enhancing information, such as improving design aspects of new products, in an effort to achieve more efficient production. Since workers usually did not receive any payment for attending such circles, it is clear that they were not formed as part of written labor contracts.[2] Moreover, the information shared and the human capital accumulated through such OJT was likely to be of little use outside a specific firm. It is unlikely that workers would have been prepared to invest their own spare time in order to achieve productivity improvements without sufficiently credible employment protection.

Put differently, this means that Japanese manufacturing firms successfully managed to persuade employees that they would not be easily dismissed, leading to productivity gains that allowed firms to compete in international markets through the mechanisms just described. This effect is amply documented in numerous case studies by Koike (1983) and this link between employers' commitment to long-term employment and high worker productivity has subsequently been confirmed in an empirical study by Kato and Morishima (2002) using micro data of a large survey. Studies examining the role of long-term employment from an international, comparative perspective, led by the one by Hashimoto and Raisian (1985), have repeatedly shown that the return to tenure is much higher in Japan than in the United States and that long-term employment is much more common in the former than the latter. In addition, as shown in Bognanno and Kambayashi (2009), different from the United States, in Japan, wage losses from job change are strongly related to age and tenure. Although providing only indirect evidence, these findings are clearly consistent with the notion that employers in Japan have established a commitment not to dismiss workers easily, while workers voluntarily engage in productivity-enhancing activities.

In this context, examining the role of "dismissal regulation" in Japan can provide important clues regarding the formation of institutional arrangements that safeguard investment in human capital. Such an examination also provides a starting point for future research as to why and how labor markets differ from markets for goods and services.

3 Dismissal regulation in Japan and the doctrine of abusive dismissal

In order to understand the legal constraints it imposes on economic agents, this section provides an overview of the establishment of "dismissal regulation" in Japan.

Japan's legal tradition since the nineteenth century is largely based on continental European law, particularly German law, and as such is mainly based on the statutory law system. Because statutory laws do not cover all possible contingencies, they, just like in other countries, are complemented by judicial precedents set by the courts. Japan's labor law is similarly subject to such a dual legal framework. On the one hand, the Labor Standards Act sets clear national minimum standards, specifying, for example, in Article 32 that "an employer shall not have a worker work more than 40 hours per week, excluding rest periods" and that "an employer shall not have a worker work more than eight hours per day for each day of the week."[3] On the other, there are few specific statutes governing procedures concerning the conclusion, change, or termination of labor contracts. To make up for this lack of legislation, Japanese courts have gradually constructed their own case law since 1945. The most important is the case law for dismissing employees, the Doctrine of Abusive Dismissal (Kaikoken Ranyo Hori).[4]

Although there has been some academic debate about whether the doctrine has impeded economic activity by imposing excess costs on employers (see, e.g., Ohtake *et al.* 2002), there is little empirical evidence to determine whether it has actually interfered with employment adjustment. One of the main reasons for this is the lack of data,[5] but another reason is the interpretation of the doctrine from the perspective of economics. Economists implicitly assume that the doctrine represents a monetary tax on employers (or severance transfers from employers to employees). From a legal perspective, the doctrine merely provides a social norm, since employers can adjust their number of employees without any additional payment as long as they follow the doctrine. Thus, the doctrine imposes additional costs in some cases but not in all. To reconcile the two perspectives, legal and economic, it is useful to examine how the doctrine was established and what role it has played in actual disputes.

Based on the principle of contractual freedom, Japan's Civil Code allows the dismissal of employees at any time, if the contract is open-ended. Article 627 states: "If the parties have not specified the term of employment, either party may request to terminate at any time. In such cases, employment shall terminate on the expiration of two weeks from the day of the request to terminate." Thus, with regard to the termination of labor contracts, the Civil Code imposes only procedural conditions (i.e., two weeks' notice), but no substantial conditions, such as compensation, etc. What is noteworthy is that the Civil Code makes no distinction between termination of employment by the employer (dismissal) or by the employee (resignation).

Although Article 627 of the Civil Code has not been changed since its enactment in 1896, changes in the economic and political environment have led to the addition of supplementary regulations on the termination of employment by employers. For example, according to the Labor Standards Act of 1947, workers suffering from a job-related illness and women on maternity leave cannot be dismissed (Article 19), and an employer wishing to dismiss an employee must give at least 30 days' advance notice or, when not giving 30 days' notice, pay the average wages for a period of at least 30 days (Article 20).

The Act on Securing, etc. of Equal Opportunity and Treatment between Men and Women in Employment of 1985 prohibits, in Article 6, discrimination against workers on the basis of sex with regard to dismissal, while Article 7 of the Labor Union Act of 1949 states:

> The employer shall not [...] discharge or treat in a disadvantageous manner a worker for the reason such as the worker's being a member of a labor union, having tried to join or organize a labor union or having performed justifiable acts of a labor union.

Leaving the world of pure contractual freedom of the Civil Code behind them, these labor laws restrict employers' conduct with regard to the discharge of employees. It is important to note that these statutes protect workers in specific situations (e.g., when suffering a job-related illness, being on maternity leave, engaged in union activity, etc.) but do not provide general dismissal rules.

As a result, Japanese courts have gradually established their own case law. Legitimate justification for regular dismissals is required, or otherwise the dismissal may be regarded as an abuse of the individual's rights and judged invalid. This case law is called the "Doctrine of Abusive Dismissal." This doctrine distinguishes two categories of dismissal, depending on the reason. The first is "normal dismissal" where an employee is dismissed for specific individual reasons, while the second is "economic dismissal" where there are no individual reasons for dismissal but rather the dismissal is due to the employer's circumstances. No-fault layoffs usually fall under the second category. In the case of "normal dismissals," the Supreme Court decided in 1975 that:

> Even when an employer exercises its right of dismissal, it will be void as an abuse of the right if it is not based on objectively reasonable grounds so that it cannot receive general social approval as a proper act.[6]

Two years later, the Supreme Court stated again that:

> Even where there are normal reasons for a dismissal, an employer does not always have the right to dismiss. If, under the specific circumstances of the case, the dismissal is unduly unreasonable so that it cannot receive general social approval as a proper act, the dismissal will be void as an abuse of the right of dismissal.[7]

Thus, even if a worker is dismissed for individual reasons, the unilateral termination of an open-ended labor contract by the employer must satisfy additional conditions, that is, the dismissal must be "objectively reasonable" and "socially acceptable." In addition, the courts, by using their authority to request an explanation (*shakumeiken*), can require the defendant (i.e., the employer in a dismissal case) to prove that the unilateral termination does not constitute an abuse of rights. Because it is difficult for employees to verify the employer's behavior and/or intent, this reversal of the burden of proof in practice is one of the most important aspects of the doctrine.

The meaning of "objectively reasonable" and "socially acceptable" of this doctrine is illustrated most clearly by referring to the leading case on economic dismissals, which is the Tokyo High Court case of *Shimazaki* v. *Toyo Sanso* from 1979,[8] with the Supreme Court specifying the following four assessment criteria four years later:

1 The employer must provide a reasonable explanation to the court of the need to reduce the number of workers.
2 The dismissal must be the last resort to adjust labor input.
3 The selection of the persons to be discharged should be proper.
4 The dismissal procedure should be reasonable.

These four criteria are sometimes referred to as the Doctrine of Economic Dismissal in order to distinguish them from the two simple conditions of "objectively reasonable" and "socially acceptable." They do not specify, however, what kind of employer actions will be deemed acceptable by the courts. A detailed examination of actual judgments in layoff cases between 1975 and 1984 is provided in Kambayashi and Hirasawa (2008a), which seeks to clarify which actions of employers the courts did or did not recognize as acceptable behavior.

Generally, the interpretation of the first criterion regarding the necessity of reducing the number of workers is that the layoffs must be carried out with sufficient consideration of business needs. Up until the first half of the 1980s, as the doctrine evolved, judgments were based on "whether or not the firm would go bankrupt without an adjustment of the number of employees."[9] Since the latter half of the 1980s, with the doctrine having matured, the courts have tended to leave it up to employers to decide the need for adjusting the number of employees, but have examined whether the reasoning used by employers was logically consistent.

The second criterion, that dismissal must be the last resort, means that dismissals are justified only when other methods of labor adjustment are not available. Textbooks on labor law suggest that courts will examine efforts to avoid layoffs such as the solicitation of voluntary retirements, a halt on new recruitment, or transferring workers to other positions, and determine whether these efforts on the whole satisfy the second criterion. The basis on which courts actually assess such efforts is still ambiguous. Let us consider as an example, the treatment of solicitations for voluntary retirement. Under Japan's life-time employment system, solicitations for voluntary retirement appear to be a common way to avoid dismissals and therefore appear to be a good example. In Kambayashi and Hirasawa (2008a), we examined 54 court cases concerning economic dismissals during the period 1975–1984. In 16 of these 54 cases, the courts ruled that the dismissals were invalid because employers did not make sufficient efforts to avoid dismissals. In eight of these 16 cases, however, the firms actually did solicit voluntary retirements, illustrating that such solicitation is not sufficient to meet the last-resort criterion. On the other hand, there were 34 cases in which employers did not solicit voluntary retirements. In 15 of these 34 cases, the courts accepted the employers' justification of the layoffs; and in 12 of these 15 cases, the courts explicitly stated that the employer had satisfied the last-resort criterion without any solicitation of voluntary retirements. Thus, the solicitation of voluntary retirements is not always necessary to meet the last-resort criterion. In sum, although the solicitation of voluntary retirement is probably the most common way to avoid dismissals under Japan's life-time employment system, court rulings do not provide an unambiguous indication as to how important such efforts are.

Next, the purpose of the third criterion is said to be the elimination of arbitrary dismissals. In actual cases, employers that, for example, had chosen to lay off married female employees with two or more children[10] or used no criteria whatsoever[11] were defeated because the selection of the persons to be dismissed was deemed to be not proper.

Finally, the fourth criterion implies that employers have to explain the necessity of layoffs to workers and/or unions with or without collective agreements.

In actual cases, the courts essentially judged efforts to have been insufficient only when employers did not explain the reasons for layoffs at all.

Overall, the Doctrine of Economic Dismissal provides some guidance with regard to acceptable employment adjustment procedures. Yet, there remains some ambiguity with regard to the strictness with which the specific criteria are applied. Although in economics, dismissal regulations are typically treated as a tax and the effects are assessed using statistical data and estimation techniques, the approach chosen here to examine the economic effects of the Doctrine of Abusive Dismissal is to analyze its role in actual dispute resolution.

4 Leading cases in the doctrine of abusive dismissal

One of the most important roles of courts is, of course, to resolve disputes, and case law is the result of such resolutions. With regard to the Doctrine of Abusive Dismissal, court decisions have been examined and polished through 30 years of scholarship, into the legal principles outlined in the preceding section. It is also instructive to examine how these principles were arrived at and the conflicts that the courts had to resolve in the process. The following are brief summaries of some of the leading cases that have contributed to the Doctrine of Abusive Dismissal.

The first leading case is that of *Ichikawa* v. *Nihon Shokuen Seizo Co.*, in which the employer dismissed a worker who had been expelled from the union. The reason for the expulsion from the union was serious political disagreements within the union. Informed that the plaintiff had been expelled from the union, it was quite natural for the employer to dismiss the expelled worker because there was a union shop agreement between the employer and the union. The worker went to court not to contest the expulsion from the union but the dismissal from the firm; the defendant in this case was not the union but the employer. After examining the case, the court decided that the expulsion from the union had been unfair; therefore, the dismissal based on the unfair expulsion from the union was held void. To arrive at this decision, the court invoked the fundamental principle of the Civil Code (Article 1) that "no abuse of rights is permitted," and concluded that even when an employer exercises his right of dismissal (dismissal based on the union shop agreement in this case), this will be void as an abuse of rights if "it cannot receive general social approval as a proper act." And in this particular case, it was clear that the true cause of the dispute was the conflict among workers.

The second leading case is that of *Kochi Hoso Co.*, in which a broadcasting company dismissed a radio announcer because he had been late for work twice within two weeks and as a result the company had to skip, once completely and once partly, its ten-minute news program. The court questioned several officers in relation to the two missed broadcasts and it emerged that the person charged with ensuring that the announcer reported to work on time had also been late and that there had been other occasions in the past not involving the plaintiff, when broadcasts were missed. The plaintiff, however, was the only person in the company who had been dismissed. Thus, the court ruled that the dismissal was unfair because there was no reason that only the plaintiff should have been dismissed and none of the other employees who had been guilty of the same behavior. In sum, the court concluded that if, in the specific circumstances of a case, the dismissal is "unduly unreasonable so that it cannot receive general social approval as a proper action, the dismissal will be void as an abuse of the right of dismissal."

Finally, the third leading case to be taken up here is *Shimazaki et al.* v. *Toyo Sanso*. This case is a typical example of no-fault layoffs caused by technological progress. The company operated in an industry, the gas industry, whose competitiveness had gradually declined during the 1960s and 1970s because of technological changes. The managers decided to close one of its factories and dismissed almost all of the employees working there. The employees argued in court that the company could have avoided layoffs by transferring employees to other factories in the same company which were still expanding in those days. The district court followed the employees' argument and decided that the layoffs were void. In contrast, the high court did not regard the employer under any obligation to transfer workers and concluded that the layoffs were effective. It is in this ruling that the Tokyo High Court presented the four criteria outlined above that should be satisfied for no-fault dismissals. The ruling was subsequently approved by the Supreme Court. In an interesting twist, even after the Supreme Court decision, the actual dispute continued for ten more years and ended in a settlement, in which the two parties agreed that, although the courts had ruled that the dismissals were effective, the layoffs had been unjustified and half of the plaintiffs (six persons) would be reinstated under their original job titles in the company.

In Kambayashi and Hirasawa (2008b), we tried to shed light on the details of the case through direct interviews with the plaintiffs. The study shows that the main reason for the dispute was a split in the union. Specifically, the union was split into two factions, with the minority faction having its base in the factory that was to be closed – something that was not observable to outsiders. In the interviews, the plaintiffs indicated that there was a strong sense that they had been singled out for "political" reasons and, therefore, decided to go to court. Unfortunately, Toyo Sanso employed the union shop system and the minority faction could not withdraw from the union. Because negotiations between the firm and the union were all conducted by members of the majority faction, the minority faction did not have an avenue for direct negotiations with the firm and the only place to resolve grievances was the courts. The courts were unable to bridge the rift, since in examining the negotiation process between the firm and the union they did not distinguish between minority and majority union factions. Ultimately, by force of circumstances, the only issues addressed in the courts were whether it would have been possible to transfer these employees and similar, related questions. The main issues of the dispute, however, were how to re-establish direct communication between the company and the minority faction and address the sense among those in the minority faction that they were being laid off for "political" reasons. Thus, the courts failed to deal with the true issues and, as a result, the court ruling did little to resolve the actual dispute.

The disputes in these three leading cases essentially focused on industrial relations and the fair and equal treatment of employees. When there were multiple unions (or union factions) within the same firm as was common during the 1970s, it was quite natural for employers to try to expel extreme groups from the firm. Under these circumstances, disputes could become quite severe and end up in court when employees suspected that layoffs were not motivated by genuine business reasons and were not implemented in a fair and equitable manner but instead were based on "political" reasons and implemented in a discriminatory fashion. In sum, the Doctrine of Abusive Dismissal arose from industrial relations conflicts.

These observations are confirmed in Kambayashi and Hirasawa (2008a). As mentioned earlier, the study focuses on 54 cases of layoffs between 1975 and 1984. Of these, 34 cases (64 percent) were in the manufacturing sector, 13 cases (25 percent) in the service sector, five cases in educational institutions, and four cases in the health and welfare field. This distribution of the cases reflects the pattern of industrial disputes overall.

The 54 cases involved 469 employees in total, so the average number of employees per case is 8.7. The number of plaintiffs varied substantially, with 21 cases (39 percent) being single plaintiff cases, while 11 cases had more than ten plaintiffs. The biggest dispute was the case of *Hiroshima Glass Kogyo Co.*, in which 128 plaintiffs participated. To put these figures in perspective, it is useful to compare them with more recent ones reported in Kambayashi (2008). Examining 55 Tokyo District Court cases between 2000 and 2004, this study finds that the average number of plaintiffs in these cases was 2.1, and 37 cases, or 67 percent, were single plaintiff cases. Comparing this with the 8.7 plaintiffs per case and the much smaller percentage of single plaintiff cases (39 percent) for the cases between 1975 and 1984 suggests that the earlier cases had a strong element of collective conflict.

The subject matters of the cases also indicate that the disputes were of a collective interest nature. Of the 54 cases between 1975 and 1984, 28 cases (52 percent) were brought for "unfair labor practices." Article 7 of the 1945 Labor Union Act enumerates various types of acts that are prohibited as unfair practices. For example, employers can neither discharge a worker "because the worker is a member of a union" nor "refuse to bargain with the representatives of its employees without proper reasons." The fact that those cases were brought for "unfair labor practices" indicates that the underlying disputes were based on collective action. Thus, during the period when the Doctrine of Economic Dismissal evolved, roughly half of all no-fault dismissal cases were based on collective action. In contrast, of the 55 Tokyo District Court cases between 2000 and 2004, only eight cases (15 percent) were brought for "unfair labor practices."

One way to interpret the four criteria of the Doctrine of Abusive Dismissal is that they are intended to foster communication between employers and labor unions rather than to provide concrete norms to guide behavior. In fact, as shown in Kambayashi and Hirasawa (2008a), since the 1980s, labor-management relations have generally improved. In addition to the decline in left-wing radicalism, better communication between management and employees, in particular, the sharing of information by management regarding business situations plays a role. This means that employees are better informed with regard to the business circumstances facing the employer and are therefore less likely to interpret layoffs as politically motivated or arbitrary. With effective communication between management and labor, mass layoffs are less likely to become a source of discord. In fact, as shown in Muramatsu and Kambayashi (2008), mass layoffs since 1997 have not resulted in severe disputes between dismissed workers and employers.

5 Recent rulings by the Tokyo District Court and Article 18-2 of the Labor Standards Act

The analysis in the previous section suggested that the main function of the Doctrine of Abusive Dismissal was to encourage communication between management and labor to achieve "relational fairness" between employers and employees. Recent years have seen a number of rulings by the Tokyo District Court that have deviated from earlier rulings, and it is interesting to have a closer look at these cases.

Between 1998 and 2000, the Tokyo District Court issued several rulings which seem to depart from the traditional interpretation of the Doctrine of Abusive Dismissal. For example, in the case of *Kadokawa Bunka Shinko Zaidan*, the judge stated that because employers are essentially free to dismiss workers, the onus lies on the plaintiff to provide evidence proving the abuse of rights, and concluded that the dismissals were justified.[12] This stands in clear contradiction to the principle of reverse liability of the Doctrine of Abusive Dismissal. On the other hand, in the case of *National Westminster Bank*, the court argued that:

> The so-called four criteria for economic dismissals provide a classification of factors to be taken into consideration when determining whether a dismissal that can be thought to fall into the category of economic dismissals constitutes an abusive dismissal; they do not give rise to legal requirements in the sense of having the legal consequence that each criterion must be met; rather, each decision on abusive dismissal must be based on a comprehensive consideration of the specific circumstances of each individual case.[13]

Legal circles in Japan, accustomed to the traditional interpretation of the doctrine, were surprised by these decisions. The Labor Lawyers Association of Japan (*Nihon Rodo Bengodan*), for instance, condemned these decisions as changes to the Doctrine of Abusive Dismissal. The decisions were also widely reviewed in legal journals, with many scholars criticizing their inconsistency with previous rulings.

Apart from the legal arguments, it is also worth considering how the challenge to the Doctrine of Abusive Dismissal by the Tokyo District Court can be interpreted from an economic point of view. One possible explanation for the rulings is that the Tokyo District Court was reacting to recent changes in Japan's labor market and tried to reshape the doctrine.

Because it is too early to interview the plaintiffs, defendants, and judges of these cases, it is necessary to rely on indirect evidence from various statistical sources. The first observation from statistical sources is that there has been a continuous decrease since the 1980s, in collective disputes. According to the Survey on Labour Disputes, the estimated unionization rate decreased from 30.8 percent in 1980 to 25.2 percent in 1990 and 21.5 percent in 2000. The number of collective disputes, which in 1980 had stood at 4,376, also decreased to 2,071 in 1990 and 958 in 2000, even though Japan experienced a prolonged period of unprecedented economic malaise during the 1990s. These figures illustrate that the collective labor movement in Japan has been in decline. The second observation is that Japan's economic structure has changed. The Population Census shows that the share of production workers among employed persons decreased from 36.4 percent in 1980 to 35.1 percent in 1990 and further to 32.9 percent in 2000. In contrast, the share of office workers increased from 29.8 percent in 1980 to 34.4 percent in 1990 and 35.5 percent in 2000, overtaking the share of production workers. Thus, many of the labor disputes in the manufacturing sector that made up a large proportion of court cases when the Doctrine of Abusive Dismissal was established are unlikely to arise today, and many of the cases arising today are likely to differ from those 30 or 40 years ago.

The third observation is that human resource management practices have gradually changed. In the past, the typical labor contract at a Japanese company was open-ended and almost perfectly incomplete. Based on such a "carte blanche," the employer assigned the employee to various positions and jobs. On the other hand, the employee accumulated wide-ranging, firm-specific human capital through the experiences of OJT acquired in each position. More recently, however, many companies have started to introduce narrowly defined promotion ladders within certain positions and jobs. The General Survey on Working Conditions, for example, indicates that the share of companies which have introduced such specific career ladders increased from only 7.1 percent in 1981 to 19.5 percent in 2002.

These changes in the labor market mean that the content of dismissal cases filed in courts is likely to have changed considerably since the original cases on which the Doctrine of Abusive Dismissal was developed. In fact, examining dismissal cases filed with the Tokyo District Court between 2000 and 2004, Okuno and Hara (2008) find examples of cases that do not clearly fit the existing dichotomous distinction between "economic dismissals" and "normal dismissals," implying that the traditional distinction in Japanese legal scholarship may be becoming meaningless. In addition, the favorable start of the recently introduced industrial tribunal system shows that, in disputes involving individuals, disagreements between employers and employees regarding the true reason for dismissal do not play as large a role as in collective disputes. Rather, the main point of contention in individual disputes often appears to be financial issues given the dismissal (Muramatsu and Kambayashi 2008). In such cases, the usefulness of the Doctrine of Abusive Dismissal, which was established to resolve collective disputes been management and labor, may be limited (Kambayashi 2009). Based on these considerations, it could be argued that the dissenting rulings by the Tokyo District Court may represent a rational response to recent labor market changes and the fact that the focus of cases has shifted from collective disputes to individual disputes revolving around questions of financial compensation.

What is even more interesting, though, is that there have not actually been more rulings in the courts deviating from the Doctrine of Abusive Dismissal in the past decade or so. The reason for this is the revision of the Labor Standards Act in 2004, which now formally includes the Doctrine of Abusive Dismissal in the form of Article 18-2, which states: "A dismissal shall, where the dismissal lacks objectively reasonable grounds and is not considered to be appropriate in general societal terms, be treated as a misuse of that right and invalid." Although the article was added only in 2004, the debate in the years leading up to its addition is likely to have affected court decisions. When discussion on the article began, the original proposal prepared by the government contained an additional sentence, stating: "An employer may dismiss a worker where his right to dismiss is not restricted by this Law or other laws." This part of the proposed article was deleted during deliberations in the Diet, as it was feared to have the declaratory effect of encouraging dismissals.

One of the foci of Diet deliberations was the burden of proof. As seen in Section 3, under the Doctrine of Abusive Dismissal, it is incumbent on employers to prove that a dismissal is not abusive. In the original government proposal, however, the burden of proof lay with employees who needed to show that a dismissal was abusive. The Diet agreed that the purpose of legislation was not to change the case law but to widen it, and deleted the sentence, adding instead that "this new article shall not change the practice in the courts." If the original proposal had been enacted, the dissenting rulings of the Tokyo District Court might have been leading cases of the "modified" Doctrine of Abusive Dismissal. As it happens, however, the Diet deliberations further clarified that the enactment of the doctrine did not alter the practice of the case law. This confirmation of case law is likely to have affected subsequent rulings by the Tokyo District Court, since, in fact, no further dissenting rulings can be found following the amendment.

6 Concluding remarks

According to North and Thomas (1976), how to secure the investment when an economy grows is important. The insecurity of human capital investment is also a potential obstacle for underdeveloped countries. One of the most important candidates to restore confidence and to induce workers to invest their own human capital is a legal regulation on job security. In this chapter we focused on the evolution of legal regulation on dismissals in Japan; that is, the Doctrine of Abusive Dismissal.

By examining each court case, we found it was a spontaneous order which had grown out of the adjudication of industrial conflicts, resolving disputes revolving around mass layoffs. The Japanese legal regulation on dismissal is neither designed nor controlled by the government as a tax should be subject to. Moreover, as shown in Muramatsu and Kambayashi (2008), the effect of the doctrine has been on fostering communication between management and labor regarding business conditions of certain firms. The collective agreement on the environment is likely to lead them to agree collectively with the fairness of mass adjustment of workers. It may have helped to smooth the rapid adjustment of employment in Japan after 1997, which did not result in severe labor disputes. Even though more than one million workers were dismissed during the financial crisis, most of them did not feel their own dismissals were unfair enough to bring them into the court; in other words, they did not recognize the dismissals were a serious breach of contract and the workers who were not dismissed did not, in turn, consider the company deviated from the normal path.

The guidance provided by the doctrine contrasts with the direct constraints imposed on the contents of labor contracts by the Labor Standards Act. Such direct intervention in the labor market with regard to the price and quantity of labor – through minimum wages and statutory working hours – may be effective in developing countries where the primary aim is to ensure a national minimum level of worker welfare. However, uniform regulation by administrative fiat is unlikely to automatically lead to cooperation in the workplace and informal investment in specific human capital. Particularly when circumstances are idiosyncratically uncertain and labor contracts are essentially incomplete, it may be better to encourage micro-level spontaneous agreements between stake holders than to take a prescriptive, top-down approach.

On the other hand, although the doctrine may have enhanced the collective agreement, the Doctrine of Abusive Dismissal may not always have been useful in mediating the individual dismissal cases. When a worker is discharged due to a personal reason, the collective agreement does not always wipe away his rational doubt of unfair practice. In fact the labor market transition since the 1990s has caused to grow such individual conflicts. The dissenting rulings by the Tokyo District Court could have been the leading cases in the adaptation of the doctrine to changes in the labor market. On the contrary, the revision of the Labor Standards Act, as well as the deliberations in the Diet which have turned the doctrine into law, have rigidly fixed the application of the doctrine and may reduce its flexibility of interpretation to adjust to changing circumstances.

It is generally agreed that while case law has the disadvantage of being slow to respond to changing circumstances, it has the advantage of imposing a stable legal order independent of political vicissitudes. This is why we often find that legal protection of financial investments has been stronger and financial development faster in the Anglo-Saxon countries than in Continental Europe. In addition, it could be argued that the example of Japan's Doctrine of Abusive

Dismissal shows that case law also has the advantage of greater flexibility, especially when relevant circumstances are in a gradual transition, because each ruling must be sensitive to marginal changes. This contrasts with political decisions, which are likely to reflect the average change.

Given these considerations, a further examination of Japan's Doctrine of Abusive Dismissal can offer instructive insights in assessing the appropriate role of the legal framework in labor markets.

Notes

1 This chapter is based on a paper co-authored with Koichi Hamada titled "Kaikoken Ranyo Hori: Hanrei Hori to Keizai no Mekanizumu (The Doctrine of Abusive Dismissal: The Economic Mechanism of Case Law)" presented at the 2006 conference of the Japan Law and Economics Association held at the National Graduate Institute for Policy Studies (GRIPS), Tokyo. The author benefitted greatly from comments from the editors of this volume as well as from Ken Togo, Fumio Ohtake, participants in the above-mentioned Japan Law and Economic Association conference, and participants in a workshop held at the University of Tokyo on November 27, 2007. The findings and data presented in this chapter largely draw on collaboration with Kyota Eguchi, Masato Hara, Junko Hirasawa, Ryoichi Imai, and Hisashi Okuno-Takeuchi in the preparation of the edited volume titled *Kaiko Kisei no Hou to-Keizai* (The Law and Economics of Dismissal Regulation). The author is deeply grateful for their cooperation and consent to use the material from the volume for this chapter.
2 See case studies for the 1960s and 1970s in Koike (1977). Such practices continued even in subsequent decades, as shown in case studies by Aoki *et al.* (1989) and Inoki and Koike (1987; 2004).
3 Translations of Japanese laws, unless otherwise noted, are from the Ministry of Justice website (online, available at:www.japaneselawtranslation.go.jp).
4 Some of the case laws have been included in the Labor Contract Act newly legislated in 2007.
5 Considering that long-term employment naturally delays the employment adjustment and the doctrine covers all of Japan equally, it is difficult to identify the effects of the doctrine apart from the effects on long-term employment.
6 Judgment of April 25, 1975, *Ichikawa* v. *Nihon Shokuen Seizo Co.*, Supreme Court, vol. 29, Minshu, pp. 456–458. Translation from Sugeno (1992), p. 402.
7 Judgment of January 31, 1977, *Kochi Hoso Co.*, Supreme Court, vol. 268, *Rodo Hanrei*, p. 17. Translation from Sugeno (1992), p. 402.
8 Judgment of October 29, 1979, *Shimazaki* v. *Toyo Sanso*, Tokyo High Court, vol. 30, *Ro Minshu*, p. 1002.
9 Several judgments use the exact same phrase. Examples include the judgment of December 24, 1975, *Hamada* v. *Omura-Nogami Co.*, Omura Branch, Nagasaki District Court, vol. 98 *Hanrei Jiho*, p. 813, and the judgment of April 25, 1979, *Kawamoto et al.* v. *Hosokawa Seisakujyo Co.*, Sakai Branch, Osaka District Court, vol. 48, *Rohan*, p. 331.
10 Judgment of September 12, 1975, *Umezu et al.* v. *Koparu Co.*, Tokyo District Court, vol. 17, *Hanrei Jiho*, p. 789.
11 Judgment of April 25, 1979, *Kawamoto et al.* v. *Hosokawa Seisakujo Co.*, Sakai Branch, Osaka District Court, vol. 48, *Rohan*, p. 331.
12 Judgment of November 29, 1999, Tokyo District Court, *Rohan*, no. 780, p. 67.
13 Judgment of January 21, 2000, Tokyo District Court, *Rohan*, no. 782, p. 23. Author's translation.

References

Acemoglu, D., Johnson, S., and Robinson, J. (2001) "The Colonial Origins of Comparative Development: An Empirical Investigation," *American Economic Review* 91(5), pp. 1369–1401.

Aoki, M., Koike, K., and Nakatani, I., (eds.) (1989) *Nihon Kigyo Gurobaruka no Kenkyu* (Studies on Globalization of Japanese Firms), Tokyo: PHP Kenkyusho.

Becker, G. (1993) *Human Capital: A Theoretical and Empirical Analysis, with Special Reference to Education*, third edition, Chicago: University of Chicago Press.

Bognanno, M. and Kambayashi, R. (2009) "Trends in Worker Displacement Penalties in Japan: 1991–2005," mimeo.

Glaeser, E., and Shleifer, A. (2002) "Legal Origins," *Quarterly Journal of Economics* 117(4), pp. 1193–1229.

Hashimoto, M. and Raisian, J. (1985) "Employment Tenure and Earnings Profiles in Japan and the United States," *American Economic Review* 75(4), pp. 721–735.

Inoki, T. and Koike, K. (eds.) (1987) *Jinzai Keisei no Kokusai Hikaku* (International Comparison of Human Capital Formation), Tokyo: Toyo Keizai Shinposha.

Inoki, T. and Koike, K. (eds.) (2004) *Howaito Kara no Jinzai Keisei* (Human Capital Formation of White Collar Workers), Tokyo: Toyo Keizai Shinposha.

Kambayashi, R. (2008) "Tokyo Chisai-no Kaiko Jiken (Dismissal Cases in the Tokyo District Court)," chapter 7 in R. Kambayashi (ed.), *Kaiko Kisei-no Hou-to-Keizai* (The Law and Economics of Dismissal Regulation), Tokyo: Nihon Hyoronsha, pp. 219–246.

Kambayashi, R. (2009) "Funso Kaiketsu Seido to Shudanteki Komyunikeshon (The Labor Disputes Resolution System and Collective Communication)," chapter 9 in K. Tsuru, Y. Higuchi, and Y. Mizumachi (eds.), *Rodo Shijyo Kaikaku* (Reforming Labor Markets), Tokyo: Nihon Hyoronsha, pp. 215–234.

Kambayashi, R. and Hirasawa, J. (2008a) "Hanreishu kara Miru Seiri Kaiko Jiken (Layoff Disputes As Seen from Law Journals)," chapter 3 in R. Kambayashi (ed.), *Kaiko Kisei no Hou to Keizai* (The Law and Economics of Dismissal Regulation), Tokyo: Nihon Hyoronsha, pp. 53–116.

Kambayashi, R. and Hirasawa, J. (2008b) "Aru Kaiko Jiken no Sugata (Aspects of a Dismissal Case)," chapter 1 in R. Kambayashi, (ed.) *Kaiko Kisei-no Hou-to-Keizai* (The Law and Economics of Dismissal Regulation), Tokyo: Nihon Hyoronsha, pp. 15–30.

Kato, T. and Morishima, M. (2002) "The Productivity Effects of Participatory Employment Practices: Evidence from New Japanese Panel Data," *Industrial Relations* 41(4), pp. 487–520.

Koike, K. (1977) *Shokuba no Rodo Kumiai to Sanka* (Labor Unions and Participation in the Workplace), Tokyo: Toyo Keizai Shinposha.

Koike, K. (1983) "Kaiko kara Mita Gendai Nihon no Roshi Kankei (Current Industrial Relations in Japan from the View Point of Dismissals)," in C. Moriguchi, M. Aoki, and T. Sawa (eds.), *Nihon Keizai-no Kozo Bunseki* (An Analysis of Japan's Economic Structure), Tokyo: Sobunsha, pp. 109–126.

Muramatsu, K. and Kambayashi, R. (2008) "Kaiko Funso no Keizai Bunseki (An Economic Analysis of Dismissal Disputes)" *Nihon Rodo Kenkyu Zasshi* (Japanese Journal of Labor Studies) 581, pp. 66–76.

North, D. and Thomas, R. (1976) *The Rise of the Western World: A New Economic History*, Cambridge: Cambridge University Press.

Ohtake, F., Ohuchi, S., and Yamakawa, R. (eds.) (2002) *Kaiko Housei wo Kangaeru* (Considering Dismissal Regulation), Tokyo: Keisohshobo.

Okuno, H. and Hara, M. (2008) "Seiri Kaiko Saibanrei no Bunseki (A Legal Analysis of Economic Dismissal Cases)," chapter 4 in R. Kambayashi (ed.), *Kaiko Kisei no Hou to Keizai* (The Law and Economics of Dismissal Regulation), Tokyo: Nihon Hyoronsha), pp. 117–156.
Sugeno, K. (1992) *Japanese Labor Law*, Seattle: University of Washington.

7 Conditions of corporate progress as seen through post-war Japanese business history

*Kōnosuke Odaka**

1 Interview records (OH) as contemporary economic history materials

The purpose of this chapter is to consider characteristics of the personnel resources of Japanese corporations and their organizational configurations. Our considerations are based on actual business history records following World War II, and the examination of practices that are intimately connected with the business strategies of production/manufacturing organizations.

The phrase "corporate strategy" usually brings to mind the concepts of new business development, the decision to bring in reforms, new axes on an organizational matrix, the acquisition of capital, and the methods of corporate buyouts and mergers, etc. This chapter, however, focuses not on externally oriented strategies, but on internal corporate policies relating to the allocation and training of employees and the corporate philosophies underlying those concepts.

Materials used here are "oral history" (OH) records that were the results of interviews with the following seven persons, all of whom at one time in their career histories, engaged in top-level management of corporations:[1]

> Taki Osamu: Senior engineer at IHI (Ishikawajima-Harima Heavy Industries, later President, Tokyo Kokusai Chūzō Gijutsu Consulting (Tokyo International Foundry Technology Consulting);
> Okuda Kenji: Director, Personnel Training and Research Division, Nippon Kōkan (now JFE Steel Corporation, a leading manufacturer of steel), later Professor of Industrial Sociology, Faculty of Economics, Sophia University;
> Nakahara Tsuneo: Director, Department of Research and Development, Sumitomo Electric Industries, Ltd., a leading manufacturer of electrical machine products, ceramic parts, wire, steel materials, laser products, etc.; later Vice-President and Advisor of same;
> Ishimaru Norio: Chief Executive Officer, Denso, a large manufacturer of electric and electronic auto parts and components, later Senior Advisor of same;
> Kumamoto Yūzō: Superintendent, Takaoka Plant, Toyota Motor Corporation, General Accounting Manager, Kuozui Motors Ltd. (a joint venture with Toyota Motor Corporation in Taiwan to produce automobiles), later member of the Executive Board, Toyota Motor Corporation;

Ikebuchi Kōsuke: Superintendent, Takaoka Plant, Toyota Motor Corporation, Vice-President of same, later Senior Advisor to the Board of same; and Wada Akihiro: Vice-president, Toyota Motor Corporation, Chairman, Aisin Seiki Co. Ltd., a large manufacturer of automobile components, housing and home appliances, etc., later Director, Mitsubishi Heavy Industries, Ltd.

The interviews are an attempt at enriching other historical materials by gathering oral records of the memories (in particular, work histories) of the interviewees. These attempts will provide valuable historical insights which cannot be gained elsewhere. Since they are case studies, however, generalizations based on their contents cannot be easily made. The present writer uses the OH records noted above as materials to uncover clues (or perhaps working hypotheses) that allow him to know better the characteristics of personnel and organizational strategies in post-war Japanese corporations. In that sense, this chapter provides opportunity for a more full-scale analysis.[2]

2 Ideas and practices of quality control (QC)

Quality control and the introduction of the Deming Prize

The first working hypothesis we gather from the OH records regarding the internal strategies of corporations, is that the ideas and practices of quality control (QC, or total quality control, TQC), were crucial factors that helped the industrial products of post-war Japan attain market reputation for their high product quality, both inside and outside the country. This can be observed from our OH records for the iron and steel, machinery and electrical equipment industries. Moreover, the undeniable effects of QC also spread not only among major corporations, but also in small and medium corporations as well, and, following the turn of the century, into the distribution industry.[3]

The Deming Prize has functioned as an important social vehicle to popularize the notion of quality control. Upon application by a company and after careful evaluation, the prize was awarded to those corporations which improved their performance through QC activities.[4] As the Deming Prize gained authority in the Japanese business world, it contributed to an increasing awareness of the importance of product quality and to the spread of the QC movement by stimulating a "tournament consciousness" among corporate employees.

According to Kumamoto Yūzo, the introduction of quality control at Toyota Motor Corporation may be attributed to the risk awareness of Toyoda Eiji, executive manager (and later president) of same (Kumamoto OH 2007: 44–45, 104–105). In the late 1950s, it was only a matter of time before the liberalization of trade and capital took place. Toyoda, with the expectation that the Japanese business environment would surely change, felt that he must do something to allow Toyota Motor Corporation to survive, and beyond that, not to lose out to US corporations. He possibly felt that the future of the company was in danger unless the then-prevailing production efficiency and product quality control were drastically transformed. A direct consequence of this feeling was the decision to introduce QC (later, TQC) into the culture of Toyota Motor Corporation.

By the same token, soon after the war, the importance of quality control in the production process was realized at Sumitomo Electric Industries. Then President Kitahara Kazue believed that the company's growth would be doubtful if better product quality could not be assured prior to the achievement of economies of scale (Nakahara 2005: p. 111).

Significance of the introduction of quality control

What is to be noted here is that the introduction of quality control was prompted not so much for improving production efficiency but rather for upgrading managerial awareness at the highest levels (Kumamoto OH 2007: 57–60). As a result of QC seminars, as pointed out by Kumamoto, the division managers (*buchō*) of Toyota Motor Corporation came to realize for the first time, the importance of making decisions with the corporate objectives of the entire company in mind instead of only optimizing the activities of a particular department.

An important historical fact is that the introduction of QC was made prior to the start of the process of mass production, i.e., before the arrival of the high-growth era; this was particularly true in the case of Toyota Motor Corporation.[5] Following this, Toyota vigorously promoted the introduction of the concept and methods of QC for its parts supplying companies at every opportunity possible. For example, Yutaka Seimitsu Kōgyō, which manufactures hypoid gear tooth plates, a key component in the manufacture of automobiles, was given instruction in QC by Toyota beginning in 1968. This was combined with the former's own initiative to reduce defective products – named the QZ movement; commonly called ZD (zero defects) movement – which helped the company to greatly reduce its production costs (Yutaka Seimitsu Kōgyō 1979: 46–55). Similarly, Central Motor Co., in an effort to effect its "leaping further forward" movement, set its corporate sights on the quality control award of Toyota Motor Corporation. After strenuous effort Central Motor Co. achieved its objective in 1979 (Sentoraru Jidōsha Kabushiji Kaisha (Central Motor Co., Ltd.) 2001; pp. 67, 69).

Since the high growth era, the unit price of Japanese machine products, including cars, declined more rapidly than those of comparable products manufactured abroad, as did the average domestic price (CPI, or consumer price index). In this sense, it was clear that Japan had gained international competitive ability. The high reputation of Japanese equipment attained after the high growth era may be ascribed not so much to their relative inexpensiveness, but rather to their high *realized* values that were sealed by their commendable quality (e.g., superior functionality, uniform quality, minimized malfunctioning, the quality of repair and maintenance services, etc.). Herein lay the secret of why the export of Japanese equipment (including cars) continued to expand, even though the low value of the yen (the cheap yen) of the high growth era had vanished after the 1980s.

3 Ideas and application of production management

Toyota Production System (TPS)

The second working hypothesis is that, in addition to QC, the idea of production control, originally introduced from the United States, made a crucial contribution to improvement in production efficiency in the post-war Japanese economy. Particularly notable is that the (so-called) Toyota Production System (TPS) in the mass production of machinery was institutionalized by Ōno Taiichi of Toyota Motor Corporation in his pursuit to eliminate the three *M*s, i.e., *muda* (waste), *muri* (overloading), and *mura* (inconsistency).

TPS is made up of six factors (Kumamoto OH 2007: p. 183). They are as follows:

1   Standardized tasks;
2   Pull system;
3   Just in time;
4   Single-product flow with workload equalization;
5   Visual control; and
6   Stoppable lines.

"Standardized tasks" means describing work procedures in words, thereby enabling anyone to grasp the basic elements of his/her production tasks once individual attributes of employees' task performances have been eliminated.

The "pull system" is also known as the "supermarket method." This involves having the workers retrieve the finished products of the preceding process as they become necessary, thereby eliminating the need for inventory of interim products that used to be stored in the factory (with the only exception being automobile dealers, for whom the presence of stock is vital (Kumamoto OH 2007: p. 183)).

"Just in time" is the other side of the post-process retrieval described in (2) above, and refers to receiving and using a small quantity of machine parts as required for immediate production. The concept is said to have dated back to the experience of Toyoda Kiichiro in the United Kingdom before World War II, who jumped on a train "just in time" as it was leaving a station (Toyoda 1985: 89–90).

"Single-product flow with workload equalization" is another way of expressing a condition for successfully manufacturing and producing a relatively small quantity of each of many types of models on a production line (Kumamoto OH 2007: 91–92). In sharp contrast to the classical assembly-line method where a single model is produced in large quantities at a low cost, small-quantity, multi-product assembly-line production requires the standardization of processing time of a worker regardless of the variety of products flowing on the conveyor. In order to attain this objective, the workload of the workers needs to be "equalized," which entails the periodic reshuffling and reorganization of work and/or job assignments. In other words, the method calls for flexibility in the division of work with the consequence that work assignments expand when production quantity is reduced, and vice versa. The concept of TPS depends crucially on the ease of frequent reformulation of work assignments.

"Visual control" makes it possible for every person in the factory to grasp immediately in visual form (and in real time), what is happening in the factory. This is an aspect of the corporate belief that the incidence of flawed products can be best prevented, and production efficiency most enhanced, if and when employees' self-initiated decisions/actions are encouraged. Specifically, it involves placing signs known as "*andon*" (originally, the Japanese for "paper lanterns"), in various places around the factory so as to allow all relevant personnel to share production information such as production goals, production flow and level of completion.

Finally, "stoppable lines" refers to the authority given to employees on the workforce to stop production, if needed, using their own judgment. Herein is contained the idea behind the importance of workers' autonomy in production.

In sum, the TPS method of automobile production has, while being technologically identical to its counterparts in the United States, displayed a high degree of uniqueness in its day-to-day operations.

Spread of the Toyota Production System (TPS)

As the TPS explained above attracted wide attention as one of the important factors that had brought about the impressive growth of Toyota Motor Corporation since the 1960s, it started to be applied and adopted first by Toyota-related corporations, and then by other firms in manufacturing and other industries.

For example, when Ishikawa Gasket Co., Ltd.,[6] a manufacturer of automobile gaskets, increased the variety of its products in 1982, it seized the opportunity to bring in TPS. Until then, they had stored in their factory, a number of different types of parts that were used for manufacturing their gaskets; this was changed to a completely unified production method through an order-based, "just-in-time" procedure. The adoption of the system shortened lead-time. The production process that used to take 64 hours before the 1980s was shortened to less than eight hours by 2003. Moreover, the company became even more aggressive in the 1990s in employing TPS. The five-step, pressing processes for gasket production, improved its efficiency drastically when the speed of changing molds, which used to require a number of hours in the 1980s, was reduced to 15 minutes by 2003.

New distribution awareness reflected in production management

In the 1970s Japanese retail trading went into a new era, as a network of franchised middle-sized retail shops spread throughout the country. One of its early adopters, Seven-Eleven Japan, which came originally from the United States in 1974, grew especially rapidly in the 1980s when it successfully introduced an on-site information-processing network of order ledgers. This was a computer-ized information system whereby sales vouchers in all the branch stores were automatically relayed to the central office (Ogawa 2001). The system helped all the franchised, branch stores make daily sales plans by reviewing their local sales records and placing new orders which reflected the regional characteristics of their customers. The system enabled member shops to not only minimize the inventory of their merchandise, but also better respond to customer preferences.

In the time of classical economists, including Marx, retail trade was not regarded as value-creating, but as a mere addendum to the production of phys-ical output. By contrast, Summit, a network of large-sized retailing supermar-kets, developed its new sales strategy on the basis of its founder's theory that the retail trade process might be conceptualized in exactly the same manner as that of manufacturing production.[7] According to this theory, all retail processes, such as the selection and procurement of merchandise from wholesalers, sales prepa-ration (cleaning, measuring, wrapping, price-tagging, etc.), storing, displaying, book-keeping and so on, could be analyzed in a similar fashion to that of machine production. This is possible provided that the work procedures as well as the merchandise are sufficiently standardized so that the basic idea of the divi-sion and coordination of labor becomes applicable. The Summit stores intro-duced the ideas of production and quality control in a similar manner to that used with TPS, and the result was minimized merchandise inventory, modernized merchandise display, computerized work schedules, improved employee work morale, and heightened customer satisfaction.[8] Herein lay one reason that the company succeeded in achieving higher efficiency and an above-average earnings-sales ratio.

These examples illustrate that a similar methodology to TPS is applicable to the seemingly different sales procedures of retailing. The similarity may be extended to other parts of the economy such as information transmission (ITC) and construction industries, as long as they are composed of discrete work processes.

4   Matrix-form of organizational management and its variations

The third working hypothesis we derive from OH records is that higher corpor-ate efficiency and re-vitalization may result from a matrix-form of organizational management.

The clashes of vertical and horizontal axes at Toyota Motor Corporation

According to the Ikebuchi OH, the work of the line and the staff personnel in the factory organization of Toyota Motor Corporation are interwoven to form what can be termed a matrix (Ikebuchi OH 2008: 50–53). If one draws on the vertical axis, the production processes lines of manufacturing an automobile (lines such

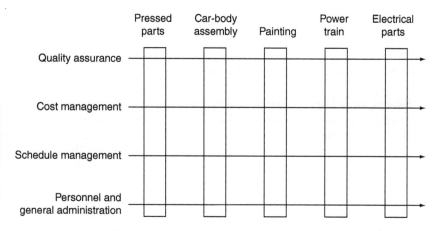

Figure 7.1 Relationship between "lines" (vertical) and "staffs" (horizontal) in automobile factories (drawn by the author on the basis of Rōdō etc. (2006: 5)).

as stamping, painting, assembling, etc., for each model of the vehicles produced) and on the horizontal axis, personnel and production management lines, the two axes are interwoven to form the matrix to which Ikebuchi referred (Figure 7.1).

Human friction often occurs at the meetings points where the vertical and horizontal axes of the matrix cross over. The vertical axis concentrates its top priority in production, and it is crossed by the horizontal axis with critical comments and/or suggestions for improvement from the point of view of the entire company, causing floods of arguments from different parts of the factory. According to the Toyota management philosophy, however, that is as it should be. By deliberately creating a mechanism where different perspectives mesh and clash, it expects improvements and new techniques to emerge.

> In this way we can identify problems early. Whenever different opinions clash at the crossing points of vertical and horizontal axes, we immediately go there and take action ... so the problems come up immediately to the surface, and we squash them. That's the Toyota way.
>
> (Ikebuchi OH 2008: 50–51)

This differs from the formal principle of "matrix organization," a method of assigning an employee to two related departments within a company. Such an assignment may create serious problems because the employee has two superiors from whom to take orders (Besanko *et al.* 2007: ch. 16). All Toyota employees who face confrontations have but one superior and debate from their own perspectives with the commonly shared purpose of attaining the best result for the company as a whole.

In order to encourage mutual understanding and cooperation between production workers and engineers, Toyota established (by July 1958) a section known as *gijutsu-in shitsu* (Engineers' Room) on the factory floor (from a proposal by Ōno Taiichi), where engineers in charge of manufacturing processes and of production equipment (i.e., the horizontal axis) were positioned to work alongside the workers on the shop floor (i.e., the vertical axis), especially when new models were introduced (Ikebuchi OH 2008: 14, 43–53, 62–71).

> Back in the old days, workers and engineers would often disagree, and that was the end of the story. What we have done here, in contrast, was to fill the hole between them.... [In the old days it was] as if neither side would come out from their homes and cross over the "river" between them. What we did was ... to build a wharf so that a ferry could go across [the river].
>
> (Ibid.: 44)

For instance, when Mr. Ōno Taiichi (on the horizontal axis) saw that the stamping section (on the vertical axis) took 90 minutes to replace molds in the 1970s, he ordered the section members to upgrade production efficiency and reduce operating costs by completing the task in ten minutes. Naturally the immediate reaction from the shop floor must have been something like, "You gotta be kidding!" Nevertheless, the line experimented with a number of different methods, and achieved the goal in a little under a year (Kumamoto OH 2007: 18–19).[9]

Matrix-form organizational management, MITI style

The matrix style of organizational management was also practiced at the Ministry of International Trade and Industry of the government of Japan (known as "MITI" for short, and now renamed the Ministry of Economy, Trade and Industry or METI).[10] In the period 1973–2000, its organizational units were of two distinct types, namely those facilitating the growth of Japanese manufacturing industries (the "vertical" axis) and those concerned with the realization of the general principles of industrial and international trade policies (the "horizontal" axis). MITI staff referred to the former as *genkyoku* (literally, "original bureaus"), which consisted of the Machinery and Information Industries Bureau, the Basic Industries Bureau, the Consumer Goods Industries Bureau, the Agency for Natural Resources and Energy, the Small and Medium Enterprise Agency, the Patent Office, and the Agency of Industrial Science and Technology. These bureaus were responsible for the introduction and the implementation of policies for each industry, such as the basic material, machine, and consumer goods industries. On the other hand, the latter, non-*genkyoku* units handled principle core issues, which established the basic stance of government policy and were applicable to all industries, horizontally cutting across the "vertical axis," i.e., the Industrial Policy Bureau, the International Trade Policy Bureau, the International Trade Administration Bureau, and the Location Suburbs Bureau.

The senior chiefs of the general affairs sections of both horizontal and vertical bureaus formed the Law Review Committee, and assembled periodically at the Secretariat of the Minister (*Daijin Kambō*) to vigorously debate the current execution and future plans of trade, industry and commercial policies.

It is interesting to note that the career paths of MITI bureaucrats facilitated the formation of industrial and commercial policy. MITI staffs, having graduated from universities and duly passed the qualifying examinations for government officials, were assigned and re-assigned either to vertical or horizontal bureaus every two to three years. They learned their jobs through on-the-job training (OJT). They might also work at external, MITI-related organizations or local MITI bureaus. While carrying out a variety of such tasks, they would, by osmosis, develop the habit of thinking flexibly about trade and industrial policy issues from a macro viewpoint, taking into account the entire Ministry's policy objectives.

Dokō Toshio's method of education

Dokō Toshio was a noted engineer, one time CEO (1950–1964) at IHI (Ishika-wajima Heavy Industries) and then at Toshiba Electric (from 1965), who, after having served as Chairman of the Japan Business Federation (*Nippon Keidanren*), spent his final years as Don of the Second Ad hoc Commission on Administrative Reform (*Rinji Gyōsei Chōsakai*, or *Rinchō* for short). He was a unique businessman who left behind many anecdotes. His outstanding characteristics were already evident when he was at IHI in the 1950s (Taki OH: 7–10). When defective products come out of a foundry shop, for instance, the normally reproved person is the one who is directly in charge of the forging process. But Dokō was different:

> Suppose I turned out a defective casting: its quality was poor, you see; and I would be made to re-do the process. As a result, the final merchandise would miss its deadline. When that happens, the common practice is that it would be me, and only me, who would be held responsible and reprimanded by supervisor in charge of the foundry shop. But Mr. Dokō was not so....
>
> [When] soot was found in the cast and the deadline missed, he would first talk to the chief in charge of the machine shop, [which was to work on the forged product], asking when the soot had got in, when the product had been shaved, completed, and taken away, etc. At the start of the inquiry the supervisor of the machine shop could not answer anything as he knew nothing about the details.... [But, as] Mr. Dokō inquired about all such details, everyone eventually came to know what had taken place in the machine as well as foundry shops.
>
> (Taki OH: 7–10)

As the top management acted in this manner, a system was set up such that relevant information regarding both prior and posterior-processes would be shared by superiors in all respective shops. According to Taki, this was the way Dokō trained work-site supervisors.

[If] a fault appeared again ... [...], he would say to the machine shop attendant, "make up for the time you've wasted," but nothing to the foundry operator. He would also ask the former, "How long was it since the casting arrived at the machine shop?" "When did you join this company?...You should know from your experience that a cast product may contain some soot or has some defects every so often. That being the case, you should have anticipated such unexpected events to take place at any time, and allowed extra time when you placed an order to the foundry shop. If a machine product misses its deadline, it's the machine shop's responsibility, not the foundry's." Mr. Dokō was very mad when he said this.

(Taki OH: 7–10)

It was Dokō's idea that supervisors in different departments should exchange information with each other, and learn about the work in the neighboring departments prior to making production plans of their own. Moreover,

Mr. Dokō, when he designed a product himself, would go down to the factory site and observe where technical difficulties lay and what expertise was required for overcoming the problems, e.g., what design would be easier to work at, how to avoid defective products in the factory. (Ibid.)

The factory was vitalized, as neighboring supervisors were obliged to communicate and share information. In this sense Dokō's production management had commonality with the concept and practice of "matrix" organization.

Technical information sharing at Sumitomo Electric

Immediately after World War II, as Sumitomo Electric Industries started to work towards reconstructing its sites, it was a standard practice in US factories that engineers determined the principles and work rules, and factory workers were to carry out their jobs in faithful obedience to these. But Sumitomo Electric thought differently. While the company respected the knowledge and experience of its engineers, it wished at the same time to make the best use of the accumulated experience and practical knowledge of its factory workers, who were invited to make suggestions and/or proposals for reforming production processes and factory management. Because of this practice, however, the company, which had introduced quality control (QC) after the war ahead of other Japanese corporations, failed to win the Deming Award when it applied for it for the first time. The company's emphasis on the participation and proposals of factory workers was apparently counter to the tenor of the award at that time (Nakahara OH 2004: 56; 2005: 112).

At the R&D division of Sumitomo Electric Industries, the exchange of information on new findings was exceptionally free and active. According to the Nakahara OH, Sumitomo Electric researchers, while engaged in thorough studies of important core principles and the analyses of observations and experiments in the laboratory as well as at their production sites, documented their outcomes by passing around daily memos containing ideas, hints, and other relevant facts. Everyone in the division shared the precious new research information in this manner (Nakahara OH 2004: 79, 130–131).

> When I plan to merge two new things, I need to know about them quite well before I execute the task successfully. Should I skip this preparatory step, the results will lack precision and be short-lived: I won't be able to get much in the way of research outputs, although they may not be total failures. So, I need first to familiarize myself with both the things thoroughly; when they are registered safely in my head, I can merge them easily and simply.
>
> (Nakahara OH 2004: 130–131)

For large industrial Japanese corporations, it was fashionable in the 1980s to set up independent research institutes (often termed the company's Central Research Laboratory). Sumitomo Electric Industries did not follow suit, however; it firmly believed that research and development could be best carried out in concert with the production site, with direct and frequent exchanges of information and personnel between the two (Nakahara OH 2004: 122).

Denso's development philosophy

Denso, which has grown rapidly as a manufacturer of automobile electrical parts e.g., headlights, lamps, air-conditioners, etc., has been exceptionally eager to develop its own technology (Ishimaru OH 2006: 204).[11] (The word "technology" here includes product design and development, production technology and sales.) While it takes years for new technologies to bear fruit, the changeover from old to new technologies also requires time and careful, advance planning. Hence no time can be wasted in preparing for the technology changeover: each day is a valuable occasion for education and training.

There are two notable factors that sustained Denso's new technology development. First, "Denso has been incredibly superior in production technology" (ibid.: 203) as evident from its history. The company was confident that its newly developed technology would gain wide support from its end users.

Second, the company's engineering and technological strength has come neither from those who possessed instantly usable expertise, nor from specialists with a doctoral degree in narrow fields of knowledge, but from "those who mastered basic fundamentals in the company's production technology," and "those who were highly motivated to respond to the need of rapidly changing technology" (ibid.: 205–206). Realizing that mastering new concepts and methods involves intellectual adventures and conceptual jumps, Denso searched for appropriate instructors from both inside and outside the company. This was a time-consuming process because it was not always easy to identify truly appropriate instructors. In any event, the company had come to realize that it "required a proper training system to prepare the employees for changing their jobs and/or specialties at a short notice" (ibid.: 206).

Not all the contents of the training are directly connected with our products; they are instead more akin to the basic principles of science and technology. We have requested the trainers to deliver theoretical lectures, closer to master's and/or doctor's levels.

(Ibid.: 207)

The task of training has been not just forming a horizontal network of the insiders and outsiders of the company, but building an intellectual matrix space that extends the time axis from now into the future.

Automobile design engineers

Multi-field learning is very important for automobile design engineers, according to Wada Akihiro. If they acquire practical knowledge on a wide range of different specialties, often by way of friendly competition between neighboring fields, they would not only make progress in their own assignments and improve efficiency, but also come up with fresh designs or radical, eye-opening inspirations (Wada OH 2008). For these reasons, newly-recruited design engineers at Toyota Motor Corporation, fresh out of college,

Were made to acquire the expertise of closely related areas other than their own ... In the case of engine designs, for instance, there are quite a few specialties to learn about: there are, starting from basic combustion process, the intake system, the air exhaustion system, the suppression of noise and vibration, and so on. We instruct them to master all of these as quickly as possible.

(Ibid.: 81–82)

Among design engineers, there is also a work-related exchange with the production technology department. Automobile production constantly involves the introduction of new models and improvements in specifications, which creates fresh problems both large and small. A closely-knit team interaction between the production factory floor and the design engineers (in the head office) would be the best answer to deal with them quickly and properly. Thus in the late 1950s and early 1960s, a system was introduced whereby engineers in charge of product design and development (called RE or "resident engineers") (Kumamoto OH 2007: 96) were stationed in the factory. When new models were launched, since proposals for improvement and/or revisions were often made by shop-floor workers, calls for instant responses from the designing department (even decisions to change the design in some cases) were made. The "software" departments of styling and design cooperated and liaised with the "hardware" departments engaged in production processes, ensuring that there were no work-related information gaps between them.

The authority of the Toyota production rank-and-file workers, or their ability to make their associate engineers listen to their opinions, while informal, was an undeniable factor that led to the establishment and the success of the RE system.

At Toyota, the personnel on the production floor are extremely strong, just as it must have been in the days of Mr. Ōno [Taiichi]. By "strong," I mean they are masterly in production skills and knowhow, such that we engineers must guard ourselves not to be laughed at behind our back. We have made our best effort since our youth so as to avoid their commenting, "Hey, who made this idiotic design, causing all these problems for us?"

(Wada OH 2008: 95)

Similarly, production engineers would come "on board" to visit the design technology division, to discuss the necessity and desirability of design changes in order to facilitate the ease of production (ibid.: 97, 191–193).

Mutual co-working for task execution in the chemical industry

At Nippon Shokubai Co., Ltd., a manufacturer and seller of petrochemicals such as ethylene oxide and derivatives, acrylic acid and acrylic acid ester, a unique form of task collaboration takes place by overstepping the boundaries of the division of labor.[12] That is to say, the production engineers would work closely with process operators in the factory. "This is our solution to fill the gaps of information created by continuous progress and changes in technology between production and planning departments," explained a company engineer.

For example, the engineers in charge of plant design frequently go out to the factory and talk with the operators, since the latter are most knowledgeable about production processes in the factory, and would often suggest improvements or solutions to problems. In addition, whenever a difficulty arises in the production process, everyone concerned gathers immediately in accordance with the motto, "Safety First, Production Second," to discuss and decide countermeasures. "Co-working" of personnel with a variety of expertise is the secret to the successful operation of a factory where technology changes frequently.

For instance, a new catalyzer is developed every so often on the basis of a new hypothesis developed by the supervisory engineers. If promising, the company sets up a pilot plant, which carries out the experiment and evaluates the new product under the optimal temperatures and reaction speeds determined by the R&D engineers. The operation of the pilot plant is another area where the participation and close collaboration of experts from wide-ranging specialties is essential, i.e., laboratory researchers, production engineers, and veteran operators on the shop floor.[13]

5 On Adam Smith once again

The cases we have reviewed in Sections 2 through 4, while varying widely in their environmental and historical background, share three common features: (*a*) frequent information exchanges between sections of diverse organizational cultures; (*b*) the presence of tension and friction between different parts of organizations – differences that often lead to improvements in production performance;

and (*c*) emphasis on the best practice as viewed from the company or the factory as a whole. In the following, we shall attempt an intellectual adventure on the basis of these observations.

The world of Lego vs the world of co-working

The engineering characteristics of discrete production processes, consisting of processing and assembly of parts and components, are exemplified in machinery manufacturing, and are precisely portrayed in Adam Smith's theory of the division and collaboration of labor (Smith (1776/1998): book I, ch. 1).

There are differences by country (or by period) as to how exactly the division and the collaboration of labor are practiced. The work of production process in machine factories in the United Kingdom and the United States from the 1960s to the 1970s was typically subdivided into finely demarcated, specialized job categories. In theory, the economic value of a worker would correspond, in a one-to-one fashion, with the market value of his or her accomplished work. The final product was a collation of the work of these subdivided jobs.

In contrast to this, in the production method at Toyota Motor Corporation during the same period, while sharing the same engineering characteristics as in the United Kingdom and the United States, there was no such one-to-one correspondence, because the workers were engaged in a plural number of jobs (i.e., "multitasking") in response to the needs of production. The labor compensation did not correspond one-to-one to the type of job either, and was determined on the basis of the economic value of the overall production process, with due consideration added to the degree of maturation and responsibility. What is even more interesting here is the close cooperative relationship between engineers and production workers, as explained in both the Kumamoto and Wada OHs.

Judging from the above difference between the United Kingdom/United States and Japan regarding the division and collaboration of labor, there are at least two approaches for applying Adam Smith's theory, which may be termed the "Lego method" and the "co-working method," respectively.

With the "Lego method," a physical good may be divided, in the same way as Legos, into a number of parts in such a way that the former is a simple sum of the latter; the parts that make up the good are precisely fitted to each other with no gaps in between them. This is a world where the whole is the union of standardized, individual parts. In contrast to this, the world of the "co-working method" is composed of parts that have overlapping portions with their neighbors (Figure 7.2).

In ideal-typus "Lego-method" organizations, the employees working in different fields exist in their own worlds, work quite independently of their fellow employees in neighboring sections with little work-related co-operation and/or information exchange between them. Each of their areas of specialty is marked with clear boundaries that no one dares to overstep. In ideal-typus "co-working world" organizations, in contrast, exchanges and co-operation of work between neighboring specialties are common and taken for granted. As a result, job

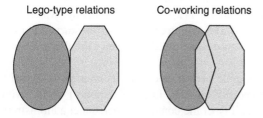

Figure 7.2 The "Lego method" and the "co-working method".

boundaries are not strictly observed, which means that friction (debates and tensions) may ensue at times inside the organization, but this is regarded as a chance for improvements. The contrast is observable even where production technologies are essentially the same between the two proto-types.

The historical origins of the "world of co-working"

Okuda's theory proposes the same concepts as those discussed above. He refers to the "Lego world" as "dichotomy," whereas the ruling principle of "co-working" is termed "complementarity."

According to Okuda (1999: 10–11 and Okuda OH 2008: 384–394), the origins of the "co-working" principle date back to the Edo period (1603–1868). For example, the moral philosophy (*shingaku*) of Ishida Baigan considered the employees as partners, and argued, by citing an example of a branch store operating with capital borrowed from its head office, that half of the profits earned should be returned to the lender, while 30 percent is retained internally, and the remaining 20 percent is distributed among the employees (called the "thirds payment system"). Ninomiya Sontoku, too, held the non-authoritarian notion that people were equal despite their differences in societal roles, and that social reform would be unworkable if it was directed in a one-way, top-down fashion. His methodology on agricultural renovation proved successful as it stoked the voluntary desire of leaders of the movement (progressive farmers or headsmen) to increase output, according to Okuda.[14]

"Complementarity" crossing the ocean

In the early 1980s GM suggested to Toyota Motor Corporation the restoration of its Fremont Plant in California, which had been closed since 1982, as a joint enterprise between them.[15] With serious US–Japan car trade friction high at the time, while the US government requested voluntary restraints on the export of Japanese cars, the Japanese government saw the proposal as a godsend, since it considered the plan would contribute to the resolution of the trade friction. Initially Toyota was not enthusiastic about the idea, but eventually agreed to establish a joint venture with GM that was later named NUMMI (New United Motor

Manufacturing Inc.), an authentic assembler of Toyota models (Kumamoto OH 2007: 159–179; Ikebuchi OH 2008: 74–112). The new company, which began operation in 1983, having adopted TPS with tremendous effort, turned out to be a great success until it finally closed down in 2009 when GM faced a serious financial crisis.

A cornerstone of NUMMI's good performance was its attempt to embed the "co-working (complementary) world" into the "Lego (dichotomy) world," whose success was dependent on the ability of the company's personnel administration to be able to maintain managerial freedom in making job assignments as it saw fit. The NUMMI workers, having been assured of stable, long-term employment, were, instead of being assigned to subdivided, specialist tasks (like at GM), grouped to form multifunctional "work teams" that attended to multiple job tasks. Moreover, their wages were essentially the same irrespective of their job content (called "job competence") or their individual performances (called "contribution").

One important pre-condition in implementing the Toyota Production System is "workload equalization," as pointed out in Section 3 above. Lego-style, strict job jurisdiction makes "equalization" untenable by precluding managerial flexibility in work assignments. The initial hesitation of Toyota to establish NUMMI must have been due to some uncertainty felt on this point (see Ikebuchi OH 2008: 75–82). If this interpretation is correct, the most significant moment in Toyota's decision to accept GM's invitation was when the United Autoworkers Union (UAW) agreed to the abolition of one-to-one correspondence between job specification and wage rate at NUMMI.

According to an international comparison by Professor Koike Kazuo (2008) of the factory operations of Toyota Motor Corporation, conducted over a number of years since the 1960s, the principle of TPS worked marvelously in all four countries of Japan, Thailand, the United Kingdom, and the United States (NUMMI). When a new car is developed, design engineers, production and manufacturing engineers, and floor-shop workers exchange their views candidly, frequently and openly with regard to anything related to the products or the production processes. Whereas minor changes are agreed to and made on the spot, relatively serious suggestions for revisions are reported back to the chief design engineer (called the *shusa*) for final decisions. While some differences remain in the practice of PST by country, the key components of multiple task orientation (i.e., emphasis on attaining the breadth and depth of technical abilities) are universal. More specifically, (a) the production workers are authorized to act in response to at least some aspects of abnormal or irregular happenings, and (b) engineers in three different areas (design, production and manufacturing operations) all participate in product design, production-line planning, and the operation of product lines from the very first stage of product development (ibid.: 266).

Naturally, there are differences in the manner of operation of TPS among countries. For example: (a) wages paid to production workers at NUMMI are the same regardless of job, with no incentive to improve work performance; (b) there is a rule of seniority in the United States, governed by trade unions, under which workers with longer service are given priority for promotion; and (*c*) the UK unions resist the implementation of assessment-based pay schemes. Despite these differences, however, the basic principles and characteristics of TPS are all maintained in these countries. This consistency is due to careful effort by Toyota management to adhere to the principle of flexible organizational management (or the principle of organizational "complementarity"), whereby the intermingling of diverse categories of multi-skilled workers is encouraged.

6 Implications of observations

As a result of the crisis consciousness held by business leaders in post-World War II Japan regarding the competitive edge of their products, quality control (QC) was brought in and established ahead of mass production. The practice of rational management systems (including TPS) was made popular especially among large corporations, but not restricted to them. Implementing this practice resulted in increased efficiency. In some cases the new style of management was accompanied by "matrix-style" organizational configurations, which enhanced information exchange and helped energize the workplaces. The risk awareness (or psychological uneasiness) of the business leaders led to the progress of their work organizations by way of quality improvement and increases in production efficiency, etc., provided that their organizations withstood financial and other strains. They sowed the seeds for reforms and breakthroughs for their organizations by active organizational planning, on- and off-the-job education and training, and making use of internal exchanges of both personnel and information.

At the same time, behind these new developments, it must not be forgotten that there are historical legacies. In particular, the system of flexible work assignment in accordance with the degree of sluggishness in market demand for the final product, i.e., a system that is sustained by information sharing in the workplace, presupposes that the employees will continue to work at the same workplace for an unspecified period of time. In other words, behind these examples exists a long-term, stable employment system. The system of management and the basic philosophy behind it are linked closely to the way the people and the organization act in latent anticipation. Systems introduced from overseas would rarely lead to the same results as those at their original place unless they were subjected to the proper adjustments.

According to a survey that compared the research and development staff at automobile manufacturers in Japan and the United States in 2005, production principles akin to TPS did not function as well as expected at a plant in the United States (Rōdō Seisaku Kenkyū Kikō (Japan Institute for Labour Policy and Training) 2006). They failed to achieve a sufficient degree of cooperation between engineers and factory workers, which was absolutely necessary for bringing in a "team concept" and measuring "*kaizen*" (a Toyota word meaning creative arranging) (Kumamoto OH 2007: 147).[16] This failure occurred because approximately half the technical staff (called "supervisors"), who existed in far greater numbers than in Japan and were in charge of assigning and adjusting jobs and monitoring work at the plant, were hired using spot contracts and dispatched from outside of the surveyed company. They were technical experts, but not sufficiently familiar with the unwritten rules and customs of the factory itself, and consequently could not fulfill their tasks as well as expected.

Changes are taking place in the composition of the domestic labor market in Japan. In the Ishikawa Gasket information quoted earlier, a large number of Brazilian *Nikkei* (persons with Japanese ancestry) were employed in as early as 2003 and given a semi-regular status at the company.[17] In another survey conducted at automotive parts suppliers in 2006, it was not unusual to find cases where more than half the employees were foreign nationals.[18] When an increasing proportion of employees leave after relatively short periods, some changes are required in TPS.

Changes can also be seen in circumstances surrounding research and development, the source of corporate dynamism. For example, at Sumitomo Electric Industries a total of 30 years was necessary for the research and development cycle of power cables and optical fibers to reach its end, ten years for the conceptualization and design of its prototype product, another ten years for its promotion in the market, and an additional ten years for its profit making and invested-fund recovery (Nakahara OH 2004: 120). Moreover, monopolistic public enterprises (such as Japanese National Railways, Nippon Telegraph and Telephone Public Corporation) which provided relatively abundant research funds, no longer exist in the contemporary world of information technology where the speed of reform is rapid in highly competitive markets under increasingly unregulated social environments.

At any rate, many aspects of the socioeconomic approaches that functioned in the twentieth century will no longer be valid in the future, necessitating a radical transformation and "leap forward" for corporations in the country. One might say that the modern age is bringing "new uncertainty" that must be overcome through reforms in technology, organization, and underlying corporate philosophies.

7   Closing remarks

What I have introduced in this chapter are the characteristics of a few exemplary techniques of organizational operation that were developed over the post-World War II history of Japanese corporations. These came about as a result of efforts to adapt and optimize, in their own way, production technologies originally introduced from overseas. These could be described as the products of the Japanese corporate culture.

Some time has passed since calls were made in this country for the necessity of reforms in business management in the age of globalization. In fact, the time when the Japanese economy is reliant on introduced technology has long gone. In modern and contemporary Japan, endogenous social and economic reforms progress only at a sluggish pace. The financial Big Bang, for instance, proceeded extremely slowly in this country. In contrast to this, transformations are rapid when an imperious stimulus suddenly arrives from outside, temporarily suspending the existing systems and habits. The Meiji Restoration, the defeat in the Pacific War, and the first oil shock, are examples of such stimuli. Added to the list are the current global financial crises that started with the American sub-prime crisis and the substantial changes that are required in energy use due to the global climatic changes. Because of rising crisis consciousness, Japanese corporations in the 2010s will be under pressure to make drastic changes in their production organizations and business strategies.

Attempts to overcome the limits of business organizations are always welcome, but what is needed for Japanese enterprises is not merely griping about the slow pace of reforms, but rather identifying the essence of their organizational characteristics and clearly spelling out a strategy for developing new, value-creating, competitive technologies in a globalized world.

Notes

* Translated from Japanese by Jeremy Phillipps with revisions by the author.
1 Subjects are listed in the order of the publication of the interview records. For details, the readers are referred to the list of references at the end of the chapter, where the oral history records are listed against the authors of the interviews: Ikebuchi OH (Matsushima and Odaka 2008a); Ishimaru OH (Matsushima and Odaka 2006); Kumamoto OH (Matsushima and Odaka 2007); Nakahara OH (Matsushima and Odaka 2004); Okuda OH (C.O.E. Oral/Policy Research Project 2004); Taki OH (Taki et al. 1993); Wada OH (Matsushima and Odaka 2008b).
2 Attempts at oral history taking (OH) have existed for some time. A series of efforts was made in the United States to record the folk tales of the Native American inhabitants at the close of the nineteenth century. Following World War II, the rapid development of sound and image recording technologies made OH much easier than before. In recent years, the tedious task of gathering, preserving, and publishing the life-work of Japanese public figures (mostly politicians) has been ongoing under the leadership of Professors Ito Takeshi and Mikuriya Takashi.

OH is usually recorded in the form of dialogues between an interviewee and an interviewer. Since the role of the interviewer is to draw out the memories of the interviewee, the former should ideally investigate the subject ahead of time so that inaccurate memories or possible confusions of the interviewee can be corrected. As a matter of principle, the interviewer does not engage in debates or arguments with the interviewee.

One cannot deny the possibilities of the interviewee being mistaken about some facts, repressing some memories (especially unpleasant ones), etc. Caution is advised when OHs are used as source materials for historical study. Mikuriya (2002, 2007) presents an introduction to OH.
3 Okuda OH (2004: 204–211, 407–414) provides examples from the iron and steel industry, and Nakahara OH (2004: 55–57; 2005: 111–113) provides examples from the electrical machinery industry.
4 Founded originally by an American statistician, W. Edwards Deming, and administered by *Nikka Giren* (the Union of Japanese Scientists and Engineers). Ishikawa Kaoru was an early leading figure, who contributed to the spread of QC in Japan.
5 This was noted by Professor Ono Keinosuke in Odaka *et al.* (1988: 270–273).
6 Ishikawa Gasket, with capital of 200 million yen and total sales of eight billion yen (as of 2006), manufactures steel laminate gaskets (which were awarded the Inventors'

Prize in 1988) as well as manifolds, mufflers, gaskets, etc. At the time of the survey, the company was independent of Japanese auto part-suppliers' groupings (*keiretsu*), each of which has close ties to an automobile assembler in the country. The company instead had business connections with all the complete automobile makers (assemblers) in Japan.

The present writer expresses his deep appreciation for the cordial and detailed explanation he received about the company's activities when he and his associates (led by Professor Matsushima Shigeru) visited its Kiyohara Factory.

7 Conversely, one could argue that the essence of manufacturing activities boils down to the disseminating and storing of human services. With the progress of industrialization, some parts of these human services are substituted by capital goods, which are nothing but "canned human services."

8 This is based on the present writer's observations gained from his on-site investigations at the Mitaka City Office branch of Summit, a representative supermarket of food products (visited in 2003 and in 2004). The present author would like to express his thanks to the managers of this company for their cordial reception and detailed explanations.

9 Time needed for mold changeover was later reduced further to two to three minutes.

10 The following is based on the present writer's interviews with former members of MITI and with Professor Matsushima Shigeru.

11 President Ishimaru never cut research and development funds even during the post-bubble depression (Ishimaru OH 2006: p. 183).

12 The present writer is indebted to the engineering staff of the Chidori Plant of Nippon Shokubai's Kawasaki Factory, which Professor Shigeru Matsushima and I visited in October 2008, for their very cordial and detailed explanation of its production activities.

13 The development of catalysts has a lower rate of success than polymers. Once successful, however, it has relatively little chance of being imitated by outsiders.

14 According to Okuda, this idea may be traced back to *Jōdō Shinshū* Buddhism (as exemplified in *Tan'ishō* (*Lamentations of Divergences*), a Japanese classic in the early fourteenth century, originally authored by the Buddhist priest Shinran).

15 The biggest reason for its problems was apparently deteriorated labor relations.

16 For the members of Toyota Motor Corporation, "*kaizen*" means creative arrangement (Kumamoto OH 2007: 147).

17 Semi-regular status, since they had to return to their home country every three years due to the visa regulations.

18 According to a survey by Professor Matsushima Shigeru (conducted in 2006), Sanki Manufacturing, a maker of auto parts (exhausts, manifolds, etc.) in Nagoya, had recruited 40 of the total of 70 employees from overseas.

References

Besanko, D., Dranove, D., Shanley, M., and Schaefer, S. (2007). *Economics of Strategy*. Fourth edition, New York: John Wiley.

C.O.E. Oral/Policy Research Project (2004). "Okuda Kenji Oral History," Tokyo: Seisaku Kenkyū-in (National Graduate Institute for Policy Studies) (in Japanese).

Koike, K. (2008). *Kaigai Nihon kigyō no jinzai ikusei* (Personnel Training at Overseas Japanese corporations). Tokyo: Toyo Keizai Shimposha.

Matsushima, S. and Odaka, K. (eds.) (2004). "Nakahara Tsuneo Oral History," *Working Paper Series no. 2*, Tokyo: Research Institute for Innovation Management, Hosei University (in Japanese).

Matsushima, S. and Odaka, K. (eds.) (2005). Nakahara Tsuneo (Oral Presentation), "Sōzō-teki shikō to kakuishin-teki soshiki: Nakahara Tsuneo ōraru hisutorī (zoku)

(Creative Thinking and Innovative Organization)," *Keiei Shirin* (Hosei Journal of Business. vol. 42 no. 2, 101–127.

Matsushima, S. and Odaka, K. (eds.) (2006). "Ishimaru Norio Oral History," *Working Paper Series no. 20*, Tokyo: Research Institute for Innovation Management, Hosei University (in Japanese).

Matsushima, S. and Odaka, K. (eds.) (2007). "Kumamoto Yūzō Oral History," *Working Paper Series no. 27*, Tokyo: Research Institute for Innovation Management, Hosei University (in Japanese).

Matsushima, S. and Odaka, K. (eds.) (2008a). "Ikebuchi Kōsuke Oral History," *Working Paper Series no. 52*, Tokyo: Research Institute for Innovation Management, Hosei University (in Japanese).

Matsushima, S. and Odaka, K. (eds.) (2008b). "Wada Akihiro Oral History," Tokyo University of Science Management of Technology (MOT) Research Series 2008, Tokyo: Graduate School of Management of Science and Technology, Tokyo University of Science (in Japanese).

Mikuriya, T. (2002). *Ōraru hisutorī, gendai-shi no tameno kōjutsu kiroku* (Oral history: Oral Recording for Contemporary History). Chūkō Shinsho, Tokyo: Chūō Kōron Shinsha.

Mikuriya, T. (ed.) (2007). *Ōraru hisutorī nyūmon* (An Introduction to Oral History). Tokyo: Iwanami Shoten.

Odaka, K., Ono, K., and Adachi, F. (1988). *The Automobile Industry in Japan, a Study of Ancillary Firm Development.* Tokyo and Oxford: Kinokuniya Bookstore and Oxford University Press.

Ogawa, S. (2001). "Degitaru-ka to kigyō keiei no kakushin: ryūtsū-gyō wo chūshin ni (Digitalization and the Reform of Corporate Management: Mainly on the Distribution Industry)" chapter 2 in Odaka, K. and Tsuru, T. (eds.) *Degitaru-ka jidai no soshiki kakushin* (Organizational Reform in the Digitization Age). Tokyo: Yūhikaku.

Okuda, K. (1999). "Nibunhō-teki kankei kara sōho-teki kankei e – Complementarity wa Nihon no tsuyoi kosei de aru – (From Dichotomic Relations to Complementary Relations)" *Monthly Journal of the Japan Institute of Labour*, no. 465, April.

Rōdō Seisaku Kenkyū Kenshu Kikō (Japan Institute for Labour Policy and Training) (2006). *Jidōsha sangyō no rōshi kankei to kokusai kyōsōryoku* (Labor Relations and International Competitiveness of the Automobile Industry). Japan Institute for Labour Policy and Training Report no. 76, Tokyo: Japan Institute for Labour Policy and Training.

Sentoraru Jidōsha Kabushiki Kaisha (Central Motor Co., Ltd.) (2001). *Gojū-nen no ayumi* (Fifty Years of Progress). Tokyo: Central Motor Co., Ltd.

Smith, A. (1776/1998). *An Inquiry into the Nature and Causes of the Wealth of Nations*, London: W. Strahan and T. Cadell, 1776; London and New York: Oxford University Press, 1998, book 1, chapter 1.

Taki, O., Senda, M., and Odaka, K. (1993). "Kōdo seichō ki Nihon imono-gyō yakushin no yōin – gijutshu dōnyū kara gijutsu yushutsu e (Causes of the Breakthroughs in the Japanese Casting Industry during the High Economic Growth Period: from Importing Technology to Exporting Technology)," Discussion Paper B no. 13, Tokyo: Institute of Economic Research, Hitotsubashi University.

Toyoda, E. (1985). *Ketsudan — watashi no rireki-sho* (My Decisions: A Curriculum Vitae). Tokyo: Nihon Keizai Shimbunsha.

Yutaka Seimitsu Kōgyō Kabushiki Kaisha (Yutaka Precision Industry, Ltd.) (1979). *Yutaka Seimitsu Kōgyō nijū-nen shi* (Twentieth Anniversary History of Yutaka Seimitsu Kōgyō). Seto, Aichi Prefecture: Yūtaka Seimitsu Kōgyō, Ltd.

8 The role of education in the economic catch-up

Comparative growth experiences from Japan, Korea, Taiwan, and the United States

Yujiro Hayami and Yoshihisa Godo

1 Introduction

Many intuitive arguments hint that the pursuit of, and changes in, education in East Asia were critical for its miraculous success. Empirical studies on the macroeconomic role of education in the East Asian countries, however, have been so limited that researchers in economics are still uncertain about even such basic questions as whether and how education contributed to the East Asian economic miracle. This paucity of empirical analysis can be attributed to the lack of detailed datasets for the education "stock."

The authors constructed a nearly 100-year-long dataset of education stock for Japan, Korea, Taiwan and the United States (Godo 2005; Godo and Fukami 2005).[1] This dataset includes detailed information such as the average number of years of schooling per person (abbreviated henceforth "average schooling") by gender, by age group, and by types and levels of education (i.e., primary, secondary, tertiary and vocational).[2] The United States has led the world economy since the late nineteenth century.[3] Japan was the first non-western nation to succeed in catching-up to the advanced nations.[4] Taiwan and Korea also achieved miraculous economic successes just 15–20 years after Japan. Thus, these four countries comprise a perfect combination of characteristics for analyzing the relationship between education and economic development.

Using the authors' dataset, this chapter examines the East Asian economic miracle from the viewpoint of human capital. In order to describe the characteristics of the miracle, this chapter invents a new terminology – "military-style, heavy industrialization." This phrase refers to the situation where a mass of homogeneous, not very highly educated, young people collaborate methodically in factories.

The next section outlines the authors' methodology of estimating the educational stock. Section 3 briefly reviews Japan, Korea and Taiwan's economic catch-up processes. Based on the authors' dataset, Sections 4, 5 and 6 examine the macroeconomic role of education during the heavy industrialization periods in Japan, Korea and Taiwan, respectively. Section 7 discusses the implication of the time lag between educational and economic catch-up that this chapter finds for these three countries. Section 8 studies the failure of Japan's education policy, which resulted in prolonged economic stagnation after the ending of the "Japanese economic miracle." Section 9 offers implications of Japan, Korea and Taiwan's experiences for today's developing countries.

2 Measuring the average level of education

Average schooling can be calculated by accumulating the total enrollment of corresponding years and ages after adjusting for changes in the population due to immigration and mortality. For reasons of simplicity, this chapter assumes that there are no differences in education level between immigrants and domestic citizens and there is no correlation between school career and mortality.

Average schooling for persons of all ages between x and y years old in year t, $AS_{x-y,t}$, is calculated by the following equation:

$$AS_{x-y,t} = \frac{\sum_{u=x}^{y} \sum_{w=0}^{u} \frac{G_{u,t}}{G_{w,t+w-u}} N_{w,t+w-u}}{\sum_{u=x}^{y} G_{u,t}}$$

where:

$N_{w,t}$ = Total school enrollment of persons at the age of w years in year t, and
$G_{w,t}$ = Total number of persons at the age of w years in year t.

Average schooling for the working-age (age 15–64) population can be calculated for the case of $x = 15$ and $y = 64$. By taking the data of enrollment by levels of education (primary, secondary and tertiary), average schooling can be estimated for levels of education as well. The problem is that the classification of levels of education differs according to time and country. This chapter employs the definition used by the US Department of Education: the primary level, the secondary level, and tertiary level correspond to grades 1–8, grades 9–12, and beyond grade 12, respectively. Likewise, average schooling of vocational education can also be estimated, as shown in Section 3.

Table 8.1 summarizes the estimated results of average schooling of the working age population and the enrollment ratio for the school age (age 6–20) population. While Japan, Korea and Taiwan fell significantly behind the United States in the pre-war period, the gap diminished rapidly in the post-war period. Although there remain gaps of two to three years among these four countries as of 2000, there are almost no differences in the enrollment ratio. Thus, the gaps in average schooling in the working age population will eventually converge to the same level for the four countries.

Figure 8.1 shows the gender gaps of education measured by the female/male ratio of average schooling. No significant gender gap ever existed in the United States, at least for the period analyzed here. In contrast, Japan, Korea, and

Table 8.1 Human capital accumulation through educational investments in the USA, Japan, Korea, and Taiwan

	Enrollment ratio[a] (%)				Average schooling[b] (yrs/psn)			
	USA	Japan	Korea[c]	Taiwan	USA	Japan	Korea[c]	Taiwan
1890	40	26	n.a.	n.a.	6.5	1.3	n.a.	n.a.
1900	40	38	n.a.	4	7.2	2.0	n.a.	0.4
1910	62	43	8[d]	6	7.7	3.3	n.a.	0.5
1920	68	51	11	14	8.3	4.3	0.6	0.6
1930	73	58	16	18	9.1	5.6	0.8	1.0
1940	74	62	38	34	9.8	6.5	1.1	1.6
1950	78	70	n.a.	32	10.5	7.6	n.a.	2.5
1960	85	75	56	57	11.3	8.7	3.3	3.6
1970	87	78	68	65	12.0	9.8	4.8	5.1
1980	85	87	77	73	12.8	10.7	6.9	7.3
1990	87	85	80	81	13.5	11.5	9.0	9.1
2000	89	87	89	86	14.0	12.3	10.5	10.9

Sources: Godo (2005), Godo and Fukami (2005).

Notes
a For persons age 6–20 years.
b Average number of years of schooling per person in the working-age population (persons age 15–64 years).
c Korea before 1945 means all the Korean Peninsula. Korea thereafter means the Republic of Korea (South Korea).
d 1912 value.

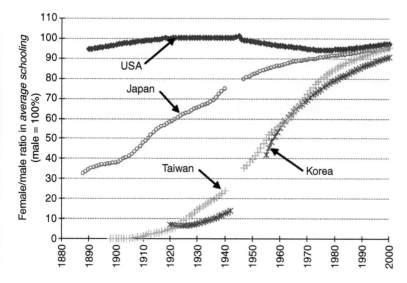

Figure 8.1 Changes in the female/male ratio in average schooling,[a] Taiwan (1898–1940, 1947–2000), Korea[b] (1920–1945, 1955–2000), Japan (1888–1940, 1953–2000), and the USA (1890–1990) (sources: Godo 2005, Godo and Fukami 2005).

Notes
a Average number of years of schooling per person in the working-age group (persons age 15–64 years).
b Korea refers to the whole Korea (all the Korean Peninsula) until its independence from Japan (in 1945) and the Republic of Korea (South Korea) thereafter.

Taiwan had large gender gaps in the early period. These gaps rapidly closed over a century of modern economic growth. As a result, females' average schooling is now almost par with males' average schooling in all four countries.

Figure 8.2 shows how the gender gap in Japan, Korea, and Taiwan decreased as the level of education increased overall. Korea's path is amazingly close to Japan's. Taiwan's path is also similar to Japan's and Korea's. Taiwan's path is higher than Japan's and Korea's after 1970, which means that Taiwan's educational development was less biased in favor of males.

It seems reasonable to hypothesize that certain aspects of Confucian ideology and traditions in Japan, Korea and Taiwan may have confined women to a subordinate role, which deprived them of the opportunity to receive higher education in the earlier period. It is very likely, however, that economic circumstances mattered more than religious or cultural ideals. Factories of certain industries require heavy manual labor, in particular in the early period of industrialization. Thus, it may be reasonable for those countries to have used their limited resources for males' education first. Obviously, more investigation is necessary concerning the reason for the gender gap, but that exploration is beyond the scope of this chapter.

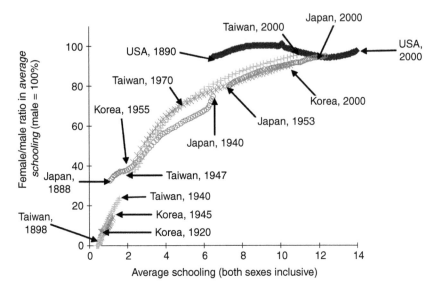

Figure 8.2 Changes in combination of average schooling[a] and the female/male ratio in average schooling, Taiwan (1898–1940, 1947–2000), Korea[b] (1920–1945, 1955–2000), Japan (1888–1940, 1953–2000), and the USA (1890–2000) (source: Godo 2005, Godo and Fukami 2005).

Notes
a Average number of years of schooling per person in the working-age population (persons age 15–64 years).
b Korea refers to the whole Korea (all the Korean Peninsula) until its independence from Japan (in 1945) and the Republic of Korea (South Korea) thereafter.

3 Overview of the process of economic catch-up

Before looking at details of the authors' dataset, it is useful to have a quick review of the East Asian success story, as shown in Figures 8.3 and 8.4 and in Table 8.2.

Figure 8.3 shows the convergence of per capita GDP among the four countries. In the pre-war period, Japan, Korea and Taiwan fell far behind the United States. Those three countries, however, achieved marvelous economic progress in the post-war period. The speed of catch-up is particularly impressive during 1950–1970 in Japan, during 1965–1995 in Korea and during 1960–1990 in Taiwan. These periods are regarded as the core of the East Asian "miracle."

Figure 8.4 views economic convergence from a different perspective. This scatter diagram shows the inverse of physical capital productivity on the vertical axis and the inverse of labor productivity on the horizontal axis, and plots the unit isoquants of the conventional macro production function. Thus, Figure 8.4 shows the change in macroeconomic efficiency and physical capital–labor ratio.[5] As can be seen, both macroeconomic efficiency and the combination of conventional

Table 8.2 The percentage of population aged 15–39 in the total population and the percentage of manufacturing sector in the total labor force in Japan, Korea, and Taiwan

	Percentage of population aged 15–34 in the total population			Percentage of manufacturing sector[a] in the total laborforce		
	Japan	Korea[b]	Taiwan	Japan	Korea[b]	Taiwan
1910	38.1	40.3	43.9	14.0	1.2[c]	7.8[d]
1920	37.5	38.7	39.7	18.3	1.7	8.8
1930	38.3	37.9	39.0	17.1	1.9	9.8
1940	38.1	38.2	37.3	22.5	4.2	10.9
1950	39.3	n.a.	40.7	n.a.	7.0	13.9[e]
1955	40.2	34.0	38.4	20.7	7.6	15.1
1960	42.2	36.7	37.5	25.0	8.2	17.1
1965	44.8	36.9[f]	37.7	27.9	10.4	18.5
1970	43.8	37.7	38.4	29.2	14.3	22.5
1975	40.6	40.9	41.3	28.0	19.1	28.6
1980	38.6	43.1	43.4	26.5	22.5	33.7
1985	37.0	45.3	45.0	26.7	24.4	34.1
1990	35.3	47.4	45.2	25.3	27.6	32.3
1995	34.4	46.4	44.4	22.4	23.6	27.2
2000	33.6	47.2	42.6	20.6	20.2	28.1

Sources: For Japan, Godo (2005), Government of Japan (various issues). For Korea, Godo (2005), Pyo (2001), Bank of Korea (various issues). For Taiwan, Godo and Fukami (2005), Moon (2002), Director-General of Budget, Accounting and Statistics (various issues).

Notes
a Includes mining.
b Korea refers to all the Korean Peninsula until its independence from Japan (in 1945) and the Republic of Korea (South Korea) thereafter.
c 1911 value.
d 1908 value.
e 1951 value.
f 1966 value.

inputs of the three Asian countries were also rapidly converging to the level of the United States in the post-war period.[6]

Table 8.2 shows the change in the industrial structure and demography in the three Asian countries. The right side of Table 8.2 indicates that the "miraculous" periods coincide with the periods of expansion of the manufacturing sector. Interestingly, the expansion in that sector also coincides with the expansion of the percentage of younger working age (age 15–39) people in the total population (the left side of Table 8.2). In sum, Table 8.2 provides a simple but persuasive picture of the East Asian miracle; the miracle occurred because of the increase in factory production that relied on truly abundant supplies of young workers.

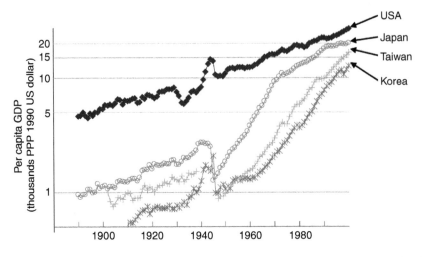

Figure 8.3 Comparison of per capita GDP among Korea[a], Japan, Taiwan, and USA (sources: Godo 2005, Godo and Fukami 2005).

Note
a Korea refers to the whole Korea (all the Korean Peninsula) until its independence from Japan (in 1945) and the Republic of Korea (South Korea) thereafter.

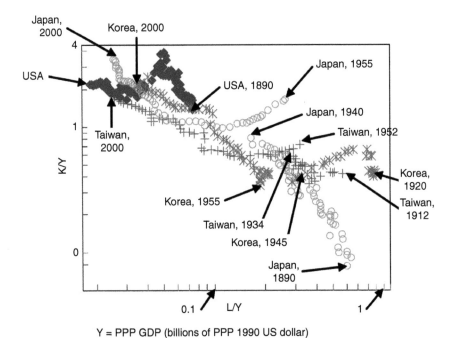

Y = PPP GDP (billions of PPP 1990 US dollar)
L = labor (thousand persons)
K = physical capital (billions of PPP 1990 US dollar)

Figure 8.4 Labor input per GDP versus physical capital per GDP (sources: Godo 2005, Godo and Fukami 2005).

4 Japan's catch-up with the United States

To observe the relationship between educational and economic catch-up, we employ the framework of the macro production function. A standard macro production function with human capital is defined as follows:

$$y = f(k, h),$$

where: y = per capita GDP; k = physical capital–labor ratio; and h = average schooling.

Assuming that the United States is in the vanguard of world economies, this chapter uses two indicators for the degree of economic catch-up, and one indicator for the degree of educational catch-up. The Japan/US ratio in per capita GDP and the physical capital–labor ratio are indicators of economic catch-up; and the Japan/US ratio in average schooling is an indicator of educational catch-up.

Figure 8.5 traces the changes of these economic and educational indicators since the late nineteenth century. As can be seen, there is a sharp contrast between the pre-war and the post-war periods. In the pre-war period, Japan's per capita GDP stagnated at 20 to 30 percent of the level of the United States.[7] Japan's physical capital–labor ratio remained less than 10 percent of the level of the United States throughout the pre-war period. Those findings demonstrate that Japan did not start economic catch-up in the pre-war period. Simultaneously,

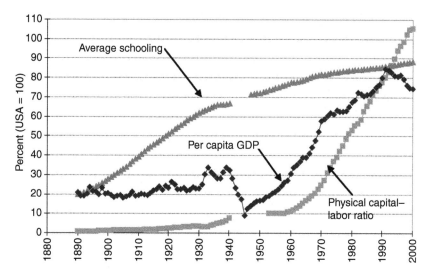

Figure 8.5 The Japan/USA ratios in average schooling[a], per capita GDP[b] and physical capital–labor ratio[c].

Notes
a Average number of years of schooling per person in the total working-age population.
b GDP is measured in PPP 1990 US dollars.
c Labor is measured by total employment. Physical capital is measured by gross nonresidential non-military capital stock at the beginning of year.

however, the educational indicators reveal that Japan had already started its educational catch-up with the United States as early as the late nineteenth century and steadily narrowed the gap throughout the pre-war period.

In contrast to the pre-war period, Japan experienced rapid economic catch-up in the post-war period. After the end of the Pacific War, the Japan/US ratio in per capita GDP and in the physical capital–labor ratio increased sharply.[8] It is well known that aggressive investments in physical capital propelled the economy in the Japanese high growth era. Strong effective demand caused by aggressive physical capital formation created rapid GDP growth, and this rapid GDP growth in turn stimulated further investments in physical capital. This virtuous cycle is known by the famous phrase – "one investment produces another investment."

Japan's educational catch-up spiraled downward in the post-war period. This trend is not surprising because the Japan/US ratio had already reached nearly 70 percent at the beginning of the post-war period. Around 1990, Japan almost caught up with the United States in both education and the economy.

Figure 8.5 describes Japan's economic doldrums in the 1990s. In this period, while Japan increased its physical capital–labor ratio faster than the United States, Japan's income gap compared to the United States widened. Japan seems to have been chasing the dream of high economic growth even in the 1990s when the virtuous cycle of "one investment produces another investment" no longer applied. Many researchers recognize the East Asian miracle for the rich endowment of its education stock.[9] The post-war portion of Figure 8.5 supports this popular view. Since human and physical capitals are complementary, Japan's high education level in the early post-war period guaranteed a high return to physical capital investments. This high return triggered the virtuous cycle of "one investment produces another investment." The pre-war portion of Figure 8.5, however, raises a tough question: why did Japan not achieve economic catch-up in the pre-war period? A nearly 60-year-long time lag exists between the starting point of educational catch-up and that of economic catch-up. How to understand this time lag is an important question for researchers.

One possible answer can be found in the threshold hypothesis presented by Lau *et al.* (1993). They argue that education will be full-fledged only after the education stock in the nation surpasses a certain critical level.

If the threshold hypothesis is true, why does such a threshold exist? In order to investigate this issue further, this chapter proposes the concept of "military-style, heavy industrialization." This phrase refers to the situation in which a mass of homogeneous laborers with a mediocre level of education work together methodically at factories (instead of military camps). Scale economies function in heavy industry. In addition, developing countries do not need to invent new production technologies by themselves because the advanced technologies already exist in developed countries. Thus, "military-style" should be regarded as a quick way for a developing country to initiate heavy industry by borrowing technology from the advanced nations. In the case of "military-style, heavy industrialization," it is obvious that the economic catch-up does not start unless a homogeneous education extends to a certain majority of the population. This chapter considers that the East Asian economic miracle was a result of this "military-style, heavy industrialization."

The Japan–US gap by levels of education in Figure 8.6 displays interesting features about Japan's educational catch-up. The catch-up of primary education comes first. Next is secondary education, and tertiary education is last. This sequence looks natural. The movement of the Japan/US ratio in tertiary education is remarkable. This ratio increased sharply from the mid-1920s to the early 1940s. This was triggered by the University Order of 1915 whereby the government allowed the establishment of private universities (before that, the nine Imperial Universities were the only universities that the government authorized). The surge of university graduates coincides with the period of Japan's heavy industrialization and military expansion to Manchuria. In these years, demands for technocrats and bureaucrats (for managing the colonial regimes) expanded. Thus, the hike in the Japan/US ratio in tertiary education matched these surging demands.

An even more impressive feature is that the Japan/US ratio in tertiary education remained constant from the 1950s to the 1980s. It means that the catch-up in tertiary education stagnated for as long as 40 years. This contradicts the common view, Kohama and Watanabe (1996), that the expansion of tertiary education promoted post-war Japan's economic miracle. This common view should be re-examined carefully in two senses. First, a simple comparison of the number of annual graduates from universities in the pre-war period with that of the post-war period may not be informative because almost all the nations in the world

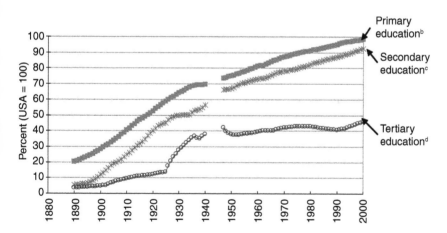

Figure 8.6 The Japan/USA ratios in average schooling[a] by levels of education (source: Godo 2005).

Notes
a Average number of years of schooling per person in the working-age population.
b Schooling of first and eighth grades.
c Schooling of ninth to twelfth grades.
d Schooling of beyond twelfth grade.

(including even the countries that showed poor economic performance in the post-war period) increased their graduates after World War II. Thus, it is overly simplistic to attribute post-war Japan's economic success to the increase in the number of university graduates. Second, researchers should pay more attention to the fact that advanced countries, in particular the United States, have heavily invested in tertiary education since the 1940s. The US government provided financial assistance to ex-servicemen and sponsored science research (partly with the intention of military use) in universities. The civil rights movement in the United States in the early post-war period also opened up more opportunities in tertiary education for girls and African Americans.

In fact, Japanese business leaders in the early post-war period often opposed the expansion of tertiary education.[10] Japan, a latecomer to industrialization, had been a labor-abundant society until around 1960. The business leaders wanted low wage, blue collar workers rather than high wage, highly educated workers. In addition, secondary education received priority in the government's educational expenditures because the enrollment in lower secondary schools surged. This surge came from the extension of compulsory education from six to nine years in 1947 and the baby-boom of the early 1950s.

Even after the 1960s, the government continued its restrictive policy on the expansion of tertiary education until around 1990. This is mainly because the government feared that the expansion of tertiary education would result in the deterioration of its quality (although many researchers are skeptical about whether this restrictive policy was actually effective in maintaining quality).[11]

Japan's tertiary education policy changed around 1990 from suppression to expansion. The government allowed more flexibility for universities in setting enrollment quotas and curricula. As a result, as Figure 8.6 shows, Japan's catch-up in tertiary education started around 1990.

The authors' dataset provides comprehensive information on Japan's vocational education as well. The definition of vocational education differs according to researchers. This chapter defines vocational education as "post-compulsory education at schools (or in courses) that provide mainly vocational training." Post-secondary education is not included in vocational education in this chapter.[12] Figure 8.7 shows the historical change in enrollment of vocational education (flow data). The government initiated the Vocational Education Order in 1897, and various types of vocational schools were established. One of the most popular vocational schools in the pre-war period was the Vocational Supplementary Schools (VSS). Accepting graduates from elementary schools, VSS provided reviews of elementary education and practical knowledge for farming, manufacturing and merchandising. While most of the VSS started as a result of local people's initiative, the government gradually increased its commitment. According to the regime shift towards war, the government reformed VSS to Adult Schools. Adult Schools provided a mixture of military and vocational training for youngsters who were not promoted to middle school after graduation from elementary school. The expansion of Adult Schools resulted in the sharp increase in vocational school enrollment in the 1920s and 1930s as seen in Figure 8.7.

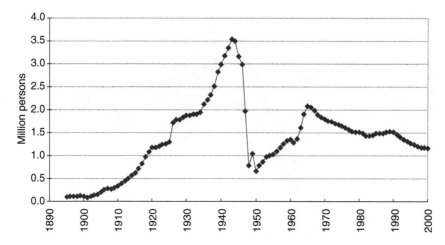

Figure 8.7 Enrollment of vocational education[a] in Japan (source: Godo 2005).

Note

a Vocational education is defined as post-compulsory education at the schools (or courses) that provide mainly vocational training. Higher education is not included. The concrete list of vocational schools (or courses) is given in Godo and Hayami (1999).

In 1947, the Japanese education system was reformed. The new system employed the so called "6–3–3" system: three years at junior high schools were added to the six years of education at elementary schools to form the new compulsory education system; the upper secondary education was unified into three-year-long senior high schools. There are two types of senior high school: vocational high school and general high school. Most of pre-war Japan's vocational schools, including the Adult Schools, were abolished in 1947. Vocational high school education was provided mostly in vocational high schools in the post-war period.[13] Gender discrimination in schooling opportunities was eliminated. This system has remained essentially unchanged through current times.

Because of the abolishment of the Adult School in 1947, the enrollment in vocational education dropped sharply from 1945 to 1950; then the enrollment in vocational education increased again from 1950 to 1968. After that, the enrollment gradually decreased throughout the 1970s. Interestingly, the enrollment was kept almost constant in the 1980s, and began a downward trend again in the 1990s.

The stock data of vocational education provides insights concerning post-war Japan's miraculous economic growth (Figure 8.8). Average schooling of vocational education for the entire working age population had been at a plateau during the high growth era (from the early post-war period to around 1970). This implies that the vocational education stock made a significant contribution to post-war Japan's miraculous economic growth. Education researchers often criticize pre-war Japan's military training in Adult Schools. It has been suggested

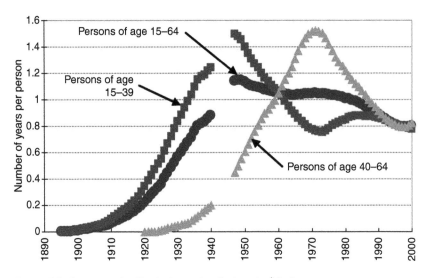

Figure 8.8 Average schooling[a] of vocational education[b] in Japan.

Notes
a Average number of years of schooling per person in the working-age population.
b Vocational education is defined as post-compulsory education at the schools (or courses) that provide mainly vocational training. Higher education is not included. The concrete list of vocational schools (or courses) is given in Godo and Hayami (1999).

that military training is far from an ideal education. This chapter neither rationalizes nor advocates for military training. Instead, we want to present the objective view that those who received military and vocational education in Adult Schools during the pre-war period held the destiny of the Japanese economy in the high growth era.

Figure 8.8 also shows average schooling of vocational education for younger workers (aged 15–39) and older workers (aged 40–64) separately. As can be seen, the vocational education stock in the younger generation exceeds that in the elder generation until 1960, and the pattern reversed after that: 1960 coincides with the year when the Japanese economy turned from a labor-abundant economy to a labor-shortage economy.[14] Thus, Figure 8.7 tells a plausible story: the labor-intensive industries led the Japanese economy based on young workers who had received ample vocational training until around 1960. After that, with the leadership of veteran workers and middle and upper level managers who had vocational knowledge and experience, Japanese manufacturers remodeled themselves to produce higher value added products.[15]

5 Korea's catching up with the United States

As is the case with Japan, this chapter explores the Korea/US ratios for education and economic indicators in Figures 8.9 and 8.10. These figures exhibit interesting

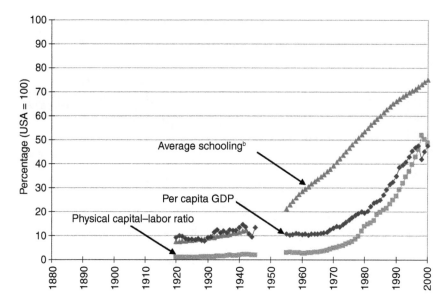

Figure 8.9 The Korea[a]/USA ratios in average schooling,[b] per capita GDP[c] and physical capital–labor ratio[d] (source: Godo 2005).

Notes
a Korea in the pre- and post-war periods refers to all the Korean Peninsula and the Republic of Korea respectively.
b Average number of years of schooling per person in the total working-age population.
c GDP is measured in PPP 1990 US dollars.
d Labor is measured by total employment. Capital is measured by gross nonresidential non-military capital stock at the beginning of year.

similarities between Japan and Korea. First, educational catch-up precedes economic catch-up. Second, the order of educational catch-up by level is also the same as Japan's case: primary level is first, the secondary level is second, and the tertiary level is the last. Third, the catch-up in tertiary education stagnated in the 1970s, when Korea sped up its heavy industrialization. In fact, the regime of President Park Chong-hui (1961–1979) severely controlled the number of enrollments in universities.[16] Instead, the regime was devoted to the expansion of primary and secondary education under the slogan of "eradication of the illiterate." As is the case of Japan's early pre-war period, President Park Chong-hui considered that low wage, blue collar workers were more useful for Korea's industrialization than high wage, highly educated workers.

In spite of these similarities between the two countries, Korea achieved the educational catch-up in a shorter period than Japan. In Japan, the economic catch-up started in the middle of the 1950s, nearly 60 years after having started its educational catch-up in the late nineteenth century. The Japan/US ratios in average schooling, per capita GDP and physical capital–labor in the middle of the 1950s were 0.7, 0.3 and 0.2 respectively. In Korea, the economic catch-up started in the middle of the 1960s. It was nearly 30 years (half of Japan's case)

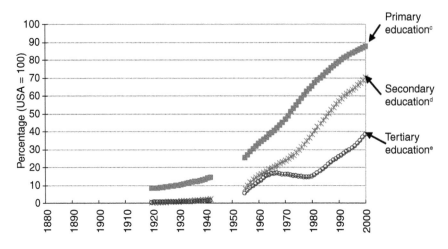

Figure 8.10 The Korea[a]/USA ratios in average schooling[b] by levels of education (source: Godo 2005).

Notes
a Korea refer to the whole Korea (all the Korean Peninsula) until its independence from Japan (in 1945) and the Republic of Korea (South Korea) thereafter.
b Average number of years of schooling per person in the working-age population.
c Schooling of first and eighth grades.
d Schooling of ninth to twelfth grades.
e Schooling of beyond twelfth grade.

after Korea had started its educational catch-up with the United States around the 1930s. The Korea/US ratios in average schooling, per capita GDP and physical capital–labor ratio in the middle of 1950 were 0.3, 0.1, and 0.05 respectively, which are much lower than Japan's starting points. Korea's delay in the catch-up of tertiary education (nearly ten years) was also much shorter than Japan's (nearly 40 years).

Thus, it is legitimate to argue that Korea's catch-up had a shorter "runway" and a higher rate of "ascent" than Japan's. Korea's economic development has often been described as "a compressed version of Japan's."[17] This chapter's analysis also shows that Korea's educational development can be described as "a compressed version of Japan's."

6 Taiwan's catching up with the United States

Figures 8.11 and 8.12 show Taiwan/US ratios in educational and economic indicators. The biggest difference between Japan and Korea are that the Taiwan/US ratio in per capita GDP exceeded that of average schooling in the pre-war period (Figure 8.11). Japan and Korea did not have such a period. This phenomenon can be attributed to the fact that agriculture (in particular sugar production) led the Taiwanese economy in the pre-war period. Taiwan's agricultural GDP grew almost parallel to Taiwan's overall GDP over 1915–1930 (Mizoguchi and

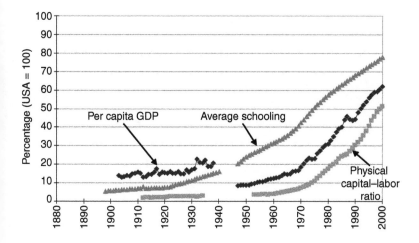

Figure 8.11 The Taiwan/USA ratios in average schooling[a], per capita GDP[b] and physical capital–labor ratio[c].

Notes
a Average number of years of schooling per person in the total working-age population.
b GDP is measured in PPP 1990 US dollars.
c Labor is measured by total employment. Physical capital is measured by gross nonresidential non-military capital stock at the beginning of year.

Umemura 1988). This is in sharp contrast to Korea's and Japan's cases where the share of agriculture in GDP decreased significantly during the same period. Many economists assert that education is less important in agriculture than in modern industries.[18] This may be the reason that pre-war Taiwan's per capita GDP was so high compared with its educational level.

In the post-war period, when the leading industry in Taiwan changed from the agricultural to the manufacturing sector, Taiwan's educational catch-up preceded its economic catch-up, just as in the cases of Japan and Korea. Still, the gap between the educational and economic catch-up was smaller in Taiwan compared with both Japan and Korea. Japan and Korea experienced some periods when the Japan/US (or Korea/US) ratio in average schooling was over 30 percentage points higher than that in per capita GDP (Figures 8.5 and 8.9), but Taiwan never experienced such a period (Figure 8.11).

It should be noted that, compared with Japan and Korea, post-war Taiwan's industrialization did not rely heavily on the process industries such as shipbuilding and iron and steel refineries that needed huge amounts of physical capital. Instead, medium- and small-sized enterprises led Taiwan's industrialization. Thus, Taiwan's industrialization relied less on physical capital stock than Japan's and Korea's. This results in the fact that the Taiwan/US ratio in per capita GDP constantly exceeded the physical capital–labor ratio in Figure 8.11.

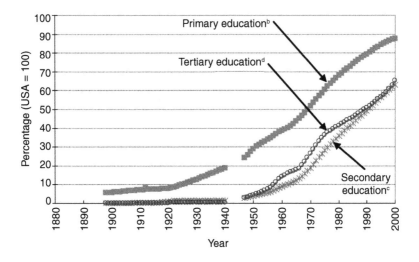

Figure 8.12 The Taiwan/USA ratios in average schooling[a] by levels of education (source: Godo and Fukami 2005).

Notes
a Average number of years of schooling per person in the working-age population.
b Schooling of first and eighth grades.
c Schooling of ninth to twelfth grades.
d Schooling of beyond twelfth grade.

Another of Taiwan's unique characteristics is that secondary education and tertiary education caught up with the United States almost at the same speed. There was no delay in catching up in tertiary education. This is a big difference from Japan's and Korea's experiences.

The above observations indicate that Taiwan's experience of catching up was smoother than Japan's and Korea's in the following three senses: (*a*) the gender gap diminished faster in Taiwan (as was mentioned in Section 2); (*b*) the gap between educational and economic catch-up was smaller in Taiwan; and (*c*) Taiwan had no delay in catching up in tertiary education.

While Korea and Taiwan experienced high economic growth in similar periods by borrowing advanced technologies from the United States and Japan, why do these two countries differ in the pattern of educational catch-up? This chapter's understanding is that this difference in educational catch-up comes from the difference in the type of economic entities which bore the task of technology-borrowing. In Korea, huge conglomerates, called *chaebol*, introduced advanced technologies from the West (including Japan), while in Taiwan, medium and small scale entrepreneurs did the introduction. Taiwanese entrepreneurs were so light-footed that they started their businesses with technologies within easy reach. So, the technologies of Korean firms had more scale economies than those of Taiwanese firms. Thus, the demands of Korean firms for a mass of homogeneous, mediocre educated workers were much stronger than those of Taiwanese firms. Since Taiwan relied less on the process industries that require heavy manual labor, Taiwan's educational development was also less biased in favor of males.

7 Implications of the time lag between educational and economic catch-up

The analysis in the previous sections found that educational catch-up preceded economic catch-up in all three East Asian countries. This finding implies that it took a long period for a latecomer country to start up industrialization. Even if a country invests in education today, it will take time to increase its educational stock. In addition, there is a time lag between educational and economic catch-up. Such a long "gestation" period may not be affordable by today's developing countries, which are often exposed to regime instability.

This time lag raises another question about those three countries' experiences: why did Japan, Korea and Taiwan invest heavily in education before their economic catch-up started? One of the reasons might be attributed to the governments' initiatives. The political leaders in the three countries emphasized the importance of education from the very early stages of development. In Japan, the post-Meiji Restoration government encouraged and persuaded (despite intimidation by the police) children to attend school as a measure of control over the country. The promotion of Adult Schools (as was mentioned above) is another example of the forcible expansion of education for ordinary families. The Government-General of Korea extended schooling as a part of the assimilation policy in the 1930s. President Park Chong-hui also stated that "the annihilation of illiteracy" was the top national priority. The Nationalist Party in Taiwan also emphasized education in order to assimilate Taiwanese with the Mainland Chinese.

More important was people's spontaneity. Many researchers observe ordinary families' enthusiasm for sending their children to schools even before the beginning of their economic catch-up. In Meiji Japan, as was mentioned above, VSS developed spontaneously nationwide. Many ordinary families welcomed the government's encouragement of Adult Schools because it meant more chances for education. Kimura (1988) asserts that post-war Korea's explosive increase in enrollment could be attributed more to ordinary families' enthusiasm for getting education than to the government's initiative. McGinn *et al.* (1980) also find that Koreans were surprisingly eager for education even in the chaotic 1950s in the wake of the Pacific War and the Korean War. Abe and Abe (1971) report that demands for education in Taiwan surged rapidly beyond the control and expectation of the Taiwanese government in the early post-war period.

Why were people in those three countries so keen on education even without sufficient macroeconomic results? This chapter's understanding is that the "screening effect" was operative here. The Meiji Restoration shuffled the Japanese society entirely. The Korean and Taiwanese societies experienced the upheaval of Japanese colonization and the Pacific War, followed by civil wars. Thus, new elite strata were formed in those countries. All the children in ordinary families had a chance to enjoy the new elite status if they had a better education than others. Conversely, people received pressure not to fall behind others in school. Thus, the private return to school was high even before the beginning of economic catch-up. This is illustrative of the "screening effect." Usually, researchers use the term in a negative connotation. In Japan, Korea and Taiwan, however, the "screening effect" helped their societies to endure the heavy burden of a long "gestation" period of educational investments.

8 Japan's long-term stagnation after the completion of the catch-up growth

If the Japanese miracle was based on the borrowing of advanced technology from abroad at the end of World War II, the speed of its economic growth would have inevitably decreased as the technology gap between Japan and the advanced economies (typically the United States) closed as a direct result of successful technology borrowing. Thus, it is easy to understand why the period of miracle growth did not last very long. One question remains: Why, in the 1990s, did the Japanese economy slide into the worst recession among the major industrialized countries?

A clue to answering this question can be found in Figure 8.6. Figure 8.6 shows that, during the miracle period, educational catch-up continued to progress mainly at the primary and secondary levels, while no significant catch-up occurred at the tertiary level. The percentage of Japan's average tertiary schooling relative to that of the United States remained virtually constant. This observation implies that Japan was able to borrow world class technology with no concurrent investment in upgrading (high-level scientists and engineers) its human capital base relative to the United States. This may not be an anomaly, considering the conditions surrounding Japan at that time. Since advanced technologies were abundantly available abroad, Japan did not need to spare its own resources to develop them. A high rate of economic growth could thus be readily achieved with a relatively small cadre of high-level scientists and engineers who could adjust foreign technology to domestic use. A more critical question would have been how to secure a supply of laborers who could understand the basics of the translated technology and use it effectively with the instructions of a hierarchical management in a large-scale factory system.

The allocation of large budgets for middle-level education at the expense of higher level education was probably efficient for maximizing the economic growth of Japan in the post-war catch-up process. The high growth performance of the Japanese economy at that time depended on the availability of advanced technology abroad which could readily be borrowed by a relatively small number of high-level scientists and engineers. This backlog was certain to be exhausted as the advanced foreign technology was successfully borrowed. When Japan closed its technology gap vis-à-vis the advanced industrial economies at the end of its successful economic catch-up in the 1980s, it required new and original technologies to compete with other industrial economies in the world market. Much larger and higher quality human capital is necessary for producing innovative ideas and designs at home than borrowing them from abroad. The Japanese government failed to prepare a human capital base during the miracle growth period. The very success of the miracle growth mechanism relied on the translation of foreign technology for domestic use by a small number of scientists and engineers who had survived the Pacific War. That "translation of foreign technology" was then used effectively by laborers with middle-level education at relatively low costs and blinded the eyes of Japanese entrepreneurs and policy makers to the need for additional higher level human capital at the end of the catch-up process.

The present stalemate of the Japanese economy is but one of the many examples in which a system that proved to be very effective in promoting economic growth at a certain stage of development turned out to be an obstacle to further growth at another point in time. Since precedent cases of economies able to escape from these constraints are quite rare in history, the prospect of the Japanese economy regaining its vigor in the competitive global arena appears to be rather bleak. The high performing economies currently comprising the East Asian economic miracle, with essentially the same mechanism as the Japanese miracle, may have a better chance to escape from being trapped in a vicious cycle if they can learn from Japan's failure. In this regard, the current strategy of Singapore to build world class education and research systems to support a transition of its economic center of gravity from labor intensive to knowledge intensive industries before the catch-up growth process is completed might represent a promising model for developing economies to sustain economic growth beyond the stage of catching up.

9 Conclusion

This chapter asserted that the East Asian economic successes can be characterized as "military-style, heavy industrialization." Roughly speaking, their societies were rich in middle-level educated, homogeneous laborers during their miraculous economic growth periods. These laborers worked together methodically in factories (instead of military camps).

Japan, Korea and Taiwan succeeded in forming uniform societies, which were suited for "military-style, heavy industrialization," through long-range educational investments. The "screening effect" helped those countries to endure the long "gestation" period between the educational and economic catch-up. The well-timed suppression of the opportunities of tertiary education by the Japanese and Korean governments was effective in achieving their rapid heavy industrialization. The heavy investments in vocational education in pre-war Japan bore fruit in the post-war high growth era.

In today's developing countries, expansion of secondary and higher education tends to receive higher priority than the pursuit of universal education.[19] This is different from the pattern of educational development in Japan, Korea and

Taiwan where the catch-up in primary education preceded the catch-up in secondary and tertiary education.

All the findings of this chapter are potentially relevant to today's developing countries, which aim to imitate East Asian success. Obviously, the situation of developing countries in the twenty-first century is different from the experiences of the East Asian countries in the twentieth century. First, in contrast to the ethnically homogeneous societies of Japan, Korea and Taiwan, many of today's developing countries suffer seriously from multi-ethnicity problems. Since the curricula of elementary and secondary education are closely related to lifestyle, the simple expansion of education without due consideration of ethnicity may provoke conflict between governments and local citizens. As this chapter has argued, Japan, Korea and Taiwan succeeded in forming a mass of homogeneous laborers that was suitable for rapid industrialization. In multi-ethnic countries, such a strategy may not work. Second, in the twenty-first century, the emphasis on increasingly heavy industry may not be synonymous with economic development as it was in the twentieth century. It is important to note that heavy industry has been reducing its percentage in World GDP since the middle of the 1970s (World Bank 2008). The non-manufacturing sectors such as IT industries may instead lead the economy of developing countries in the twenty-first century. If so, "military-style, heavy industrialization" may not be an appropriate development strategy for today's developing countries. Still, it may be a necessary, if shortened, phase; and clarifying the characteristics of twentieth-century-style economic development remains important for academicians and non-academicians who are concerned with development policies in today's developing countries.

Notes

1 "Korea" in this chapter refers to Korea as a whole (all the Korean Peninsula) until its independence from Japan (1945) and to the Republic of Korea (South Korea) thereafter.
2 The earlier versions of the authors are available at Godo and Hayami (1999), Godo (2001), and Yamauchi and Godo (2004).
3 The United States has been at the top of the world economy since around 1890 (Maddison 1995).
4 It is a popular view among researchers that after the Meiji restoration of 1868 Japan needed 20–30 years to complete its "transition" from a feudal to modern state. For example, see Ito (1992: 16).
5 The southwest direction in Figure 8.4 means higher macroeconomic efficiency. The northwest (or southeast) direction means more labor-saving (or labor-using) and capital-saving (or capital-using) technology.
6 An exception is the 1990s in Japan. In spite of increases in the physical capital–labor ratio, Japan had almost zero economic growth during the 1990s.
7 The ratio increased barely 10 percent in the 1930s. This period should be seen as unusual because the United States was experiencing the aftermath of Black Thursday and Japan enjoyed a short-lived economic boom brought on by the military expansion in China.
8 It should be noted that physical capital–labor ratio is a stock term while per capita GDP is a flow term. Physical capital investments (flow data) surged almost simultaneously as per capita GDP did.

9 For example, see World Bank (1993), Asian Development Bank (2001), and Hayami and Godo (2005).

10 See Kaneko and Kobayashi (1996: 141–145).

11 Many Japanese universities were established in the large cities which had suffered from overpopulation during the high growth era. Thus, the alleviation of congestion in the large cities was another reason for suppressing tertiary education.

12 This chapter's definition of vocational education is the same as in Godo and Hayami (1999) who provide a concrete list of all aspects of vocational education.

13 Technical College, another type of vocational school, was established in 1962. For the post-war period, only vocational high school and technical college are counted as vocational education in this chapter.

14 Minami (2002).

15 Panasonic, Sony, and Honda are good examples.

16 See, McGinn *et al.* (1980) and Kim (2000).

17 See Watanabe (1992).

18 For example, see Lockheed *et al.* (1980), Yang (1997), Otsuka and Place (2001) and Fafchamps and Quisumbing (1999).

19 For example, see Szirmai (2005: 238).

References

Abe, M. and Abe, H. (1971) *Taiwan to Kankoku no Kyoiku Kaihatsu* (Educational Development in Taiwan and Korea), Tokyo: Institute of Developing Economies.

Asia Development Bank (2001) *Education and National Development in Asia*, Manila: Asia Development Bank.

Bank of Korea (various issues) *Economic Statistics Yearbook*, Bank of Korea.

Directorate-General of Budget, Accounting and Statistics, Executive Yuan, (various issues), *Yearbook of Manpower Statistics Taiwan Area*, Republic of China.

Fafchamps, M. and Quisumbing, A.R. (1999) "Human Capital, Productivity, and Labor Allocation in Rural Pakistan," *Journal of Human Resources*, 34(2): 396–406.

Gerschenkron, A. (1962) *Economic Backwardness in Historical Perspective*, Cambridge, MA: Harvard University Press.

Godo, Y. (2001) "Estimation of Average Years of Schooling by Levels of Education for Japan and the United States, 1890–1990," FASID Development Database (Foundation for Advanced Studies on International Development, Japan) 2000–2001.

Godo, Y. (2005) "Revised Annual Estimates of Average Years of Schooling for Japan, Korea and the United States," mimeo.

Godo, Y. and Fukami, S. (2005) "New Estimates of Average Years of Schooling for Taiwan," mimeo.

Godo, Y. and Hayami, Y. (1999) "Accumulation of Education in Modern Economic Growth; Comparison of Japan with the United States," *ADBI Working Paper 4*, Asian Development Bank Institute.

Government of Japan. Ministry of Public Management, Home Affairs, Posts and Telecommunications. Statistics Bureau (various issues), *Annual Report on the Labour Force Survey*, Tokyo: Japan Statistical Association.

Hayami, Y. and Godo, Y. (2005) *Development Economics* (third edition), Oxford: Oxford University Press.

Ito, T. (1992), *The Japanese Economy*, Cambridge, MA: MIT Press.

Kaneko, M. and Kobayashi, M. (1996) *Kyoiku, Keizai, Shakai* (Education, Economy and Society), Tokyo: Society of the Promotion of the University of the Air.

Kim J. (2000) "Historical Development" in: J.C. Weidman and N. Park (eds.), *Higher Education in Korea: Tradition and Adoption*, London: Falmer Press.

Kimura, M. (1988) "Kankoku (Chosen) ni-okeru Shoto Kyoiku no Fukyu, 1911–1955 nen" (Diffusion of Primary Education in Korea, 1911–1955), *Asian Studies*, 34(3): 3–22.

Kohama, H. and Watanabe, M. (1996) *Sengo Nihon Keizai no 50 nen* (Economic Development in Post-War Japan), Tokyo: Toyo Keizai Shimpo-sha.

Lau, L.J., Jamison, D.T., Liu, S., and Rivkin, S. (1993) "Education and Economic Growth: Some Cross-Sectional Evidence from Brazil," *Journal of Development Economics*, 41: 45–70.

Lockheed, M.E., Jamison, D.T., and Lau, L. (1980) "Farmer Education and Farm Efficiency: A Survey," *Economic Development and Cultural Change*, 29: 37–76.

McGinn, N.F., Snodgrass, D.R., Kim, Y., Kim, S., and Kim, Q. (1980) *Education and Modernization of the Republic of Korea, 1945–1975*, KDI Working Paper 7806 (Korean Development Institute).

Maddison, A. (1995), *Monitoring the World Economy*, Paris: Development Centre of Organization for Economic Co-operation and Development.

Minami, R. (2002) *Nihon no Keizai Hatten* (Economic Development of Japan) (third edition), Tokyo: Toyo Keizai Shimpo-sha.

Mizoguchi T. and Umemura, M. (1988) *Basic Statistics of Former Japanese Colonies, 1895–1938: Estimates and Findings*, Tokyo: Toyo Keizai Shimpo-sha.

Moon, D. (2002) *Taiwan*, Asia Information Center, Institute for International Development of Takushoku University (ed.), *Higashi Ajia Choki Tokei* (Long Term Economics Statistics for East Asia), Tokyo: Keiso Shobo.

Otsuka, K. and Place, F. (2001) *Land Tenure and Natural Resource Management: A Comparative Study of Agrarian Communities in Asia and Africa*, Baltimore, MD: Johns Hopkins University Press.

Pyo, H. (2001) "Economic Growth in Korea (1910–1999): A Long-term Trend and Perspective," *Seoul Journal of Economics*, 14: 1.

Szirmai, A. (2005) *The Dynamics of Socio-Economic Development: An Introduction*, Cambridge: Cambridge University Press.

Watanabe, T. (1992) *Asia: Its Growth and Agony*, Tokyo: Institute for Economic Development and Policy.

World Bank (1993) *The East Asian Miracle: Economic Growth and Public Policy*, Oxford: Oxford University Press.

World Bank (2008), *The World Development Indicators CD-ROM*.

Yamauchi, F. and Godo, Y. (2004) "Human Capital Accumulation, Technological Change and International Spillovers: Comparative Growth Experience from Japan, Korea and the United States," *FASID Discussion Paper Series on International Development Strategies 2004–05–01* (Foundation for Advanced Studies on International Development, Japan). Online, available at: www.fasid.or.jp/chosa/kenkyu/senryaku/kaihatsu/pdf/discussion/2004–05–001.pdf.

Yang, D.T. (1997) "Education and Off-Farm Work," *Economic Development and Cultural Change*, 45(3): 613–632.

9   The "Yoshida Doctrine" in the post-Cold War world[1]

'Pre-emptive' minimalist strategy in a multipolar world

Koichi Hamada and Seiko Mimaki

1 Introduction

There has been a lot of debate over the sources of post-war Japan's economic development. This chapter focuses on the most prominent legacy, the "Yoshida Doctrine." The "Yoshida Doctrine" is the expression of Japan's minimalist defense posture, which was chosen by Prime Minister Shigeru Yoshida (1878–1967) and was maintained as a fundamental policy by successive cabinets. Practically speaking, the acceptance of this doctrine was to drive Japan into fast economic recovery at the expense of heavy security dependence on the United States.

In contrast to the fact that the other major powers achieved their status by a more or less balanced combination of economic strength and military strength, post-war Japan focused extreme emphasis on economic objectives in foreign policy by relying on the protection of the United States. Of course, Japan had to pay various costs such as those for maintaining the use of American bases in Japan, and those that came as a result of almost blindly following American military policies throughout the world. Yet, the "Yoshida Doctrine" was a largely successful course to follow during the Cold War period. The Japanese economy prospered as a dividend of peace in the 1960s–1970s, and then achieved status as an economic superpower in the 1980s. Japan's spectacular economic growth under the "Yoshida Doctrine" was praised as an ideal model of capitalistic development for Asian developing countries (Hatano and Sato 2004).

Since the end of the Cold War, however, the assumptions underlying the "Yoshida Doctrine" have undergone significant questioning. In the 1990s, Japan found itself under severe pressure to assume a greater share of the international military burden. Japan's $13 billion monetary contribution to the Gulf War (1991) was almost ignored despite its magnitude. Indeed, having refused to dispatch military personnel to the battlefield, Japan was even accused of non-cooperation.

Faced with world-wide denouncement of Japan's "checkbook diplomacy," some "realist" politicians seriously questioned the relevance of the "Yoshida Doctrine" in a post-Cold War world. They demanded the expansion of Japan's security commitment under the aegis of the US–Japan alliance, and a relaxation of the constitutional constraints of the use of forces abroad.

In opposition to these "realists," a defender of the "Yoshida Doctrine" would emphasize that the doctrine is the best embodiment of the spirit of Japan's Peace Constitution. They never dared to discuss whether a simple extension of the "Yoshida Doctrine" would be a sufficient security strategy for Japan today, because for them the real meaning of the doctrine lies not in its efficacy as a national strategy but in its symbolic value. They rather idealistically believe that, however difficult it may be, the "Yoshida Doctrine" should be maintained as Japan's national "doctrine."

In our view, however, neither a "realist" nor an "idealist" view provides a satisfactory answer for Japan's security strategy in the post-Cold War world. A "realist" insists that the "Yoshida Doctrine" has become completely out of date in rapidly changing situations after the end of the Cold War, and Japan needs entirely new security policies. On the other hand, an "idealist" believes that the "Yoshida Doctrine" is an ideal embodiment of the Peace Constitution, and should be kept intact regardless of changes in the surrounding situation. At a glance, their arguments present a stark contrast, but they have significant common ground. They both regard the "Yoshida Doctrine" as a static rather than a dynamic doctrine. In other words, they both dismiss the possibility of its further development and new effectiveness in the post-Cold War world.

Our chapter explores a way to combine realism and idealism so as to overcome the negative legacies of the "Yoshida Doctrine," while maintaining and developing its positive legacies in the current world.

In Section 2, we briefly review the historical development of the "Yoshida Doctrine" from its birth to the present. We hope that this historical analysis will show that, even without outright revision of the "Yoshida Doctrine," post-World War II Japan has been pursuing a dynamic and flexible security policy. We also hope that our analysis will show the possibilities for Japan to cope with post-Cold War security challenges without a total denial of the "Yoshida Doctrine."

In Section 3, we question whether the "Yoshida Doctrine" has completely lost its positive impact on world security or might have new stabilizing effects. In game theoretic language, the "Yoshida Doctrine" can be called a "pre-emptive" minimalist strategy, because Japan proclaims in advance that she will keep the minimum level of military expenditure and keep it regardless of the amount of the military expenditure of others. In order to fully understand the strategic impact of Japan's "pre-emptive" minimalist strategy today, we should recognize the importance of the changing strategic situation from the Cold War regime to the post-Cold War regime; a simple bipolar world now changed to a complex multipolar world. The nature of the game also changed from a strategic substitute situation to a strategic complement situation, where players' defense policies and defense expenditures are mutually dependent. We would like to stress that when taking the multiple strategic interdependence approach into account, Japan's "pre-emptive" minimalist strategy can be an important step towards realizing a dividend of peace in East Asia.

In Section 4, we review a security dialogue which is now going on in Japan; a "realist" who advocates abandoning the "Yoshida Doctrine" and an "idealist" who denies any possibility of its modification. Then, we try to balance both views and suggest what Japan's new security strategy might be. In the final section, we present our conclusions.

2 The historical development of the "Yoshida Doctrine"

The birth of a minimalist security policy

Certainly, Prime Minister Yoshida's choice of a minimalist security policy was partially necessitated by history. In the aftermath of the devastation of World War II, the Allied Forces, which primarily reflected the will of the United States, drafted Japan's new constitution. The most notable article was, of course, Article 9, which provides for the "abandonment of the right to engage in war as a means of resolving international conflicts." Under Prime Minister Yoshida's guidance, the Japanese public accepted the draft. In fact, there was no choice but to accept it under the ongoing occupation. At that point in time, Japan was reborn as a "peace-loving nation" with its Peace Constitution.

Yoshida's diplomacy, however, was severely criticized for its cowardliness including Japan's acceptance of almost complete dependence on the United States for its security. Since then, his diplomacy has increasingly been regarded as a symbol of national humiliation.

It was Masataka Kosaka's essays, written in the 1960s, that redeemed Yoshida's honor. Kosaka is one of the most influential scholars in post-war Japan, and his political view is known as "realism." In his "Saisho Yoshida Shigeru ron" (Prime Minister Yoshida Shigeru: An Interpretation) printed in *Chuo Koron* in 1964, he pointed out that Yoshida's choice of the minimalist security policy was a carefully calculated "strategy" for damaged Japan to survive the severe Cold War realities and lay the foundation for its economic recovery (Kosaka 1964). After the war, Japan had neither resources nor the will to engage in military encounters, and Yoshida thought that Japan should focus its limited resources on economic development by keeping its security commitments to the lowest acceptable level.

While praising Yoshida's realistic choice to put economics first, Kosaka also emphasized that the minimalist security policy should be a temporary policy for a weakened Japan to achieve sufficient economic recovery. In subsequent articles Kosaka called more and more attention to the fact that Yoshida himself recognized that Japan's minimalist defense policy should be abandoned with the fulfillment of its main objective (Kosaka 1967).

Actually, Yoshida was clearly aware of Japan's future security role in the international community. In his 1959 essay, Yoshida criticized SEATO (Southeast Asia Treaty Organization), which excluded Japan, and instead suggested FETO (Far Eastern Treaty Organization), which is the Asian counterpart to NATO (North Atlantic Treaty Organization) led by Japan (Yoshida 1962, pp. 37–42).

After Japan achieved sufficient economic power in the 1960s, Yoshida became increasingly skeptical of the continuation of the minimalist defense posture. In a 1962 speech at the America–Japan Society, he said,

Today, many people still devote their energy solely to economic development. They seem to misunderstand the objective of Japan's "economics-first" policy in the past years. Having achieved sufficient economic power, Japan should now have its own military force not only for guaranteeing national security but for contributing to Asian regional stability and the common defense against the Communist threat. We should no longer fail to share our fair "burden" with the United States. We should fulfill our duty to defend the Western bloc with our own military force.

(Yoshida 1963, pp. 202–207)

The birth of the "Yoshida Doctrine"

It was not Yoshida but Prime Minister Hayato Ikeda (1899–1965) that changed the minimalist security policy into a fundamental and inviolate "doctrine" for Japan. Though Ikeda, one of the most fervent disciples of Yoshida, faithfully acceded to Yoshida's policies, he never shared Yoshida's ultimate vision of Japan's active role in the arena of international security. Under the Ikeda administration (1960–1964), Japan enjoyed a higher growth rate than most countries in the world including the victor countries of World War II. Japan's remarkable economic recovery urged some US politicians to question its continuation of the minimalist security policy. Nevertheless, Ikeda repeatedly stressed the impossibility of increasing Japan's defense spending to more than 1 percent of GNP.

After achieving remarkable economic development in the 1960s, however, Ikeda could no longer justify Japan's minimalist security policy in terms of its economic weakness. Instead, he emphasized that Japan's minimalist security was a fundamental "doctrine" dictated by its Peace Constitution. He added that, even if the surrounding situation had drastically changed since the end of World War II, Japan could not abandon the doctrine (Nakajima 2006, pp. 195–200). As Japan began to challenge US economic dominance, Japan's minimalist security policy came increasingly under fire. During the 1970s–1980s, Japan was the largest creditor country in the world, and recorded huge trade surpluses with the United States. Conversely, the United States was suffering from huge government deficits. As the US–Japan trade conflicts became more severe, burden-sharing became a serious and real issue between the two countries.

Typically the US allies' burden-sharing efforts are measured in terms of defense spending as a share of GNP. Yet, the low defense spending does not mean that Japan was also "free-riding" in other realms.[2] We agree with the following remark by Mark A. Boyer:

Although a nation may appear to be free-riding on the security contributions of other alliance members with reference to a particular type of alliance contribution, this should not lead one to assume that this same nation will be free-riding in all categories. Rather, apparent free-riding should lead the researcher to examine other types of alliance contributions to discover where that nation is specializing in contributions.

(Boyer 1989, p. 723)

Without any reliable security policy other than US protection, the fulfillment of burden-sharing was an absolute obligation for Japan. Faced with the US mounting accusation of Japan's defense "free-riding," however, Japan still did not choose to increase its military expenditure to over 1 percent of its GDP. Instead, Japan chose to offset its defense "free-riding" by sharing economic burdens.

Since 1978, Japan's host nation support to US military bases in Japan has constantly increased (Yoda 2006). It has covered the costs of facilities and housing of US bases, the salaries of local hires, the payment of utility costs for US bases, and so on. According to the 2004 annual report of the US Department of Defense, the Japanese budget for host nation support in 2002 was about $4.4 billion. This amount is prominently cited among the US allies (United States Department of Defense 2004).

In addition to host nation support, the Japanese government has regarded foreign aid policy as part of Japan's burden-sharing efforts. Indeed, in 1989, replacing the United States, Japan ranked as the top ODA (Official Development Assistance) donor nation in absolute terms (Figure 9.1).

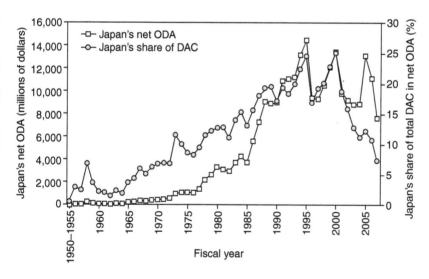

Figure 9.1 Japan's net ODA and its share of total DAC (Development Assistance Committee (source: OECD–DAC, net ODA from DAC countries from 1950 to 2007).

Note

* 1990, 1991, 1992: Including debt forgiven.

The crisis of the "Yoshida Doctrine"

Until the 1980s, Japan's efforts to offset its defense "free-riding" through economic contributions were welcomed by the United States as well as by the Japanese people. Sometimes US resentment over Japan's security "free-riding" was expressed as the demand for increased defense spending, but it was generally agreed that economic burden-sharing was a better option considering Japan's domestic and international constraints on the increase of defense spending (Shafiqul 1991, pp. 192–196).

The Japanese people also admitted that Japan should play its appropriate role in the global economic arena rather than in the security arena. In the 1989 Cabinet Office public opinion poll about Japan's contribution to international society, 52.5 percent of the respondents chose "the sound development of the world economy," and 39.1 percent chose "the economic assistance to developing countries," while only 24.6 percent chose "the area of peace and stability of the world," and 8.7 percent chose "the military contribution to the Western Alliance" (Naikakufu Seifu Kohoshitsu 1989, p. 120).

In 1985, a leading political scholar, Yonosuke Nagai, declared, "There is no other such 'abnormal' country like Japan, who has kept 1percent defense spending of its GNP despite repeated pressure from the United States to adopt military Keynesianism." Then he added, "If Japan, responding to the US–Japan Mutual Security Assistance (MSA) Act of 1951, had removed the ban on arms production and export, its spectacular economic growth in the subsequent decades would never have been realized." Finally, he proudly proclaimed, "Forever Yoshida Doctrine!" (Nagai 1985, pp. 60–68).

In the 1990s, however, Japanese economic burden-sharing efforts gradually reached a plateau. Due to the relative decline of Japanese economic power, it has become increasingly difficult for Japan to share the burden only through economic contributions. A more fundamental reason for this difficulty was, however, the mounting criticism from the international society toward Japan's "checkbook diplomacy." In the Gulf War of 1991 Japan provided $13 billion of financial support, but was excluded from Kuwait's "thanks" list after the war.

In fact, after the Gulf War, the United States has increasingly demanded greater military contributions from its allies. The US preference for military contributions over financial or other non-military contributions is clearly evident in the "The Report on Allied Contribution to Common Defense," an annual report issued by the US Department of Defense in order to measure the burden-sharing efforts of US key allies and assess them comprehensively.[3]

In the case of the 1992 report, they examined the United States and its 16 allies,[4] and measured their contributions by 11 criteria (Figure 9.2). Due to its constitutional restrictions on the use of force abroad, Japan (JA) had no choice but to contribute to non-military realms such as host nation support (line 8) and economic assistance (lines 10 and 11). Moreover, because the report, emphasizing a "fair" share of burden, assessed a nation's financial contribution on the basis of a percentage of GDP, Japan's financial contribution was ranked quite

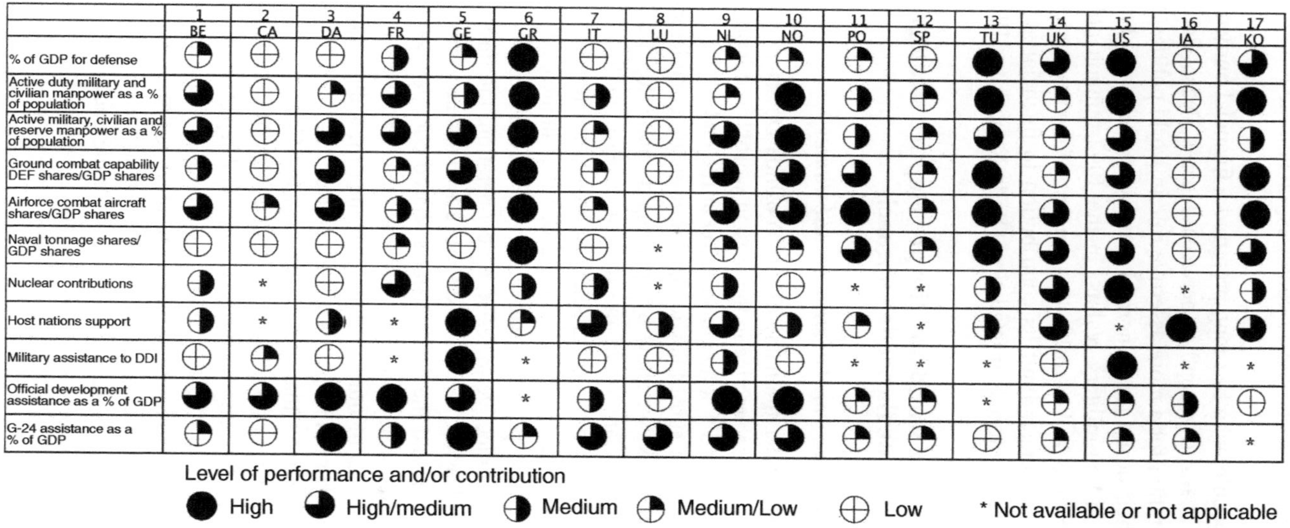

Figure 9.2

Level of performance and/or contribution

● High ◗ High/medium ◗ Medium ⊕ Medium/Low ⊕ Low * Not available or not applicable

Columns: 1 BE · 2 CA · 3 DA · 4 FR · 5 GE · 6 GR · 7 IT · 8 LU · 9 NL · 10 NO · 11 PO · 12 SP · 13 TU · 14 UK · 15 US · 16 IA · 17 KO

Row categories:
- % of GDP for defense
- Active duty military and civilian manpower as a % of population
- Active military, civilian and reserve manpower as a % of population
- Ground combat capability DEF shares/GDP shares
- Airforce combat aircraft shares/GDP shares
- Naval tonnage shares/GDP shares
- Nuclear contributions
- Host nations support
- Military assistance to DDI
- Official development assistance as a % of GDP
- G-24 assistance as a % of GDP

Figure 9.2 Country performance in selected burdensharing and force improvement areas (source: Department of Defense, Report on Allied Contributions to the Common Defense 1992).

low despite its absolute size. As a result, Japan was ranked "high" only in the realm of host nation support, and ranked "low" in most other areas. Japan practically ranked the lowest among the 17 countries, though the report never explicitly said that.

The Japanese people, who had long preferred a financial burden to a military one, increasingly realized a conflict between Japan's Peace Constitution and their national aspiration for a more assertive role in world politics. Some people openly declared their desire for a "normal country" which would not restrict its international role in non-military realms. In the 1992 opinion poll about how Japan should contribute to the world, 49.4 percent of the respondents answered that Japan should no longer limit its contribution to financial aid, and should increase its personnel contribution (Naikakufu Seifu Kohoshitsu 1992, p. 120).

3 The post-Cold War world and the pre-emptive strategy of limited arming: a game theoretic approach

The Cold War period: the world of strategic substitutes

Did defense practice under the name of the "Yoshida Doctrine" really compromise its value as a defense practice in the present world? In this section we illustrate the shift of the world's strategic situation at the end of the Cold War from the structure of strategic substitutes to that of strategic complements (Hamada 1999). In this framework, we show by applying a simple logic of game theory that the pre-emptive declaration of the limited defense, or the "Yoshida Doctrine," which was criticized as a free-rider strategy, can now be regarded as a strategy that mitigates the tension of world geopolitics in the post-Cold War era.

During the Cold War period, Japan and the United States shared a common objective, that is, the objective to resist, by cooperation, the threat of the Communist bloc. Regardless of the minute differences in stances among countries in the Soviet bloc, Japan and the United States shared common values in international politics. Therefore, the problem between Japan and the United States was how to divide the costs of mutual defense against the Communist bloc and to keep the budget of their public goods under control.

Suppose, for simplicity, that the strategy for the Communist bloc is given. There are two approaches of modeling the cooperation of defense between Japan and the United States. One approach is to assume that Japan and the United States are countries that have identical strategic objectives so that they behave as one entity to cope with the Communist bloc. The other approach is to assume that Japan and the United States cooperate in defense against the Communist bloc, but that, at the same time, each nation takes account of the trade-off between defense expenditures and non-military consumption goods, namely the trade-off between "guns and butter." They cooperate in producing defense power as an international public good, but they take explicit account of the sacrifice of private goods.

Under the first approach, the cooperation automatically achieves the identical objective, and the remaining question is to how to divide the cost of defense. In this case, even though Japan has the limitation to define the maximum for its defense expenditure, the choice of defense will be made as the optimal amount for the two countries, and then the United States has to accept a larger portion of defense costs. As economic logic that supports the Coase theorem suggests, it can easily happen, and it actually did happen between the United States and Japan, that Japan had to share a larger portion of the costs practically, not as defense costs, but as peripheral costs of defense like procurement costs, even though Japan shared officially a smaller portion of actual defense costs.

Based on the second approach, which we will mainly pursue here, the interests in both countries do not coincide completely. They care for a common benefit, a defense, with an alliance generated by mutual cooperation, but the benefit of public goods has different trade-offs value with private consumption goods in different countries. The trade-offs between guns (defense) and butter (consumption) may take different degrees of substitution in countries. Then as the classical work by Olson and Zeckhauser suggests, a country in the alliance (which consists of two countries) has the incentive to free ride on a partner's defense spending. Consequently, the amount of public goods as a whole will become smaller than the desirable amount for the alliance, and a country with a larger national scale will support a proportionately larger portion of burden than its relative size. As Olson and Zeckhauser put it, "the small exploit the large" (Olson and Zeckhauser 1966).

This can be understood well if we imagine a manor during the feudal age. As members of a manor, the feudal lord, vassals, farmers etc., have to cooperate to maintain the system of the manor, and also to protect themselves from enemies. Since the lord has a larger stake in the performance of the manor, he has more incentive and obligations to spend more and exert more energy on the maintenance of the manor. The unexpected nature of the result by Olson and Zeckhauser is that a large member spends more than an amount proportional to its relative size, and that a smaller member spends less than an amount proportional to its relative share. If we return to the economics of alliance, a larger participant assumes a burden for spending on public goods relatively more than its national scale. In the terminology of game theory, this is called the situation of *strategic substitutes*, where the expenditure of your partner substitutes for your expenditure and lightens your obligation. Olson and Zeckhauser plotted the relative expenditures of the NATO countries and found the positive relationship between the national scale and relative expenditures (Figure 9.3).

Let us consider the "Yoshida Doctrine" under which Japan limits its military expenditure at or below 1 percent of its GDP. Regardless of other countries' strategies, Japan unilaterally restricts its spending by declaring the limit of defense expenditures. We are reminded of the myth of Ulysses. Ulysses allegedly listened to the magical songs of Sirens, without consequence, by binding his body to the mast of the boat and insisting that the sailors wore ear plugs. Thus, it is not always unprofitable to pre-commit to a certain strategy. It is meaningful to consider the effect of the "Yoshida Doctrine" of pre-committing to a light arms strategy with the incentive structure of sharing burdens between the United States and Japan during the Cold War period.

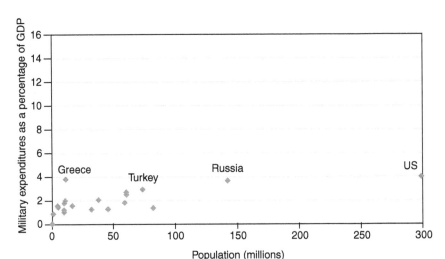

Figure 9.3 Relative expenditures in the NATO countries plus Russia (source: SIPRI data on military expenditure, 2006 world population).

Consider a simplified world consisting of three countries, A, B, and C. During the Cold War period, from the perspectives of Countries A and B, Country C is a country behind the iron curtain. Let us assume that C (e.g., the USSR), being a hostile country, is engaging in an independent defense effort regardless of defense activities of Country A (e.g., the United States) and Country B (e.g., Japan). It is mutually profitable for Country A and Country B to form a mutual alliance against Country C, and the problem is to share the burdens of co-operative defense. The effectiveness of this defense alliance is assumed to depend upon the sum of the defense efforts by A and B, that is, X_A and X_B. The effect of these defense efforts is jointly determined by the sum of defense expenditures, $X_A + X_B$.

During the Cold War period, Japan belonged to a military alliance with the United States under the nuclear umbrella extended by the Unites States. Japan was protecting itself from the threat of the Communist bloc by co-operating with the United States; the NATO countries could be said to have similar positions. Since the Communist bloc remained the Communist bloc, that is, antagonistic to allies, its militaristic effort X_C remains more or less the same regardless of the amounts that are expended by X_A and X_B. The effectiveness of the alliance to cope with the adversary bloc depends on the amounts expended by X_A and X_B. The effectiveness of the alliance thus depends on the sum of expenditures of member countries X_A and X_B. Or, the effectiveness of A's defense expenditures depends on how much its partner B spends on defense for the alliance. This is the mutual dependence model with expenditures as strategic substitutes.

Take the defense expenditure of Country A on the horizontal axis, and take the expenditure of Country B on the vertical axis so that the Stackelberg diagram

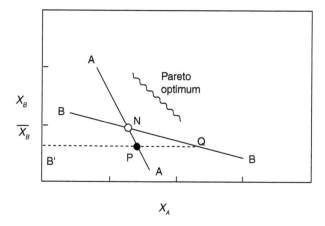

Figure 9.4 Strategic substitutes.

between Country A and Country B is drawn (Figure 9.4). Then, one obtains the reaction curves of the two countries. AA is Country A's reaction curve that indicates how military expenditures X_A change if Country B's expenditures X_B are given. Similarly, BB is Country B's reaction curve that indicates how military expenditures X_B change if Country A's expenditures X_A are given. If Country A is a large country, and Country B is a small country, Country A behaves as if the common benefits from the public goods are close to its national benefits. When Country B neglects its defense effort, the larger country tries to increase its defense spending in order to compensate for the neglect of efforts by Country B. Consequently, reaction curve AA is drawn as a steeper downward sloping graph. On the other hand, reaction curve BB of a smaller country is a relatively flatter curve. A smaller country considers that its own effort does not affect the defense of the alliance, or that a larger country will eventually protect its safety, and it acts based mainly for its own benefit (cost of defense) regardless of the value of defense for the larger country.

Two reaction curves, AA and BB, will give the Nash equilibrium N. N is easily shown to be on the lower left side of the Pareto efficient contract curve. In other words, since there are incentives to rely on the other country's effort, or since the countries try to free ride on the partner's effort, the resulting outcome stays in one area and the defense efforts fall short of the optimal amounts. Suppose under this kind of situation, Country B, like Japan, has a self-imposed restriction, by Constitution Article 9, that military expenditures cannot exceed 1 percent of GDP. In the diagram, Country B is restricted by this "Yoshida Doctrine" in such a way so as not to extend its military expenditures beyond X_B. Then the reaction curve BB will be slanted as BQB.' Country B, say Japan, bears a smaller burden, and Country A, say the United States, bears a larger burden. Thus the free-riding character of the public goods will be magnified. If this tendency continues, a larger country will become more and more reluctant to sustain the alliance. It criticizes B's free-riding, and demands an increase of expenses in forms other than the direct defense expenses bound by the constitution of Country B. Threatened by the cancellation of the alliance, Country B may start to increase its defense spending or increase indirect rewards for Country A.

These types of relationship are derived by an algebraic model as shown in Appendix 9.1. We will show the pay-off matrix illustrated by the model. Table 9.1 shows the pay-offs for two countries. The columns indicate strategies for Country A and the rows indicate strategies for Country B. The pay-off table in the second row and the first column indicates the combinations (the first for Country A, the second for Country B) of payoffs for Country A's cooperative strategy and Country B's Nash equilibrium non-cooperative strategy. The payoff table in the first row and the first column indicates the payoffs of strategic play when A and B engage in a cooperative strategy. If both countries employ cooperative strategies, mutual pay-offs will be as high as (0.605, 0.605). If one party, for example Country A, employs a non-cooperative strategy, the pay-off table at the first row and the second column indicates the payoff.

For a non-cooperative strategy, it can improve its payoff at the cost of the partner as (0.616, 0.588). If both countries employ non-cooperative strategies, the payoffs to both countries will deteriorate as (0.595, 0.595). Thus the payoffs at the second row and second column exhibit the prisoners' dilemma type of payoffs and the strategic encounter may fall into a combination of max–min strategy, that is, the lower equilibrium of the prisoners' dilemma.

The payoff in the third row and the third column, among the 3 × 3 entry, indicates the payoff when Country A takes the pre-emptive light arms strategy of the Yoshida type, and the other country takes the optimal policy against it. The pre-emptive light arms policy of one country certainly avoids the prisoners' dilemma situation for inside the system, but the payoff of the country will be hurt, compared to the optimal payoffs. In particular, the degree of free-riding of B will be aggravated.

Table 9.1 Pay-offs table of the cold war period (strategic substitutes)

(A, B)	Co-operative strategy ($x^* = 1/3$)	Nash equilibrium strategy ($x^* = 1/4$)	Response to pre-emptive strategy ($x^* = 4/15$)
Co-operative strategy ($x = 1/3$)	(0.605, 0.605)	(0.588, 0.616)	–
Nash equilibrium strategy ($x = 1/4$)	(0.616, 0.588)	(0.595, 0.595)	–
Pre-emptive strategy ($x = 1/5$)	–	–	(0.597, 0.582)

The pre-emptive light arms announcement and the strategic structure of the post-Cold War period

After the end of the Cold War, the common enemy that the United States and Japan had cooperated to defend against disappeared. The relationship between Japan and its neighbors is not simply judged like friends or enemies or like an ally or an adversary, as was the case during the Cold War period. Countries are potentially afraid of their neighbors as possible enemies, but at the same time, they depend on each other in their diplomatic and particularly in their economic relationships. The biggest strategic challenge confronting Japan today is the rapid growth of China's military power. China has developed dramatically and emerged as a powerful nation that possesses a potential to compete or sometimes to confront with Japan. This strategic structure in international politics is different from that of the Cold War period when Japan belonged to the alliance with the United States and treated China as a part of the Soviet bloc within the iron curtain.

It gives us a more complex task than during the Cold War regime to model these situations. Let B (say, Japan) and C (say, China) be two countries between which potential military conflicts may arise. Let us concentrate on the interdependence between B and C. Both B and C spend available disposable income on guns and butter, namely on defense and consumption. B or C does not consider the other to be an ally so that the increase in military spending of the other country necessitates an increase in military spending by the country. This relationship creates a strategic structure called *strategic complements*. Figure 9.5 illustrates this. The reaction curves BB and CC (CC indicates Country C's responses to Country B's military expenditure) become positively sloping in this strategic complements case, while they are negatively sloping in the strategic substitutes case.

In this strategic complements case, countries compete to increase defense spending in order not to be dominated by the other country's defense spending.

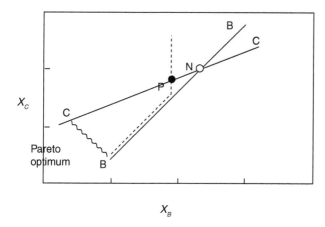

Figure 9.5 Strategic complements.

This will lead to a world with excessive spending on arms. The mutually desirable Pareto efficient combinations of defense spending lie in the lower left side of the Nash equilibrium. This situation is contrasted with the strategic substitute case where free-riding is encouraged and the Pareto efficient combinations lie in the upper right side of the Nash equilibrium.

We can clearly see the effect of a pre-emptive light arms position. Since B abstains from increasing its defense spending beyond a certain level, the reaction curve BB bends vertically. The equilibrium changes from N to P. Point P lies closer to the Pareto optimum situation. This comes from the fact that both countries could be better off if they switch from military spending to consumption spending as long as national security is guaranteed. Because of the pre-emptive action by B, the world will avoid a competitive arms race. Accordingly, the welfare of C will definitely increase. Even for Country B which initiated a pre-emptive light arms declaration, its welfare may improve. The only, sometimes deemed serious, danger for Country B is that at point P, Country B does not possess enough arms to protect itself against aggression from other countries. The payoffs from the algebraic example in Appendix 9.1 are shown in Table 9.2.

Table 9.2 can be interpreted in the same way as Table 9.1. In this case, however, since the pre-emptive strategy $x = 7/15$ $x^* = 22/45$ lies between the cooperative strategy and the Nash equilibrium strategy, the equilibrium outcome corresponding to the pre-emptive strategy and the reaction to it stays in the middle of the table. It is to be noted that if a country commits credibly to a pre-emptive strategy, the equilibrium corresponding to the pre-emptive strategy of that country and the reaction from its neighbor will achieve an equilibrium that is definitely better for the neighbor of the country, and, in some cases, better even for the country that initiates its light arms pre-emptive strategy. The payoffs in the table show that such a case exists.

Moreover, in the two-country case, it is shown in Appendix 9.1 that in the situation of the strategic complements, if the level of pre-emptive arms reduction of defense is limited, then the outcome triggered by the pre-emptive strategy is

Table 9.2 Pay-offs table after the cold war

(A, B)	Nash equilibrium strategy ($x^* = 1/2$)	Response to pre-emptive strategy ($x^* = 22/45$)	Co-operative strategy ($x^* = 1/3$)
Nash equilibrium strategy ($x = 1/2$)	(0.397, 0.397)	–	(0.437, 0.333)
Pre-emptive strategy ($x = 7/15$)	–	(0.409, 0.406)	–
Co-operative strategy ($x = 1/3$)	(0.333, 0.437)	–	(0.529, 0.529)

more desirable than the outcome of the Nash strategies for both the initiator of the pre-emptive strategy and its partner that respond to the initiator. Needless to say, this kind of improvement is only possible if the commitment to light arms is credible. The roles of diplomacy or international alliance for security are to foster the credibility of international commitments.

Let us briefly analyze the case with three-way interdependence, A (the United States), B (Japan) and C (China). Figure 9.6 depicts, on the horizontal axis, the sum of defense expenditures of A and B, that is, $X_A + X_B$, and on the vertical axis, the defense expenditures X_C. Since expenditures of A and B are strategic complements to expenditures of Country C, the reaction curve of A + B will be upward sloping.

This curve can be steeper than the upward sloping reaction curve of Country C. When Country B announces a light arms strategy, the reaction curve of A and B will be tilted similar to Figure 9.6. The resulting outcome will be point P. By the pre-emptive declaration of light arms by Japan, the military tension all over the world will be mitigated.

We can see that world tension was favorably affected by the pre-emptive action of Country B. A delicate point is, however, that Country B might be under the threat of being invaded by Country C because B gave up defense expenditures beyond a certain limit. This risk is covered by the alliance of A and B. If a light arms strategy by B reduces the competing arms expansion on the part of C, it will eventually contribute to the peace of the world.

In this strategic complements model, it is no longer true that the small exploit the large. If a small country endures a certain risk, a large country will realize its arms reduction. We see the tendency, conforming to the strategic complement case, that in East Asia today smaller countries spend relatively more than larger countries, if we abstract from the super large country, China (Figure 9.7).

In the post-Cold War world, the Yoshida line that Japan is pre-emptive in declaring a light arms strategy, is desirable because the strategic structure has

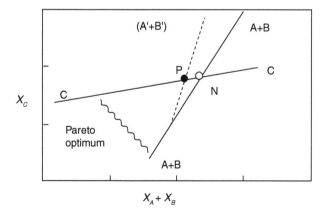

Figure 9.6 Reaction curves and pre-emptive arms reduction (three country case).

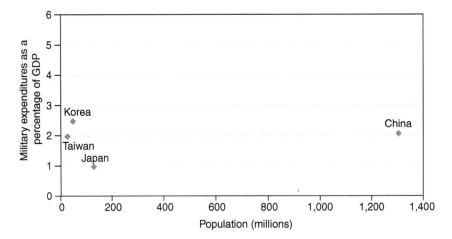

Figure 9.7 Relative military expenditures in Asia (source: SIPRI data on military expenditure, 2006 world population).

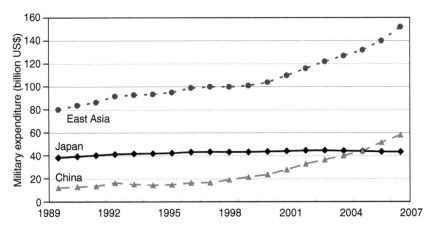

Figure 9.8 East Asia's military expenditure 1989–2007 (source: SIPRI data on military
expenditure).

changed to the type of strategic complements. The only caveat is that such a
move may endanger the security of Japan by choosing too low a level of armament. As Figure 9.8 indicates, East Asian military expenditures continue to
increase and the military tension there is growing. It is important that Japan
explore ways to keep the necessary level for its security.

4 The "Yoshida Doctrine" in the post-Cold War world

The relevance of the "Yoshida Doctrine" in East Asia today

Today, with China's rising power and North Korea a security threat, a "realist" group has become large and vocal. They loudly stress that Japan's old strategy of defense "free-riding" will no longer be tolerated. That is, if Japan continues to maintain the "Yoshida Doctrine" and refuses any military contribution to the common defense, the US–Japan alliance will be seriously endangered, and, as a result, Japan will have to guard itself against the danger of being attacked without sufficient support from the United States. They conclude that Japan must have its own adequate military force in order to fulfill the US increased demand for military burden-sharing and consequently strengthen the US–Japan alliance.

Their arguments, however, have some serious defects. Certainly, during the fight against the Soviet Union, there was a close alliance in security interests between Japan and the United States. Yet, nowadays the United States has many areas for its military interests other than East Asia; Europe, Latin America, and most notably the Middle East, and has to cope with many types of enemies all at once. Japan also has to deal more directly and individually with different neighboring countries. In short, the US–Japan alliance is no longer a panacea for Japan's security.

Moreover, in the pursuit of the "war on terror" under the Bush Jr. administration, US security strategy has become extremely militaristic and less acceptable to many Japanese. After the 9/11 terrorist attacks in 2001, the US government issued a new National Security Strategy (NSS), which justified the right of a preemptive strike to counter "rogue states" and "terrorists." When pursuing a military mission, it clearly preferred unilateral action to coordinated multilateral action. Especially after the outbreak of the Iraq War in 2003, world opinion has increasingly regarded US unilateral and militaristic foreign policy as problematic. The political costs of blindly following US military policies are becoming increasingly high.

As Figure 9.9a shows, it is a drastic increase of US military expenditure after 9/11 that has promoted world militarization. Figure 9.9b calculates a correlation between world total military expenditure (minus the United States) and US military spending. The slope of the linear regression is 0.840 and the y-intercept is 226. The coefficient of determination (R^2) is 0.70. There is a strong correlation between world total military expenditure and US military spending.

Second, the "realist" group, while paying so much attention to US-Japan relations, tends to overlook how Asian neighbors would respond to Japan's sudden discarding of self-restraint in its military expenditure.

Even after the Cold War, East Asian defense spending has been constantly rising. China especially has drastically increased its defense spending, although the precise data have been kept secret.[5] Figure 9.10a is a linear regression analysis of the relationship between East Asian total military expenditure (minus China) and Chinese military spending. Its slope is 0.382, and the y-intercept is 71. The

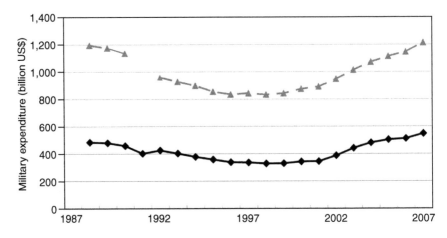

Figure 9.9a World military expenditure and US military expenditure 1988–2007 (source: SIPRI data on military expenditure).

Note
No data of 1991 total world military expenditure is available due to lack of reliable data regarding the East European military spending of the year.

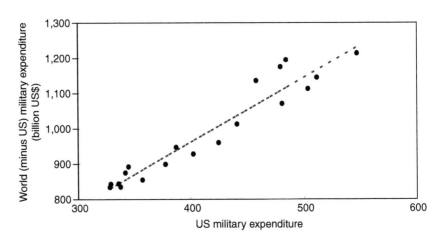

Figure 9.9b Correlation between world total military expenditure (minus the United States) and US military expenditure 1988–2007 (except 1991).

Notes
* Calculation based on SIPRI data.
The linear regression equation is $y = 0.840x + 226$ $R2=0.70$.

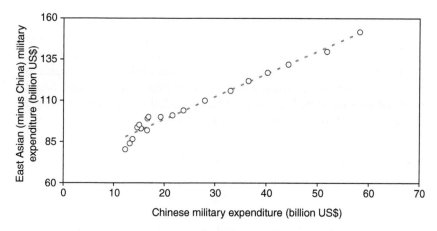

Figure 9.10a Correlation between East Asian total military expenditure (minus China) and Chinese military expenditure 1988–2007.

Notes
* Calculation based on SIPRI data.
The linear regression equation is y = 0.382x + 71   R2 = 0.71.

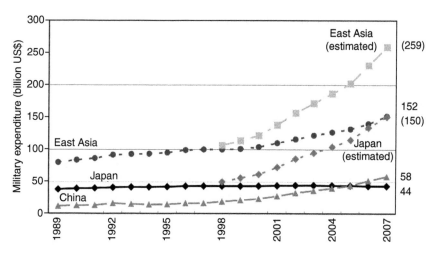

Figure 9.10b East Asia's military expenditure estimated on the supposition of arms race between China and Japan 1989–2007.

Note
* Calculation based on SIPRI data.

coefficient of determination (R2) is 0.71, which means a strong correlation between two variables.

Figure 9.10b estimates the increase of Japan and East Asian total military expenditure based on the assumption that Japan has increased its defense spending at the same pace as China's drastic increase since 1998. It was estimated that Japan's defense spending would amount to $150 billion in 2007, and the total East Asian military spending would increase to $259 billion in the same year, approximately 70 percent higher than the actual figure.

The positive legacies of the "Yoshida Doctrine"

In East Asia, many countries still cannot normalize their relations and continue to increase their defense spending. If Japan suddenly abandons its minimalist security policy and begins substantial re-armament, it would likely trigger an arms race in East Asia, which is an unwelcome consequence of the game of strategic complements. In East Asia today, Japan's "pre-emptive" minimalist strategy still contributes to preventing further deterioration and militarization of the East Asian security environment.

We admit, however, that the positive effects of Japan's minimalist security policy on East Asian stability have been quite limited; it has neither brought general disarmament nor relaxed tension in East Asia. In order to achieve a dividend of peace in East Asia, Japan should promote friendly relations between Asian counties by more active diplomacy.

Here, we can find post-war Japan's "economics first" policy as a useful tool today. For example, post-war Japan's ODA to China, by creating favorable economic interdependence between the two countries, gradually gained political influence, and then helped to normalize and stabilize the two countries' relationship (Wang 1993). We can say that, even today, Japan's ODA can still contribute to international stability and peace in many ways, especially to the improvement of the East Asian security environment.

Certainly, the Japanese people today are not enthusiastic about playing an active role in the global economic arena. As we have seen above, after the Gulf War, there has been growing doubt with regard to Article 9. Yet, the Gulf War never ended Japan's economic diplomacy. There are a considerable number of people who seek ways in which Japan might assume an influential role without violating Article 9, and pay renewed attention to ODA as a diplomatic tool.

Of course, Japan's new economic diplomacy must overcome the weakness of traditional economic diplomacy. As we have seen in Section 2, in compensation for defense "free-riding," post-war Japan rapidly increased its ODA and became the top donor nation in absolute terms in 1989. Despite its huge volume, Japan's ODA policy had long been questioned for its "non-interference" stance and "mercantilist" character, which focused almost solely on economic development and carefully avoided complicated political problems (Rix 1989/1990).

By contrast, today Japan is no longer a "Great Aid Power" (Yasutomo 1989–1990), at least with regard to the sheer size of its aid budget. Japan had substantially reduced its ODA budget during the past decade due to its severe economic situation and the relative economic development of Asian countries, which were previously the main recipients of Japan's ODA. Nevertheless, we must also pay attention to the sophistication of recent Japanese ODA philosophy. Since the 1990s, Japanese ODA policy has increasingly become aware of the link between economic assistance, political stability, and democracy promotion (Katada 2004; Inada 2005). In June 1992, the government announced the ODA Charter that articulates the four basic criteria of its aid philosophy: (*a*) environmental conservation and development should be pursued in tandem; (*b*) any use of ODA for military purposes or for aggravation of international conflicts should be avoided; (*c*) full attention should be paid to trends in recipient countries' military expenditures, their development and production of weapons of mass destruction and missiles, and their export and import of arms; and (*d*) full attention should be paid to efforts in promoting democratization and the introduction of a market-based economy and to the condition of basic human rights and freedoms in the recipient country(Ministry of Foreign Affairs 1992).

The revised ODA Charter in 2003 began with, "The objectives of Japan's ODA are to contribute to the peace and development of the international community, and thereby help to ensure Japan's own security and prosperity." Then, it emphasized the concept of human security and peace-building as an important part of Japanese ODA principles (Ministry of Foreign Affairs 2003). Here we can see Japan's mutuality as an ODA donor and the sophistication of its traditional "economics first" diplomacy.

Actually, the idea of "peace through non-military means" is not new to Japan. Due to domestic and international constraints, Japan has had to seek its national security by means other than military force. This attempt naturally led to the development of "comprehensive security," an idea that national security could not be achieved by solely militaristic means. Especially after the oil crises of 1973 revealed a growing diversity of international threats, the idea of "comprehensive security" acquired greater importance. In the late 1970s Prime Minister Masayoshi Ohira (1910–1980) first formally introduced this idea in order to describe Japan's national goal to establish balanced national power consisting of economic, diplomatic, and cultural as well as military power.

Of course, even though the idea of "comprehensive security" had already been mentioned by influential politicians more than a few times, we cannot say that the idea had been sufficiently put into practice. Its realization still remains in the future. Faced with the various security threats in the post-Cold War world, Japan is now in real need of a "comprehensive security" strategy. International security threats have become even more diverse, ranging from traditional military threats to non-traditional ones like terrorism, economic instability, and natural disasters. Dealing with them requires complex approaches. We can understand post-war Japan's search for "comprehensive security" as one of the positive legacies of the past.

The negative legacy of the "Yoshida Doctrine"

In order to realize true stability in East Asia, however, not only the promotion of further regional cooperation by economic assistance and diplomatic negotiation but the institutionalization of these cooperative relations would be necessary. Throughout the Cold War period, Asia had suffered from a lack of regional security structure analogous to NATO in Europe (Hemmer and Katzenstein 2002). It is true that after the end of the Cold War, Asia experienced extensive progress toward regional institutionalization. Yet, East Asia was left behind by the other Asian regions in organizing multilateral cooperation mechanisms.

Figure 9.11 shows a shift in military expenditure as a share of government spending of each country and region before and after the Cold War. Here, we can clearly see that East Asia today is still in a "Cold War" state. In addition to Russia and the United States, NATO countries also received a peace dividend resulting from the end of the East–West confrontation, and decreased its budget allocation for defense. By contrast, East Asian countries have devoted the same or an increased share of their public resources to military expenditure even after the end of the Cold War. The creation of a more stable multilateral framework for regional cooperation would be an important step towards ending the "Cold War" in East Asia today.

The next problem, then, is how much of a possibility exists for building a multilateral security framework to cover the entire Asian region including the East Asian countries, and how and to what degree Japan could contribute to realizing it.

During the Cold War period, Asia was divided by a deep antagonism between capitalist and communist nations, and creating a regional security system was an elusive and distant goal. The United States was clearly in favor of bilateral alliances than a multilateral security framework in Asia, and even showed hostility towards ASEAN's (Association of Southeast Asian Nations) initiatives for

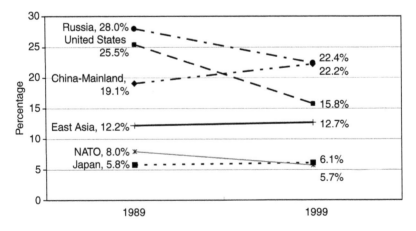

Figure 9.11 Military expenditure as a share of government spending 1989–1999.

regional security cooperation. Being afraid that a commitment to Asian regional security cooperation would weaken the US–Japan bilateral relationship, Japan never actively engaged in ASEAN's struggle for Asian security.

Yet, the end of the Cold War promoted substantial progress in the institutionalization of security cooperation in Asia. The best example was ARF (ASEAN Regional Forum), which was founded in 1994 for promoting security dialogues among not only the ASEAN countries but also the major countries outside the region such as the United States, Russia, China and Japan. Recently the United States has also gradually recognized Asian security regionalism to be a strong and irreversible trend, and future US strategy for Asia should pay due attention to this trend (Yamakage 2000, pp. 148–151).

Of course, we should note that Asian security cooperation has not yet reached the stage of collective security. Considering the situations of conflict in the region, ARF has intentionally adopted a gradual evolutionary approach which places its main focus on CBMs (confidence building measures). It may be correct to say that, at present, the Asian regional security system is a complement to rather than a substitute for the bilateral defense arrangements between the United States and its Asian allies (Hoshino 1999). At least in the predictable future, the Asian security system will continue to be a mixture of the "hub-and-spoke" security system led by the United States and the regional multilateral security system.

In recent years, however, ARF has been evolving into a more sophisticated organization. It has established a more comprehensive approach to regional conflicts, expanding its sphere of activity into those implemented by OSCE (Organization for Security and Cooperation in Europe) such as preventive diplomacy and conflict resolutions.

Have the recent developments of Asian security regionalism brought some changes to Japan's security policy? How has Japan responded to them? So far, Japan's attitude has been moderate, but not negative. Certainly the Japanese government has emphasized the significance of ARF as the "sole reliable multilateral framework for regional security in the Asia-Pacific region." On the other hand, they have stressed the limitation of ARF's role for security issues in Asia where each country has a different political and economic system, a different culture, and a different security strategy. One report issued by the Japanese Ministry of Foreign Affairs in 2007 said that there would be little possibility for ARF to evolve into a comprehensive and sophisticated security mechanism like OSCE (Ministry of Foreign Affairs 2007). The report clearly shows that the Japanese government would welcome the development of an Asian regional security system as long as it remains a "complement" to the US–Japan alliance with its emphasis on non-binding agreements and voluntary compliance. At present, this argument seems compelling. Yet, we should recognize that Japan's future security policy cannot be decided in a purely objective manner. It definitely depends on its own vision of the future Asia-Pacific order, and its own decision to realize it.

The "Yoshida Doctrine" was a well-calculated grand strategy to fulfill post-war Japan's economic and security needs, but it seriously lacked Asian perspectives. Certainly, during the Cold War, Japan's Asian policy had been under powerful external constraints largely imposed by the United States, and there was little room for Japan to develop its own security strategy towards Asia. Yet, even after the end of the Cold War, Japan seems to have prolonged the negative legacy of the past.

The recent remarkable development of the multilateral security system in Asia has carved out new possibilities for Japan to develop its own security strategy and to overcome one of the serious negative legacies of the "Yoshida Doctrine." Whether to realize these possibilities or disregard them will certainly depend upon the desires and will of the Japanese people and their leaders.

Modifying the "Yoshida Doctrine" without losing its spirit

As we have discussed above, Japan's economic diplomacy has evolved into a sophisticated one which is clearly aware of its role in world stability. We partly agree with the opinion that Japan, without any modification of the "Yoshida Doctrine," can still contribute substantially to world stability today. Nevertheless, it is also true that there has been an increasing demand internationally for Japan's more active role in the security arena, beyond the constraints of the "Yoshida Doctrine."

Actually, when we focus on the number of regional conflicts, we cannot necessarily say that the end of the Cold War brought peace to the world. The post-Cold War world has suffered successive regional conflicts which have been suppressed so as not to escalate into all-out wars. Contemporary regional conflicts have become even more problematic because of US excessive interventions in them. Today, in many cases, a regional conflict finally invites US intervention which then oversteps its appropriate limits and brings undesirable consequences.

Faced with the devastating consequences of the Iraq War, the Japanese people have become more and more suspicious of US interventions in the name of world peace. However, it is the other countries' indifference to the conflicts in remote areas that presses the United States into an excessive "police" action with a strong sense of responsibility. Can the Japanese say anything really meaningful about excessive US "police" action while they themselves refuse to play any "police" role for ensuring world stability?

Recently the domestic conditions for Japan's more active commitment to international security have been gradually fulfilled. While Article 9 itself still remains intact, a substantial number of people have been prepared for an international peacekeeping operation, including military tasks if sanctioned by a legitimate body like the United Nations.

Internationally, however, there are still many obstacles to Japan's active peacekeeping role. Asian neighbors are still deeply suspicious of the resurgence of Japanese militarism. When Japan declared the National Defense Program Outline (NDPO) in 2004, which featured more pro-active uses of force and a deeper involvement of SDF (Self Defense Forces) in international affairs, South Korea accused Japan of lacking concern for the neighboring countries who were the victims of Japan's past aggression. China also expressed "deep concern" over Japan's new defense policy (*Japan Times* 2004). The strengthening of the US–Japan alliance has stirred up China's fear of the "two against one" scenario (Xinbo 2006). Before considering a further step to loosening the legal constraints on the use of force abroad, Japan should seek its Asian neighbors' understanding of Japan's more active role on behalf of international stability.

When considering how to ease Asian neighbors' fear toward Japan's re-armament, the history of West German re-armament gives us useful lessons. As a defeated nation of World War II, post-war West Germany found itself in a situation similar to that of post-war Japan. Situated in the forefront of the Cold War, however, West Germany had to begin re-arming as early as the 1950s. At first, European neighbors, especially Germany's lifelong enemy France, were deeply suspicious of Germany's re-armament. Yet, they gradually accepted a re-armed Germany mainly because its military force was strongly tied to NATO. Now, Germany is the second largest contributor to NATO after the United States (Iwama 1993).

Contrary to the German army, Japanese SDF have been almost exclusively tied to the US–Japanese alliance. What has stirred Asian neighbors' fear is not necessarily the absolute quantity of Japan's military force but its strong bilateral nature. In fact, due to SDF's bilateral character, Japan's participation in UN peacekeeping operations has been regarded with hostility and suspicion by neighboring countries (Hummel 1996).

There have already been substantial debates over Japan's more active peace-keeping role and the possibilities of its re-armament. Nevertheless, these debates have put too much emphasis on the following two points; one concerns the inter-pretation of the Peace Constitution, that is, whether the Constitution allows Japan to participate in international peacekeeping activities or not; and the other frequently asked question is how much military contribution would actually be required to keep a good relationship between Japan and the United States. In these debates, however, one important point has been missing: the possible influ-ence of Japan's substantial re-armament on Asian security. Further discussion is necessary on how Japan's military force could contribute to enhancing Asian security, and how Japan can get Asian neighbors' consent of SDF participation in international peacekeeping activities.

The Cold War is over, and Asian security regionalism is steadily proceeding. Now is the best time for Japan to embark on the long-neglected task of connect-ing its military force to the regional framework, and thereby changing it into something more transnational and acceptable for its Asian neighbors.

5 Conclusion

Today, many people are seriously concerned with the future of the "Yoshida Doctrine," but their discussion is still often reduced to a controversy between "realists" who pronounce a death sentence on the doctrine, and "idealists" who want to maintain the status quo.

Our chapter has shown that neither pure realism nor pure idealism offers a reliable answer for Japan's security in the post-Cold War world. The end of the Cold War dramatically changed the strategic situation surrounding Japan and the simple execution of the "Yoshida Doctrine" has become increasingly difficult. Recently more and more people are leaning towards the abandonment of the "Yoshida Doctrine," saying that it has become out of date and its legacies are useless, even harmful. Then, they urge an entirely new set of policies to deal with today's security challenges.

This argument seriously overlooks, however, the flexibility of the "Yoshida Doctrine." Section 2 reviewed post-war Japan's struggle to cope with new settings without violating the 1 percent of GNP ceiling on its defense spending. Since its birth, the "Yoshida Doctrine" has constantly been faced with crises. Nevertheless, Japan has survived them by not completely abandoning it but by searching for its renewed meaning and effectiveness in a new setting. If we understand these historical dynamics of post-war Japan's policy, we may find an expanded opportunity for Japan to cope with the post-Cold War security challenges without a total abandonment of the "Yoshida Doctrine" and its positive legacies.

Section 3 compared the world strategic situation before and after the tearing down of the Berlin wall, and explored the strategic impact of Japan's "pre-emptive" minimalist policy on the post-Cold War world. Under the Cold War regime, the structure of conflicts among nations was rather straightforward, and the players' main focus was concentrated on the supply of public goods for the common defense. Here appears a game with strategic substitutes, which leads to the "small exploits large" situation, that is, a larger country tends to bear more than its proportionate fair share of the burden. In such a circumstance, Japan might be seen as a "free-rider" by its security provider, the United States.

The end of the Cold War changed the world military situation into a situation of divided interests of nations. During the Cold War era, the behavior of the Communist bloc was almost a given, and the two-country game was not so far from reality. After the end of the Cold War, however, common interests between the United States and Japan became uncertain, and each had to define its security strategy in the context of a more than three-party game with strategic complements. One of the major focuses of our thesis was that, when introducing the perspective of multiple and strategic interdependence, Japan's "pre-emptive" minimalist strategy can have a restraining effect on arms races in Asia, and thereby contribute to Asian regional security as well as Japan's national security.

It is true that we should not overlook the relevance of the "Yoshida Doctrine" for regional and world security today, but at the same time, we must also recognize a growing demand from the international society for Japan's more active commitment to world security. Regardless of the pros and cons of the ultimate revision of Article 9, Japan must now consider seriously, the possibilities and conditions for a more active peacekeeping role.

So far Japan's re-armament has been discussed almost exclusively in terms of strengthening the US–Japan bilateral relationship, but we should open up the discussion to encompass a broader perspective, especially an Asian perspective.

Our thesis suggests that in order for Japan's SDF to take a more active peace-keeping role, Japan should make them less bilateral and more transnational by linking them to the evolving multilateral security system in Asia.

Japan's search for a new security policy cannot be simplified to the question of whether Japan should be a "normal" country with sufficient military force, or remain an "abnormal" country escaping from any international peacekeeping role. When we discuss a future Japanese security policy and its role, we should pay close attention to an increasingly multipolar world and its various stakeholders with different security interests. We should also seriously take into account the ongoing changes in Asian security, especially the rise of the multilateral security system. Only with a truly global perspective can we respond to an increasingly complex world, and successfully develop a new grand strategy after the "Yoshida Doctrine."

Appendix 9.1 derivation of reaction curves and the pay-off matrix

Consider a world economy that consists of two countries. They receive the same amount of income y, which is spent either as defense spending x, x^*, or consumption c, c^*. The variables in the foreign country are denoted with asterisks. Let us assume that the welfares of the two countries are given by the social utility function encompassing security.

$$U = c^\alpha (x + \beta x^*)^{1-\alpha} = (y - x)^\alpha (x + \beta x^*)^{1-\alpha}$$

$$U = c^{*\alpha} (x + \beta x^*)^{1-\alpha} = (y - x^*)^\alpha (\beta x + x^*)^{1-\alpha}$$

Hence, $a(0 < \alpha < 1)$ is the proportion of income spent to consumption when we neglect the externality due to defense, and $\beta(-1 < \beta < 1)$ is the degree of reinforcement to security by the neighbor as in an alliance ($\beta > 0$ – – – leading to the strategic substitutes) or the degree of threat to security by the neighbor when its expenditure increases ($\beta < 0$ – – – leading to the strategic complements).

The reaction function of the home country is given by maximizing U with respect to x, given x^*.

$$x = (1-\alpha) y - \alpha\beta x^*$$

Similarly, the reaction function of the foreign country is given by maximizing U^* with respect to x^*, given x.

$$x^* = (1-\alpha) y - \alpha\beta x$$

Accordingly, the Nash equilibrium that is given by the intersection of the two reaction curves as

$$x = x^* = (1-\alpha) (1 + \alpha\beta)^{-1} y$$

The Pareto optimal, cooperative solution with equal share will be $x = x^* = (1-\alpha)$ y. Under the strategic substitutes ($\beta > 0$), the Nash equilibrium represents too small levels of defense. On the other hand, under the strategic complements of ($\beta < 0$), the Nash equilibrium represents too large levels of defense.

(1) Numerical payoffs to the strategic substitutes case:
Let $y = y^* = 1$, $\alpha = 2/3$, $\beta = 1/2$. Then the Nash equilibrium becomes $x = x^* = 1/4$ and both defense efforts fall short of the symmetric cooperation outcome $x = x^* = 1/3$. Suppose Country A takes the pre-emptive light arms strategy $x = 1/5$. If that is credible to Country B, it will take the point on the reaction curve of Country B, $x^* = 4/15$. We obtain the normal form numerical in Table 9.1 (p. 146), which is referred to in the text as well.

(2) Numerical payoffs to the strategic complements case:
Let $y = y^* = 1$, $\alpha = 2/3$, $\beta = 1/2$, as representing the strategic complements case. Then the Nash equilibrium becomes $x = x^* = 1/2$ and both defense efforts exceed the symmetric cooperation outcome $x = x^* = 1/3$. Suppose Country A takes the credible, pre-emptive light arms strategy $x = 7/15$. Country B will take the point on the reaction curve of Country B, $x^* = 22/45$. We obtain the normal form numerical in Table 9.2 (p. 148), which is referred to in the text as well.

In the case of strategic complements such that the reduction of the other's defense spending reduces the necessity of one's defense spending, *a pre-emptive arms reduction of a country sufficiently near the Nash equilibrium will improve both countries' welfare.*

The proof of this proposition follows from Figure 9.12. Figure 9.12 is a magnified picture around the Nash equilibrium around N in Figure 9.5. Country B's

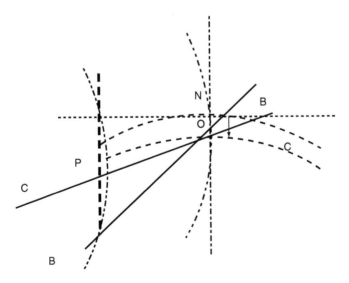

Figure 9.12 Magnified picture around the Nash equilibrium.

indifference map has a vertical tangency with BB at N. Country C's indifference map has a horizontal tangency with CC at N. Therefore, if BB is tilted by the pre-emptive strategy in the area close to the vertical line that goes through N, then the intersection of the new vertical segment indicating that pre-emptive defense spending will intersect with the reacting curve CC at the higher level of welfare for Country B. (It is required that the reduction of arms should be sufficiently small measured from the level of defense expenditures at the Nash equilibrium level.) Note that this logic may not apply for a large retreat of spending by Country B.

Notes

1 We owe a very important debt to Mr. Junichiro Mimaki (Ministry of Economy, Trade and Industry). He gave us insightful comments and generous support, especially for statistical analysis. Of course, we bear the sole responsibility for all the views and mistakes in this chapter.
2 Though post-war Japan has kept the ceiling of 1 percent of GNP on military spending, the main reason for this low percentage was the enormous size of its GNP. In fact, there was a substantial increase in the actual quantity of Japan's military expenditure throughout the period. According to Stockholm International Peace Research Institute (SIPRI), Japan is the top fifth military spender in the absolute term in 2007. See SIPRI data on military expenditure (SIPRI website. Online, available at: www.sipri.org/research/armaments/milex). Some scholars point out that a formula to calculate defense spending differs from country to country, and Japan's definition of military expenditure is not as comprehensive as that of the NATO's definition. The NATO definition include; (*a*) all spending on regular military forces, (*b*) military aid, (*c*) military pensions, (*d*) host government expenses for US forces, and host country infrastructure and staff costs. The Japanese defense budget omits (*c*) military pension. When calculated in the same way as NATO countries, Japanese military expenditure becomes well over 1 percent of its GNP, practically equal to recent German military expenditure (Dekle 1989).
3 The reports of 1995–2004 are available on the Department of Defense website (online, available at: www.defense.gov/pubs/allied.aspx).
4 The 16 allies are; the 14 NATO countries (Belgium, Canada, Denmark, France, Germany, Greece, Italy, Luxembourg, the Netherlands, Norway, Portugal, Spain, Turkey, the United Kingdom), Japan, and Korea.
5 It is generally said that China's actual military expenditure is far higher than the officially published figure. Though there are various opinions as to how much higher it is, here we use the date calculated by SIPRI, which includes the items not included in the Chinese official military budget. These items include the People's Armed Police, military pensions, military research, development, testing and evaluation, subsidies to arms production, and arms imports, and, on the revenue side, earnings from People's Liberation Army's business activities and from arms exports, some of which are used for military purposes (Wang 1999).

References

Boyer, M.A. (1989) "Trading Public Goods in the Western Alliance System," *Journal of Conflict Resolution* 33(4), pp. 700–727.
Dekle, R. (1989) "The Relationship between Defense Spending and Economic Performance in Japan," in J. Makin, and D. Hellmann (eds.) *Sharing World Leadership? A New*

Era for America and Japan (Washington, DC: American Enterprise Institute for Public Policy Research), pp. 127–149.

Hamada, K. (1999) "The Structure of Arms Races before and after the End of the Cold War: From Strategic Substitutes to Strategic Complements," in S.B. Dahiya (ed.) *The Current State of Economic Science* 4 (Rohtak, India: Spellbound Publications), pp. 1817–1832.

Hatano, S. and Sato, S. (2004) "Ajia Moderu to Shiteno 'Yoshida Dokutorin' (Yoshida Doctrine as an 'Asian Model')," *Gunji Shigaku* 39(4), pp. 4–20.

Hemmer, C. and Katzenstein, P.J. (2002) "Why Is There No NATO in Asia? Collective Identity, Regionalism, and the Origins of Multilateralism," *International Organization* 56(3), pp. 575–607.

Hoshino, T. (1999) "Nichibei Domei to Ajia Taiheiyo no Takokukan Anzen Hosho: Nihon no Shiten Kara (The US–Japan Alliance and Multilateral Security Cooperation in the Asia-Pacific Region: a Japanese Perspective)," in H. Kan, G.D. Hook, and S.A. Weston (eds.) *Ajia Taiheiyo no Chiiki Chitsujo to Anzen Hosho* (Regional Order and Security in the Asia-Pacific Region) (Kyoto: Minerva Shobo), pp. 166–185.

Hummel, H. (1996) "The PKO-Debate in Japan and Germany in Comparison," *Paper presented at Hokusei Gakuen University Sapporo, October 1, 1996*, pp. 1–13. Online, available at: www.phil-fak.uni-duesseldorf.de/politik/Mitarbeiter/Hummel/hokusei.pdf.

Inada, J. (2005) "Japan's Emerging Role in Peace-Building and Post-Conflict Reconstruction: Have Traditional Norms Changed?" *Japanese ODA at 50: An Assessment, Woodrow Wilson International Centre for Scholars Asia Program Special Report* 128, pp. 13–16.

Iwama, Y. (1993) *Doitsu Saigunbi* (German Rearmament) (Tokyo: Chuokoron-Sha).

Japan Times (2004), "China Criticizes Japan's New Defense Guidelines," December 12. Online, available at: http://search.japantimes.co.jp/cgi-bin/nn20041212a1.html.

Katada, S.N. (2004) "New Courses in Japan's Foreign Aid Policy: More Humanitarian and More Nationalistic," in S. Katada, H.W. Maull, and T. Inoguchi (eds.) *Global Governance: Germany and Japan in the International System* (Aldershot: Ashgate), pp. 183–199.

Kosaka, M. (1964) "Saisho Yoshida Shigeru ron (Prime Minister Yoshida Shigeru: An Interpretation)," in M. Kosaka (2006) *Saisho Yoshida Shigeru* (Prime Minister Yoshida Shigeru) (Tokyo: Chuokoron-Shinsha), pp. 5–75.

Kosaka, M. (1967) "Idaisa no Joken (The Conditions of Greatness)," in M. Kosaka (2006), *Saisho Yoshida Shigeru*, pp. 247–266.

Ministry of Foreign Affairs (1992) *Japan's Official Development Assistance Charter*. Online, available at: www.mofa.go.jp/POLICY/oda/summary/1999/ref1.html.

Ministry of Foreign Affairs (2003) *Japan's Official Development Assistance Charter*. Online, available at: www.mofa.go.jp/policy/oda/reform/revision0308.pdf.

Ministry of Foreign Affairs (2007) "Nihon no Anzen Hosho Seisaku ni Kansuru Gaiko Seisaku (Japan's Foreign and Security Policy)," in Gaimusho Seisaku Hyokasho 2007 (Japanese title), Foreign Policy Evaluation Report 2007 (English title), pp. 196–200. Online, available at: www.mofa.go.jp/mofaj/annai/shocho/hyouka/h19.html.

Nagai Y. (1985) "Anzenhosho to Kokuminkeizai: Yoshida Dokutorin wa Eien Nari (National Security and National Economy: Forever Yoshida Doctrine)," in Y. Nagai, *Gendai to Senryaku* (The Contemporary Era and Strategy) (Tokyo: Bungei Shunju), pp. 47–78.

Naikakufu Seifu Kohoshitsu (Cabinet Public Relations Office) (1989), *Yoron Chosa Nenkan* (Public Opinion Poll) (Tokyo: Okurasho Insatsukyoku).

Naikakufu Seifu Kohoshitsu (Cabinet Public Relations Office) (1992), *Yoron Chosa Nenkan* (Public Opinion Poll) (Tokyo: Okurasho Insatsukyoku).

Nakajima, S. (2006) *Sengo Nihon no Boei Seisaku: "Yoshida Rosen" wo Meguru Seiji, Gaiko, Gunji* (Post-war Japan's Defense Policy: "Yoshida's Policy Line" and Politics, Diplomacy and Military Affairs) (Tokyo: Keio Daigaku Shuppankai).

Olson, M. and Zeckhauser, R. (1966) "An Economic Theory of Alliance," *Review of Economics and Statistics* 48(3), pp. 266–279.

Organization for Economic Cooperation and Development (OECD) – Development Assistance Committee (DAC), *Net ODA from DAC Countries from 1950 to 2007*. Online, available at: www.oecd.org/dac/stats/dac/reftables.

Rix, A. (1989/1990) "Japan's Foreign Aid Policy: A Capacity for Leadership?" *Pacific Affairs* 62(4), pp. 461–475.

Shafiqul, I. (1991) "Beyond Burden-Sharing; Economics and Politics of Japanese Foreign Aid," in I. Shafiqul (ed.) *Yen for Development: Japanese Foreign Aid and the Politics of Burden-Sharing* (New York: Council on Foreign Relations), pp. 191–230.

Stockholm International Peace Research Institute (SIPRI), *Data on Military Expenditure*. Online, available at: www.sipri.org/.

United States Department of Defense (1992) *Report on Allied Contributions to the Common Defense*. Online, available at: www.dod.gov/pubs/foi/reading_room/447.pdf.

United States Department of Defense (2004) *Report on Allied Contributions to the Common Defense*. Online, available at: www.defenselink.mil/pubs/allied.html.

Wang, Q.K. (1993) "Recent Japanese Economic Diplomacy in China: Political Alignment in a Changing World Order," *Asian Survey* 33(6), pp. 625–641.

Wang, S. (1999) "The Military Expenditure of China, 1989–1998," in Stockholm International Peace Research Institute (ed.) *SIPRI Yearbook 1999: Armaments, Disarmament and International Security* (Oxford: Oxford University Press), pp. 334–349.

Xinbo, W. (2006) "The End of the Silver Lining: A Chinese View of the US–Japan Alliance," *Washington Quarterly* 29(1), pp. 119–130.

Yamakage S. (2000) "Tonan Ajia kara Mita 'Toa no Koso': ASEAN no Koiki Chitsujyo Keiseiryoku to Nihon (A Scheme of East Asian Order: From South East Asian Perspectives: ASEAN's Power to Create Regional Order)," in Y. Onuma (ed.) *Toa no Koso: 21 Seiki Higashi Ajia no Kihan Chitsujyo wo Motomete* (Toward a Normative Order of East Asia in the Twenty-first Century) (Tokyo: Chikuma Shobo), pp. 133–163.

Yasutomo, D.T. (1989–1990) "Why Aid? Japan as an 'Aid Great Power,'" *Pacific Affairs* 62(4), pp. 490–503.

Yoda, T. (2006) "Japan's Host Nation Support Program for the US–Japan Security Alliance: Past and Prospects," *Asian Survey* 46(6), pp. 937–961.

Yoshida, S. (1962) *Oiso Zuiso* (Random Thoughts from Oiso) (Tokyo: Sekkasya).

Yoshida, S. (1963) *Sekai to Nihon* (The World and Japan) (Tokyo: Bancho-Shobo).

10 The new model of foreign aid drawn from the experiences of Japan and the United States

Gustav Ranis, Stephen Kosack, and Ken Togo[*]

1 Introduction

Japan and the United States have long been two of the largest donors of foreign aid. For a long time, the United States has led international thinking on foreign aid, while Japan has generally deferred to the United States' lead. Although Japan's own development experience often contradicted US thinking, it has seldom pushed back. Even when Japan did register resistance, as with the World Bank's *East Asian Miracle* study, it has generally failed to follow up, content, instead, to signal its position rhetorically while continuing to follow the United States.

This hesitancy is disappointing. Today, there is appreciation, even in Washington, that structural adjustment programs adopted by the World Bank and the IMF in the 1980s and 1990s were largely unsuccessful. There is clearly a need for a new model of foreign aid. Japan has a great deal to offer this debate. It has a wealth of accumulated knowledge, borne of its own unique path to development and experiences as one of the world's largest donors.

Although "modesty" is considered a virtue in Japanese society, it should be realized that less "modesty" on Japan's part may assist the bottom billion poor in the third world.

In this chapter, we examine the historical and recent trends in foreign aid and related capital flows by Japan and the United States in a comparative context, and identify some promising areas of convergence that may provide the basis for a new, more effective model of foreign aid. In Section 2, we briefly review the experiences of Japan and the United States. In Section 3, we suggest a new model of foreign aid. The final section concludes with some suggestions for the future.

2 Aid experiences: the United States and Japan

During the Cold War

Cold War divergence in patterns of giving

Today the United States and Japan are still among the world's largest donors; together they provided nearly $35 billion to developing countries in 2008 – 30 percent of the more than $112 billion contributed by all DAC donors that year. The United States has long been the largest donor in absolute terms – it provided the most ODA in all but one of the last 48 years. Japan joined the ranks of the world's top donors relatively recently; it was a relatively small donor until the 1980s, when it moved into second place in terms of absolute size; in 1995 it was Japan that overtook the United States (Figure 10.1). In recent years the United States has retaken the absolute top spot, while Japan has fallen substantially to fifth place in 2007. The current international financial and economic crisis, however, has caused a leveling off of US ODA and a substantial decline in Japan's contribution as well.

The United States and Japan are also two donors whose generosity was driven by a strategic rationale – and for both donors that rationale initially was the Cold War. The United States' foreign aid programs had, until 1989, been seen, above all else, as a way to buy the loyalty of Cold War allies. Japan's rationale was different, though related: its aid was mainly viewed as "Cold War burden-sharing." That is, Japan's ODA was given under US pressure and was tacitly seen as a way to compensate the United States for including Japan under its security umbrella.

Japan's ODA began around 1955, in the form of a modest post-World War II reparations program for its Southeast Asian neighbors. Around this time, conflicts in Korea and Vietnam were revealing Southeast Asia as a vital strategic front in the Cold War. Thus, as the Japanese economy recovered, the United States pressured Japan to move beyond reparations to a full foreign aid program for the region. Japan responded with large aid packages for Korea, Indonesia, and the Philippines.

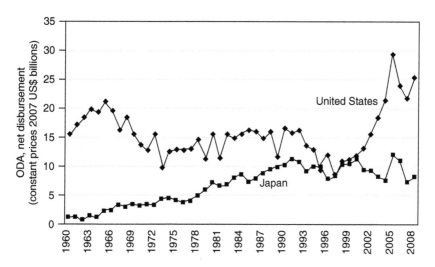

Figure 10.1 Net disbursement of ODA: United States and Japan (1960–2008) (source: OECD).

Although both countries have historically preferred to give aid bilaterally, in most other respects the United States and Japan have provided aid very differently. There are four areas of divergence: in the preference of each for program versus project aid; in the sort of projects or programs each funded; in the preference of each for giving aid in the form of loans or grants; and, finally, in the degree of "tying" aid to domestic purchases.

Japan traditionally preferred to fund specific projects rather than support country programs. Project aid often made use of politically powerful Japanese engineering firms whose influence was crucial to the continuing Diet approval of aid allocations. Also key to this preference was undoubtedly Japan's post-war development experience, in which large infrastructure projects played a central role. Japan's aid also supplemented its export-led development strategy by developing new markets for Japanese construction and engineering projects.[1] The United States, by contrast, has been more willing to utilize fast-flowing program assistance, as evidenced by its support of conditionality-laden Structural Adjustment Loans (SALs).

A related area of contrast between the United States and Japan is over the *type* of projects each donor has tended to finance. The largest proportion of US aid has gone into the so-called social sectors – education, health, water and sanitation – reflecting a bias toward providing "basic needs" and promoting "human development." By contrast, the influence of Japan's own post-war experience, plus its powerful engineering lobby, made for a natural preference for large infrastructural projects in energy, transportation, and communications, as well as

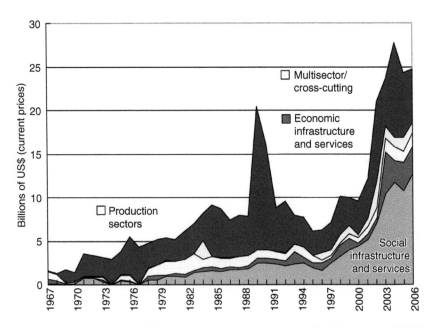

Figure 10.2 Breakdown of US aid commitments by sector, 1967–2007 (source: OECD).

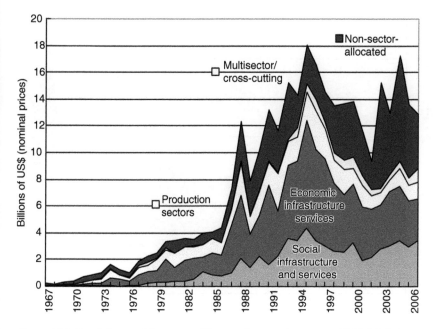

Figure 10.3 Breakdown of Japanese aid commitments by sector, 1967–2007 (source: OECD).

in some directly productive sectors: agriculture and fisheries, industry, mining, construction, trade and tourism.

The third area of divergence is in the preference for giving aid as loans or grants. Figure 10.4 shows a clear US preference for grants over loans. Japan prefers loans (Figure 10.5) although these loans have generally been highly concessional. This preference is based largely on the logic that, when countries know they are required to repay, they are more likely to allocate resources carefully.

The final area of divergence is in the degree to which each "tied" its aid to domestic purchases. Both countries are naturally under political pressure to retain the support of their exporters. In the United States this pressure has translated into the tying of most aid to the purchase of US goods and services, thereby reducing its value by an estimated 15 percent. In fact, in 1996, under pressure, the United States simply stopped reporting the tied percentage of its aid, despite formally agreeing to the OECD's Development Assistance Committee's (2001) "Recommendations on Untying ODA to the Least Developed Countries." In the immediate post-war years, Japan tied too much of its aid, as a way of increasing the benefit to its engineering companies. But with time, as Japan faced international pressure to reduce its massive trade surpluses, the tied percentage of Japanese ODA declined. By 1997, only 0.05 percent of Japanese aid was even partially tied, and none was fully tied.

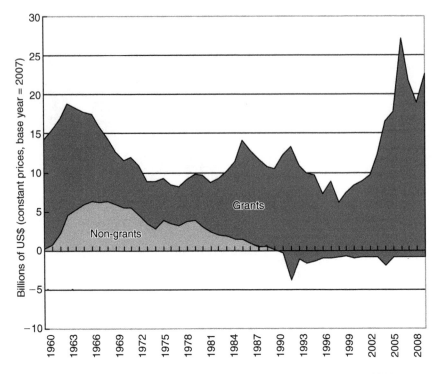

Figure 10.4 Breakdown of US bilateral aid into grant and non-grant, 1960–2008 (source: OECD).

Theoretical framework of aid

The aforementioned divergence between US and Japanese ODA patterns was a partial reflection of differences in US and Japanese attitudes concerning the ideal role of development assistance, rooted in the very different development models that prevailed in Washington and Tokyo. Yet, at least until very recently, Japan's hesitancy in pushing its intellectual position onto the international agenda meant that the United States' position remained dominant. Historically, Japan has generally accepted, if grudgingly, US intellectual leadership on aid.

The United States, until quite recently, favored aid that is interventionist: it has often come with the requirement that recipients hew to certain policies. These requirements were developed centrally, based on the development thinking in vogue at the time in the United States, and applied with only moderate variability to different countries and contexts.

Japan's posture, on the other hand, stemmed both from a reluctance to be interventionist in countries still smarting from their World War II experience and from Japan's own post-war domestic economic policies which were based on directed credit, selective assistance to promising industries, and heavy investments in infrastructure. Japan's emphasis was on "self-help" and "request-based

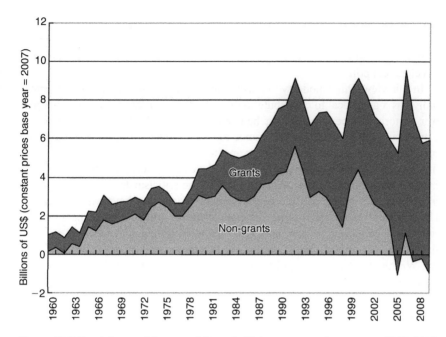

Figure 10.5 Breakdown of Japanese bilateral aid into grant and non-grant, 1960–2008 (source: OECD).

assistance," which allowed it to minimize intervention in the domestic politics and policies of recipients while still directing assistance to countries that Japan could assume were already self-motivated to help themselves. Japanese rhetoric on aid has thus long emphasized the importance of countries taking true "ownership" of their development programs, in contrast to the United States and the IFIs who have rediscovered this principle only recently (a point we discuss below).

The Washington Consensus, as its name suggests, reflected the thinking among mainly US and IFI economists, and Japan, unsurprisingly, has found fault with it. Like other critics, the Japanese saw it as an unduly rigid program, applied wholesale to countries with widely varying situations, without sufficient regard for the costs imposed on its intended beneficiaries. Yet despite reservations, Japan chose not to enter the debate forcefully. Instead, Japan offered its critique quite meekly in 1991, when the Overseas Economic Cooperation Fund (OECF), then Japan's main aid agency, published its Occasional Paper no. 1, the first such paper in its 30-year history. The paper criticized the Consensus's excessive emphasis on market-oriented approaches, which seemed contrary to the lessons of Japan's own post-war experience. Japan followed up this critique in public statements[2] and by advocating – and paying for – the World Bank's high profile *East Asian Miracle* study, which was intended to provide theoretical and empirical support for an alternative development model. Yet Japan failed to support these critiques with detailed, continuous policy engagement. While striking a mildly critical posture, Japan did not try to mobilize its own intellectual firepower to engage the powerful intellectual forces in Washington. Instead it continued, as in the past, to grudgingly follow the US lead on basic ODA and development policy.

In our view, this "modesty" is disappointing. In the first place, Japan potentially has a great deal to contribute to the debate. For instance, from its own pre-war historical experience, Japan had unique reasons for disagreeing with the Consensus – in particular, a preference for government-led industrialization and opposition to financial liberalization in the early stages of development when financial systems are generally still underdeveloped. Second, while the Washington Consensus certainly deserved some of the criticism Japan offered, it was, in practice, not nearly as rigid as the Japanese seemed to have assumed. While US advisors would often enter different contexts with the same paradigm in mind, the messiness of any individual situation would inevitably alter, often drastically, the application of policies so that two countries ostensibly undergoing Washington Consensus policy adjustment actually exhibited far more differences than similarities. Thus, both sides might have benefited had Japan recognized the fallacies of its assumptions about the Consensus and entered the debate more actively, with confidence in the value of its own experience and perspective.

After the Cold War

Convergence of aid between the United States and Japan

With the end of the Cold War much of the strategic rationale for aid seemed, for a time, to evaporate. Peace and prosperity lulled many in the OECD countries into thinking that they had little to gain, strategically or economically, by assisting the development of the world's poorer countries. The residual moral argument – that rich countries have a duty to help the poor – was never an easy sell to voters who doubted aid's effectiveness and had no trouble thinking of better uses for their taxes. There is a remarkable corollary to the loss of this strategic rationale: in a surprising number of areas it has led to some convergence between US and Japanese aid.

In Japan, three decades of steady increases in aid came to a halt in 1990 (Figure 10.1). The Cold War's end offered Japan the opportunity to reduce US influence and begin to assert itself as a development leader in its own right. But Japan had other, higher priority concerns. It faced a sustained recession in the 1990s, one made all the more daunting by a large budget deficit and ballooning obligations to an aging population. Moreover, as most donors were cutting back on their aid, the sense among the Japanese that a generous aid budget gained a country international respect also waned. Consequently, in the 1990s the Japanese aid budget stagnated; as a percentage of Japan's GNI, aid fell by nearly a third between 1990 and 1997. In recent years this decline has accelerated.

In the United States, the cutbacks in the 1990s were even sharper. Aid in constant dollars fell by nearly 50 percent between 1990 and 1997; as a percentage of US GNI, it fell by 57 percent. However, unlike Japan, in the United States this decline had a definitive end: September 11, 2001. On that day, the strategic rationale for aid made an abrupt reappearance. Aid for development played a starring role in the much-publicized US National Security Strategy Memorandum, issued later that year, in which development was elevated to one of the three pillars of US foreign policy, alongside diplomacy and defense. President Bush announced an initiative called "a new compact for development" in March, 2002, in which he pledged a 50 percent increase in foreign aid, amounting to $5 billion over 2004–2006, to fund the newly created Millennium Challenge Account (MCA), run by the Millennium Challenge Corporation. In reality, the United States more than doubled its aid between 2001 and 2005.

There has also been a shift by the United States in focus and institutions that have rather unexpectedly brought the United States closer to Japan's position. Several important developments in Japanese aid – a move away from loans for infrastructure projects toward grants, an acceptance of poverty reduction as an important goal for aid, and an increasing, if still limited, willingness to engage constructively with the international community on aid – have moved Japan closer to the United States. The result, in our view, is a significant, if incomplete, convergence between the two donors, even if neither side seems fully aware of it.

The major shift on the United States' part is a move away from interventionist aid. Traditionally, the United States has been more pessimistic about the ability of countries to act in their own interest and more willing to intervene as a consequence. But US attitudes on conditionality seem to have shifted in recent years. In tacit acknowledgement that conditionality, at least as practiced during the Structural Adjustment Loan (SAL) and even the more recent Poverty Reduction Strategy Paper (PRSP) era, hasn't been effective, the United States is increasingly shying away from *ex ante* conditionality to rewarding already well-behaved recipients. This shift has brought the United States closer to the Japanese position. A good illustration of this partial convergence is the Millennium Challenge Corporation, the biggest new US aid initiative. The MCC's structure reflects a belief that the only aid that will work is aid to countries that have already demonstrated past progress toward good governance, sound economic policies, and resulting improvements in levels of health, education, etc. The recipient must pass muster on 17 indicators of past performance, in three categories: "ruling justly," "practicing economic freedom," and "investing in people."

The MCC seems to reflect a new paradigm in Washington, which might be summed up as follows: after decades of disbursing aid to countries on the promise of future reforms, but generally disbursing the aid regardless of whether or not the country actually adopted these reforms, the United States seems to have concluded that aid simply can't influence countries that aren't already committed to helping themselves. Thus, instead of providing resources to encourage conditions to be met, the MCC is supposed to disburse only to countries where conditions have already been met.

While this philosophy is much closer to the Japanese position, it is not a complete embrace and, in fact, the Japanese have generally been critical of the MCC. In their view the MCC's requirements are as burdensome as any past conditionality, even if the point is to offer *ex post* rewards rather than requiring reforms *ex ante*. Moreover, they note that the implied severe selectivity eliminates from consideration many countries that are desperately in need of assistance (Sunaga 2004).

It is also worth pointing out that the reality of the MCC has so far seemed to deviate somewhat from the rhetoric, though the program may still be too young to be accurately assessed. First, although the MCC criteria are theoretically objective – apolitical, and strategic only in the sense that they seek to direct aid only to where it will do the most to fight poverty, and thereby terrorism – in practice the United States still does not seem to be able to keep itself from applying exceptions to its own rules, particularly in returning to its old habit of favoring its strategic allies. Second, although the initial idea for the MCC was to assist countries in doing more of the good things they were already doing, the MCC has so far preferred funding specific projects, rather than offering budgetary or program support – a shift that is likely a concession to Congress, which prefers that the products of US aid be easily identifiable. Sectorally, the grants are heavy on growth-inducing rural development, particularly in agriculture and transportation. There is little emphasis on support for technology, health, and education, which were the focus of President Bush's announcement of the MCC. And, while the MCC grants were supposed to move fast enough and be large enough to induce those who don't yet qualify to change their behavior,[3] in reality the MCC has been very slow in disbursing resources.

Japan, too, has been altering its aid delivery in ways that bring it much closer to the United States. The United States shifted its aid from loans to grants earlier and is on record urging other donors and the International Financial Institutions to do the same. In recent years the United States has received more in repayments on past loans than it has provided in new loans, rendering its net loan contribution negative (Figure 10.4).

Japan's shift to grants has been slower, but by 2004 its net loan contributions were also negative (Figure 10.5). A reason for Japan's shift away from loans is that Japan may be responding to the growing consensus that loans simply burden future generations and lead to continued pressure for additional debt relief. There is also the more mundane concern that loans are often not repaid (see Iimi and Ojima 2005). On the other hand, there is always the danger that an increased reliance on grants will reduce future resource availabilities.

From the mid-1990s, Japan began to converge with the United States in another area as well: the sectoral allocation of its aid. Japan appears to have recognized the limits of infrastructural investments not accompanied by institutional changes and improvements in human development. In addition, Japan seems gradually to have come to realize that its large volume of projects, suffering from inadequate coordination with other donors, had become excessively costly and inefficient. Instead, Japan seems to increasingly favor a more sectoral approach to aid. For example, after 1998, Japan's Ministry of Foreign Affairs pushed for a "sector/non-project grant" instrument. By 2006, the proportion of Japan's bilateral aid commitments allocated to "economic infrastructure" had fallen to 25 percent, down from 45 percent in 1997 (Figure 10.3).

In Section 2 we noted the hesitancy with which Japan presented its criticism of the Washington Consensus. But in two more recent developments in the international aid arena – the adoption of "Poverty Reduction Strategy Papers," or PRSPs, and the Millennium Development Goals, or MDGs – the signs are that Japan has become more interested in constructive engagement.

Poverty Reduction Strategy Credits (PRSCs) were adopted by the World Bank and the IMF following widespread appreciation in Washington that two decades of structural adjustment loans had been largely unsuccessful, and, in many cases, had prevented developing countries from exercising effective control over their own economies. The idea behind PRSCs is that developing countries make up their own development plan which is called Poverty Reduction Strategy Paper (PRSP) and the World Bank and developed countries then extend PRSCs to support the plan. In theory, PRSPs were to be more country-driven, an effort to give countries real "ownership" over their policies and resource allocation decisions, including all aspects of society – economic and political – in the context of a single, comprehensive, long-term anti-poverty strategy. That is the theory; in practice, PRSPs have probably done little to enhance the empowerment of developing countries or to tailor aid programs more closely to specific country needs.

Japan's reaction to PRSPs has been decidedly more positive than to structural adjustment lending. In 2000, in order to make better use of PRSP guidelines in reforming Japan's own aid programs, JICA established study committees to review its activities in various countries, and, in 2001, Japan's Ministry of Foreign Affairs explicitly endorsed a multilateral engagement with the PRSPs: "We must pay more attention to the PRSPs. It is desirable that the PRSP should serve as development guidelines shared by all donors" (MOFA 2001). In 2004, Japan's Finance Minister went so far as to recommend to the World Bank and IMF that they use PRSPs as a starting point for a general improvement in the quality of aid (Tanigaki 2004).

Signs of Japan's increased engagement are also apparent in its involvement with the Millennium Development Goals (MDGs). Major elements of the goals played a prominent role in revisions Japan made to its ODA Charter in 2003, though the charter does not explicitly name them. Still, the MDGs emphasize far more uniformity among countries than the PRSP process, and, not surprisingly, Japan has been critical of this aspect, noting that the MDGs appear to allow for little heterogeneity among countries, conditions, or priorities. Yet Japanese officials did try to critique the goals constructively, arguing for "localization" of the MDGs to fit conditions on the ground, and offering PRSPs as a possible starting point for such an effort (see, e.g., Tanigaki 2004).

Toward a new paradigm?

The multiple convergences just outlined have led both the United States and Japan toward a middle ground that, in our view, is more effective than the Cold War model, though there is still much room for improvement. Although the United States is still clearly the dominant partner, the new paradigm seems to accept lessons from the other side's viewpoint and has ended up less interventionist and more focused on human development. The real danger is that, given the current global economic malaise, both countries will be reducing the quantity of aid. Moreover, if current moves on the quality side are any indication, both countries seem to be moving towards aid structures which are both leaner and possibly more focused on short-term foreign-policy goals, to the detriment of aid effectiveness.

In the United States substantial reorganization has occurred. Both the US Agency for International Development (USAID), born in 1961, and the newborn MCC, are now under a new director of foreign assistance in the Department of State who simultaneously serves as the administrator of USAID; 18 other smaller programs within the Department of State were to be integrated to enhance the governance and effective use of aid.

This reorganization has left out some important issues. The proliferation of smaller aid programs in many of the US line ministries has not been addressed. These programs were initiated in the Clinton years and have caused much overlap and confusion in recipient countries. The accumulated number of barnacles or Congressional earmarks in the 1961 Foreign Assistance Act has substantially impeded USAID's effectiveness.

In short, past reorganization efforts may well enhance efficiency but are also likely to emphasize short-term political objectives as opposed to longer-term development objectives. The first signs were already apparent in the Bush Administration's budget request for 2008: USAID's Development Assistance money was down by almost a third, while the politically focused Economic Support Fund went up by nearly a third. It remains to be seen whether the Obama administration, which emphasized a renewed focus on development assistance during the campaign, will reverse this trend. Thus far, it seems clear that the entire subject has not received much attention.

In Japan, aid did not experience a similar boost after September 11, and Japan's post-Cold-War aid budget has ebbed and flowed. It had recovered somewhat in the wake of the Asian financial crisis but fell again immediately thereafter. In 2005, it rose once more, but mainly on the back of contributions to Iraqi reconstruction and in donations to the Asian tsunami recovery effort. Since that time, aid has continued to decline consistently, and promises to increase it – such as former Prime Minister Koizumi's announcement of a three-year, $10 billion ODA increase at the Hong Kong WTO meeting in December 2005 – have not materialized. Japan's biggest challenge is to satisfy increasingly skeptical voters that its aid is strategically important. Recent institutional changes seem to be geared toward meeting this challenge by increasing institutional efficiency and integrating Japanese aid more closely with Japanese foreign policy, while also making some efforts to increase Japan's intellectual firepower and engagement with international aid debates.

One implication of Japan's focus on the national interest has been the changing regional pattern of Japanese aid in the 1990s. In many respects, Japan's national security, economic and political interests still reside in Asia, and this regional concentration is still recognized in a new Japanese ODA Charter. Yet Japan is also beginning to cast a wider net, significantly reducing its relative contributions to Asia and increasing its relative contribution to regions it has traditionally ignored, such as Africa. At the same time, Japan largely ignored US calls for major increases in aid to the newly independent states of Central and Eastern Europe – perhaps a sign of Japan's burgeoning assertiveness.

Japan is currently implementing a series of institutional reforms intended to restructure and rationalize the number of ministries involved in aid-related policy-making. Historically, in Japan not a single ministry or executive agency has had primary control over development policy; rather, as many as 15 different ministries have been involved. Today, three main ministries still vie for control: the Ministry of Foreign Affairs (MOFA), the Ministry of Economy, Trade, and Industry (METI), and the Ministry of Finance (MOF). Their preferences generally follow their jurisdictions. MOFA advocates the use of aid to support Japan's international diplomacy by improving the economic and social conditions of low-income countries. Its increasing influence over aid policy in the 1990s is reflected in the large share of Japanese aid that is now untied. METI's view, in line with business interests, is that aid should be used to promote an expansion of trade and investment opportunities. METI's influence has waned somewhat in recent years, but it regained some influence during the recent Abe administration, which viewed development assistance more explicitly as an instrument to promote national objectives. Indeed, in recent years Japan has again begun to tie some of its aid, though it still remains at the low end of the spectrum among donors. The third main agency is the Ministry of Finance whose interest is far more basic: to maintain fiscal discipline and to use aid to maintain an orderly international financial system. This has led the MOF to push for a decline in the total volume of ODA and to argue for limiting the amount of aid allotted to any one country.

The aid bureaucracy is also in flux. Having only recently combined its two main aid agencies, the soft-loan Japanese Overseas Economic Cooperation Fund (OECF) and the hard-loan Export–Import Bank of Japan (JEXIM), under the Japan Bank for International Cooperation (JBIC), Japan further consolidated its loans and grants under a "New JICA," or Japan International Cooperation Agency, traditionally the institution responsible for basic technical assistance and training. As part of this reform, New JICA has formed a "JICA Research Institute" to improve Japan's capacity for development research. Also under discussion is the placement of the JICA Research Institute directly under the Cabinet Office, with a reduced number of ministries (from 13 down to five) involved, and with the Ministry of Foreign Affairs now in control, a potentially important shift that would surely further re-orient Japanese aid toward shorter term foreign policy objectives. However, whether such heavyweight ministries as MOF and METI will really prove willing to concede pride of place to the Ministry of Foreign Affairs remains to be seen. Past reorganization efforts have often amounted to less than meets the eye.

Regardless of the precise outcome of Japan's institutional reforms, the process thus far shows substantial similarities with what has been happening in the United States. In both countries aid, as during the Cold War, is again being viewed mainly as a political instrument to advance the foreign policy and national security objectives of the donor, objectives which may or may not prominently include economic growth and poverty alleviation in the recipient countries.

Aid and non-governmental organizations

The convergence between the United States and Japan in official development assistance is not reflected in private flows, neither those delivered through NGOs or as foreign direct investment (FDI), nor those sent home as remittances by migrant workers. This section examines NGOs; the following section takes up FDI and remittances.

The relationship between aid and NGOs is one where there remains a substantial divergence between the United States and Japan. Figure 10.6 shows net flows to developing countries through NGOs from both governments. NGOs account for a miniscule percentage of Japanese ODA, but today deliver a large and growing percentage of US aid – at least 30 percent of USAID donations. Japan has little history of private giving, and, despite recent lip-service to the value of NGOs by the Japanese government, such activities, after a period of some growth in the mid-1980s and early 1990s, have remained modest, as has government assistance to them. Most of this assistance, in fact, goes to private organizations that are closely related to corporations or government ministries. Contrast this with the United States, with its decades-old tradition of private involvement in development activities. In 2005, US NGOs provided more than 30 times as much to the developing world as Japanese NGOs. The relatively minor role played by Japanese NGOs does not necessarily inhibit Japan's aid effectiveness; however, the lack of private involvement by Japanese citizens and civil society in general in the country's foreign aid effort undoubtedly affects its waning support among the Japanese public.

NGOs have long been important players on the international stage and have grown increasingly influential since the 1990s, fueled by the assumption that they carry distinct advantages in aid delivery and by a feeling that their roots among both donor and recipient publics build support for aid at a time when support for directly delivered official aid was falling. As a consequence, official donors and the IFIs have grown increasingly willing to deliver aid through NGOs. The World Bank estimates that in 1980 international NGOs working in development received less than 10 percent of their budgets from official sources.

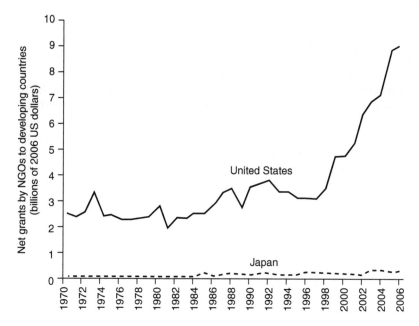

Figure 10.6 Net grants by NGOs to developing countries.

By the late 1990s, this had ballooned to 35 percent via a far larger and more influential community of NGOs (World Bank 1998). Increasingly, NGOs are now part of the aid establishment, sanctioned by governments, delivering large amounts of aid and exerting a considerable influence over aid policy. The 2005 Paris Declaration on Aid Effectiveness, for instance, was drafted using the input of representatives from more than 50 NGOs. While most NGO funding is provided by ODA, an estimated 20 percent is provided by religious and other private organizations.

The aid apparatuses of the United States and Japan have historically had far different relationships with NGOs, reflecting the widely divergent attitudes of the two governments toward the private sector. In the United States the tradition of voluntary organizations is historically strong; Alexis de Tocqueville (1841) credited them in part for the strength of American democracy. US aid policy has followed this tradition, working closely with both the profit and non-profit private sectors since it began giving aid; today the United States consistently touts the importance of "public–private partnerships." In Japan, the tradition of voluntary organizations is comparatively new and weak, and NGOs have played much less of a role, both domestically and in relation to the developing world. Yet in recent years the NGO community in Japan has grown quite a bit and the Japanese government has increased its support somewhat (see Figure 10.6).

Public–private interactions in US aid also have support from the unique US tax code.[4] Since the 1936 Tax Act, individuals and corporations have been able to deduct charitable donations from their income taxes. And beginning with Marshall Plan aid to Europe after World War II, the US government has made a conscious decision to work with the private sector to deliver assistance. In the beginning the US government relied on NGOs mostly to deliver short-term humanitarian assistance, mainly using the large US food surpluses which, after 1949, Congress authorized to be delivered as aid. However, starting in the 1970s NGOs, frustrated by decades of band-aid solutions and being made increasingly aware of conditions in the developing world by legions of returning Peace Corps and other volunteers, began to focus more on activities that promote development. Mindful of this transformation and concerned with making aid more efficient and popular at a time of declining public support, the formal US aid apparatus, in particular USAID, began making increasing use of NGOs. This was attractive to Main Street as well as Congress and permitted USAID to reduce its direct hire personnel. In 1993, the Presidential Advisory Committee on Voluntary Foreign Aid noted that US official and private aid organizations had increasingly convergent motives and recommended closer ties. Since then, many US NGOs have grown into virtual arms of the official aid apparatus, pursuing projects along the lines of official US aid policy and maintaining elaborate operations in Washington to lobby for government contracts. Initially the leveraging purpose of these partnerships was explicit. The 1986 Foreign Assistance Appropriations Act required that any NGO eligible for USAID grants or contracts had to get at least 20 percent of its funding for international activities from sources other than the US government. But, in keeping with the general trend toward outsourcing, this requirement was dropped in 2005. Yet, in contrast to the close relationship many NGOs have with the US government, other NGOs have resolutely maintained their independence and either set a cap on the proportion of their budgets they obtain from official sources, or refused government money altogether.

Although registration in the United States for non-profit status is relatively simple, registering with USAID is a cumbersome and time-consuming process, requiring a range of independently audited documents and is beyond the capacity of many NGOs. The process grew even more complex during the 1990s when, with declining support for aid among the US public, Congress attached increasingly onerous conditions to ODA. Today the mere cost of making an application to USAID for a government contract can run into tens of thousands of dollars. Such high overhead costs are a major reason why some are today questioning whether NGOs are indeed a more efficient way to deliver aid. Other reasons relate to the relative lack of accountability of NGOs, the other side of the independence coin.

The community of a little more than 500 registered US NGOs is somewhat smaller than the NGO community in most DAC countries. However, the high bar set for registering means that these figures fail to account for small unregistered NGOs active in international development, of which there are probably hundreds, if not thousands.[5] Although USAID's registration requirements are often outside the capacity of many NGOs from developing countries, USAID has made efforts to partner with indigenous developing-country NGOs, occasionally going so far as to set up endowments for their future operations.

Japan's aid has always been more centered on its public institutions. It has never shared the US tradition of private giving and support of charitable organizations, beyond the traditional Buddhist support for temples and private specialized schools for religious study. Moreover, the Japanese tax code discourages private donations. Aside from the self-employed, most Japanese do not report their income for tax purposes, but have their taxes deducted from their wages. To get a tax deduction for a charitable gift, a Japanese citizen must file special paperwork. Traditionally the only gifts eligible for such deductions were for "experimental research corporations," i.e., private entities engaged in R&D. In the 1990s, such eligibility was expanded to cover development assistance, but such organizations still face substantial hurdles. Foundations require a large capital fund and associations require a large membership base, so that eligible development NGOs are usually the creations of corporations and government ministries, in addition to a few large international NGOs with bargaining power.

As a result, the NGO sector in Japan, while growing, is still small. Today the Japanese NGO Center for International Cooperation (JANIC) estimates that only 10 percent of the few hundred NGOs engaged in international development have legal status. The Japanese NGO community dates from anti-government protests in the 1960s and 1970s and their concern with developing countries stems from such antecedents as the post-Vietnam War refugee crisis, Japan's overall increasing involvement in world affairs, and the return to Japan of Cooperation Volunteers (JOCV), who, like returning US Peace Corps volunteers, added to public awareness of development issues.[6] Some of the larger Japanese NGOs active in development are also either products of Japanese Christian organizations or branches of foreign – mainly US – organizations. In the mid-1980s, these NGOs emerged as activists, pressing for changes in Japanese foreign aid, in particular, challenging the traditional Japanese focus on infrastructure projects, which they called "faceless." They urged more of a focus on the needs of local people and for the aid apparatus to become more transparent.

This public pressure had some effect. In the mid-1980s, for example, the government began to publicize more details of its aid activities. Since the 1990s, as part of the aforementioned shift in purpose away from Cold War burden sharing and decreasing public support for aid, the government began to consider the wishes and activities of NGOs with increased seriousness. Economic recession and a series of high-profile corruption scandals in a once-revered bureaucracy further enhanced the appeal of NGOs (Hirata 2002). The government began channeling some aid through NGOs. In 1991 the government officially began cooperating with NGOs under the banner of "Visible Japanese Aid," in the hope that this would prove more creative, cost-effective and transparent (Nanami 2002).

The projects funded under this initiative were mostly small-scale, trying to take advantage of the greater flexibility of NGOs and their ability to implement grass-roots projects using appropriate technology and mindful of environmental effects. But the administrative rules governing the subsidies hampered their effectiveness. For example, unlike USAID/NGO contracts, they relied on single-year budgeting and did not cover personnel or administrative costs. Consequently, the flows remained small. According to the OECD, support to Japanese national NGOs in 2004 dollars was only US $133 million in 1990 and $212 million by 1995. More important in these early years was the "International Volunteer Savings Scheme," set up in 1991, to allow private citizens with post-office savings accounts to donate 20 percent of their after-tax interest to NGOs through the Ministry of Posts and Telecommunications. The response revealed that the lack of charitable giving by Japanese citizens had been far more the result of negative institutional incentives than a lack of concern by the public for development issues. In the first two months, 2.1 million citizens enrolled, generating ¥1.1 billion ($9.25 million) in donations. Yet this response also reveals the public sector orientation that continues to characterize even private Japanese aid: it was not until an officially-sanctioned outlet for donations was opened that Japanese began to donate in large numbers to development activities.

The role of NGOs was further institutionalized with the establishment in 1996 of the NGO–MOFA Regular Council Meeting, a quarterly gathering of officials of the Ministry of Foreign Affairs and ten representatives of the NGO community. The NGO–MOFA Council was followed in 1999 by an NGO–JICA Council, focused more on the particulars of implementation. Following a decade of irregular but growing collaboration, in 1999 for the first time, MOFA began the regular subcontracting of projects to NGOs (Hirata 2002). The number of Japanese NGOs active in international development consequently has grown substantially. In 1980, a directory noted 59; by 1993, there were 290; and by 1996, 368 (Japanese NGO Center for International Cooperation 1994; Saotome 1999). Today MOFA monitors more than 400 Japanese NGOs engaged in international activities.

Yet there are important caveats. In the first place, many of these NGOs are involved exclusively in education or are Japanese branches of international NGOs; only about 100 are engaged regularly in development as part of a wider range of activities, and only a little more than 50 have foreign aid as their main activity.[7] Furthermore, the basic definition of an "NGO" in Japan is very different from that in the United States; it is broad enough to include corporate foundations and extensions of various government ministries. Clearly "NGOs" closely linked or even created by corporations and government ministries differ from their US counterparts; yet they receive the lion's share of government aid. By the mid-1990s, the OECD estimates that only about 10–12 percent of Japanese government aid to NGOs, i.e., about $10 million–$20 million, actually went to private NGOs engaged in grass-roots activities. It is also notable that Japanese assistance to NGOs as recorded by the OECD/DAC – of which, again, assistance to grass-roots NGOs is only a small fraction – has stopped growing since the late 1990s.

Other associated flows to developing countries

Foreign aid can also play a catalytic role in attracting private capital, international flows of which have indeed dwarfed foreign aid in recent years. Figure

10.7 shows foreign aid alongside FDI (foreign direct investment) and remittances. The Asian financial crisis and the subsequent worldwide economic downturn led to a temporary reversal, but by 2003 private capital flows were again on the rise and have since far outstripped ODA as the main source of external capital from the OECD donor countries.

The United States and Japan have always been among the largest sources of private capital flows to developing countries. With rare exception the United States has been consistently the largest. In 2005, for example, the United States accounted for 39 percent of the DAC total. Japan was usually number two except in the immediate aftermath of the Asian financial crisis. Yet as a percentage of GNI, private capital outflows from the United States and Japan have been remarkably similar, both averaging a little less than 3 percent since 1968.

As to destination, not surprisingly, Japan's FDI has been concentrated in its Asian neighbors, while the United States provides more to Latin America and Central and Eastern Europe. The sphere of influence in both donor cases is undoubtedly based on some combination of geography, politics, history and the law of comparative advantage, in some order open to dispute. Undoubtedly, the ready supply of inexpensive labor in Southeast Asia was attractive to Japanese firms pushing relentlessly to lower production costs. Japanese investors did not count heavily on these same neighbors as markets for Japanese goods, which are more tailored to meeting the demands of developed country consumers. The United States, given its comparative advantage in high tech manufacturing and

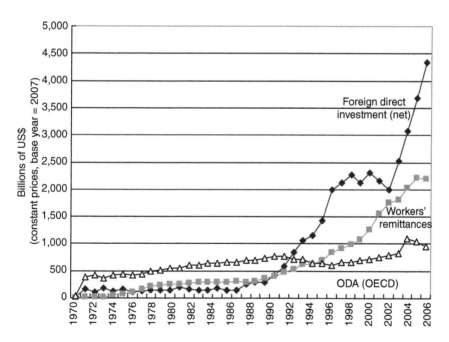

Figure 10.7 Total capital flows (source: OECD and World Bank).

services, has been more successful in selling its products to domestic consumers in developing countries, especially in Latin America, while taking tropical fruits and raw materials, sometimes produced by US firms, in exchange.

With respect to sectoral preferences, Japan's FDI has, for some time, been more or less split between manufacturing and services, while very little has been directed to agriculture and mining. The United States, by contrast, has usually invested far more in the primary sector, although in recent years new investments have also been increasingly concentrated in manufacturing and services, including transportation, tourism, construction, and financial services. Until the 1990s, Japan actually led the United States in the absolute size of investments in the service sector, but, since then, US service sector investments have skyrocketed. In manufacturing, the United States and Japan invest very similar amounts, but this, of course, reveals a strong Japanese preference for this sector, given its smaller total GNI as well as FDI.

Recent trends follow these historic patterns. While the United States has always been stronger abroad in non-price competitive manufactured goods, Japan has mostly used its overseas direct investments to lower its production costs in relatively competitive standardized manufactured goods markets. This has meant that much of Japanese FDI has been concentrated in manufacturing. This has also conditioned the nature of Japanese investments which emphasize the transfer of technology through learning-by-doing, often in a joint venture context, less likely to transfer technology wholesale, in contrast to the "turn-key" project preference often encountered in the US case. US firms are famous for utilizing secret technology and patent-protected methods of production embedded with their investments abroad, frequently using the wholly owned subsidiary vehicle.

Until recently, less-well-known, remittances – money that emigrants to developed countries send back to relatives at home – represent another increasingly important source of private capital for developing countries. Figure 10.7 shows remittances in a comparative context. Since the late 1990s such flows have far outstripped ODA as the second-largest source of foreign capital, after FDI, four-fifths of which goes to low income and lower middle income countries. And because so much in remittances flow through informal channels, their total may be as much as 50 percent higher than official data indicate (World Bank 2006).

Remittance flows also have the advantage of going directly to families, not only permitting increased consumption, but also enhanced investment and entrepreneurial activities. They are, therefore, potentially important in helping to reduce poverty. Adams and Page (2005), for example, estimate that a 10 percent increase in per capita remittances lowers the share of people living in poverty by 3.5 percent.

Both Japan and the United States represent important sources of remittances. The United States especially has long been a favored destination for immigrants. The largest group, 16.5 million adults, is made up of those coming from neighboring Latin America. More than 60 percent send money home at least four times a year, with the average person sending more than once a month. While the average Latin American worker in the United States will send home only about 10 percent of his or her income, this still constitutes anywhere from 50 to 80 percent of the recipient household's total income. While the current financial crisis has reduced these flows, Mexico alone is estimated to have received $20 billion in remittances during 2005, again, mostly from the United States and more than it received in FDI (World Bank 2006).

Japan has traditionally been far less open to immigrant labor than the United States. Nonetheless, those families whose relatives do find work in Japan send substantially more remittances than do the relatives of migrant laborers in the United States. The case of Latin America is an example. A higher proportion of the 435,000 Latin Americans currently living in Japan send money home than do the Latin Americans living in the United States – 70 percent versus 60 percent – and they send it more often, about 14.5 times a year, on average. In Japan, they are also more educated and earn an average of $50,000 a year, twice as much as Latin Americans earn in the United States, permitting them to send back twice as much – 20 percent as opposed to 10 percent of their incomes. Not unrelated is the fact that more of the money actually ends up in the hands of relatives rather than financial intermediaries, because transaction costs for remittances from Japan are just 3 percent, compared to more than 7 percent for remittances from the United States.[8]

These advantages – the larger proportion of migrants sending money home, in larger amounts, more frequently, and at lower cost – would seem to make Japan's remittances worthy of emulation. The Inter-American Development Bank has indeed declared that "the Japan to Latin America remittance market is the model for much of the rest of the world" (IADB 2005). Yet a closer look at Japanese remittances reveals that they represent a very special case, difficult to replicate. The vast majority of Latin Americans living in Japan are, in fact, descendants of Japanese who emigrated to Latin America in the first half of the twentieth century, often with the help of government subsidies, who subsequently returned. Today 1.5 million people of Japanese descent still live in Latin America, the largest concentration of Japanese anywhere outside Japan. This diaspora has generally been successful economically, as a result of which Latin Americans of Japanese descent who emigrate back to Japan are far better educated than Latin Americans who make their way to the United States. Compared to just 17 percent in the United States, 85 percent of Latin American adults living in Japan have at least a high school diploma. This superior education level is a primary factor behind the much higher incomes Latin Americans earn in Japan. This is not to say that there is nothing to be learned from the Japanese example; certainly it points to the importance of reducing the transactions cost of remittances by migrant laborers.

3 Searching for a new model of foreign capital flows

Leaving other flows such as NGO, FDI and remittances to one side, we finally return to the one issue of foreign assistance, currently under attack and most in need of change. We have previously noted signs of convergence between the United States and Japan with respect to their behavior on foreign aid. This convergence raises the possibility of a "third way" of delivering aid, which draws on the advantages of both sides. Such a "third way" will require both a lessening of Japan's historical modesty on aid, as well as a greater willingness by the United States and Japan – and indeed of donors generally – to rely on recipients themselves to develop their own development plans independently of donors, and then to hold recipients to their word by withdrawing funds if "self-conditionalities" are not met.

Japan's substantial involvement in the recent Vietnamese PRSP may be a sign that it is more willing to innovate and build on the lessons of its own development experience. The resulting paper, called the "Comprehensive Poverty Reduction and Growth Strategy (CPRGS)," heavily emphasizes investments in growth-enhancing infrastructure, alongside the traditional social sector investments in health and education. Vietnam's first two PRSPs were light on infrastructure investments: they included only investments in power lines and rural farm roads as elements of infrastructure (Kitano and Ishii 2003). The Japanese government subsequently approached the Vietnam government and the World Bank to suggest including large-scale investments in infrastructure. Japan's ideas were subsequently incorporated into Vietnam's third PRSP, which Japan co-financed (Kitano *et al.* 2004).

Initially, the Japanese government did not show much interest in Vietnam's PRSP. According to Kitano, Ishi, and Karasawa who was the representative of the JBIC at Hanoi at the time, there were two reasons for this (Kitano *et al.* 2004). The first is that the original PRSp only focused on social sectors and did not include the large-scale investment in infrastructure which was considered important for Japanese foreign aid historically. The second is that Japan found no strategic reason to co-finance the PRSC. In the case of co-financing SALs in the 1980s and 1990s, Japan had been under pressure by other donor countries to reduce its substantial balance of payments surpluses. But by the time PRSPs came into the picture, Japan was no longer under such pressure. Furthermore, the Japanese public did not support ODA as it had before. Incorporating the approach of poverty reduction through large-scale investments in infrastructure was possible because Japan was the largest ODA donor to Vietnam and had a long history of cooperation with it.

Vietnam adopted the *Doi Moi* reform policy in 1986, was able to stabilize the economic situation and began to grow vigorously by 1992. JICA initiated a country study for Japan's official development assistance to Vietnam in January 1994 and supported a research project called "Study on the Economic Development Policy in the Transition towards a Market-Oriented Economy in the Socialist Republic of Vietnam" from August 1995 to March 1998. The research project was led by Professor Shigeru Ishikawa, Emeritus Professor of Hitotsubashi University and supported by the JICA. More than ten professors and researchers from Japan, government officers of the Ministry of Planning and Investment (MPI) and researchers of the Development Strategy Institute (DSI) of Vietnam participated in the project. The main tasks of the project were to comment on the draft of the five-year plan for socio-economic development which was presented at the Eighth National Congress in June 1996, to analyze the problems emerging during the five-year plan and to propose policies to resolve the problems. According to Tran Van Tho, some of the Japanese professors who participated in the project knew well the historical development experience of Asian economies such as Japan and China. They focused on the supply-side of the economy and preferred gradualism to Washington Consensus reforms (Tho 1999). The government of Vietnam seems to have studied the development experiences of its Asian neighbors and its own economic problems and realized the importance of large-scale infrastructure investments.

There is a related project, the Japan–Vietnam Joint Initiative, through which the government of Vietnam was able to study the importance of large-scale infrastructural investments. This is a framework established in April 2003 to improve the investment circumstances of Vietnam to attract FDI. The members are the Japanese government, Nippon Keidanren (Japan Business Federation), the Japan Chamber of Commerce and Industry at Hanoi and Ho Chi Minh City, and the Vietnamese government. They identified problems of the Vietnamese investment environment, worked out action plans to resolve these problems, and monitored the results of the action plan. There is no doubt that the knowledge acquired through this initiative contributed to the preparation of the CPRGS.

As a result of Japan's involvement, Vietnam produced a third PRSP that is arguably more balanced than its first two. The original PRSP took account of the social sectors which the United States prefers based on the concept of human development. By contrast, the third PRSP, the CPRGS, included large-scale economic infrastructure investments which Japan considers very important, based on her own development experience. The catalytic role of such foreign aid to attract private capital is fully recognized in the Vietnamese CPRGS. As a sign of Japan's increasing assertiveness in the development arena, this is a positive development. Yet there is also a risk that, just as Japan has criticized the United States for offering one-size-fits-all advice to countries with very different situations and needs, Japan's advice to Vietnam may reflect an over-emphasis on infrastructure investments as a panacea for development. While Vietnam clearly benefited from Japan's advice, there is some question as to how much its new CPRGS is truly Vietnam's home-grown, and therefore fully "owned," development plan.

With this central problem of recipient "ownership" in mind, we suggest that a third model might be superior and worthy of consideration by both parties. This model does not reward countries for pledging to follow donors' advice, nor does it reward recipients for the past, as the MCC does. Instead, our third model delivers aid based on the recipient's future commitments. What distinguishes it from past efforts is an insistence on true local ownership coupled with "self-conditionality" drawn up by aid recipients themselves. Donors would, of course, have a chance to negotiate concerning the self-conditionality packages proposed. The important change is in the enforcement of compliance that self-conditionality allows: donors would restore credibility to the system by offering, and carrying out, the threat to cut off aid in the event of non-compliance. In the past, donor conditions have seldom been taken seriously, since ultimately both parties realized that the money would eventually flow, regardless of the rhetoric. Conditions frequently ignored the reality of the political economy of the recipient, and donors, facing their own political need to continue lending, found it impossible to cut off assistance. As noted, PRSPs have been as vulnerable to this problem as any past efforts, in their implementation if not in their design. Indeed, experience indicates that policy change promised under external pressure rarely "sticks." But with recipients who are in a better position to know what is possible and what is not, proposing the conditionalities themselves, with donors accepting, rather than imposing them, the possibility for real policy change would be much enhanced.

For this third model to work, it is important that the preparation of the reform package be at arm's length from the donors, allowing true local ownership. If the recipients need assistance, they must be assisted by independent third parties, not the donors. Likewise, it is important for donors to learn to be more passive, i.e., ready to provide aid ballooning over a multi-year period.[9] The World Bank seems to be taking some small steps in this direction, but the current dispute over the application of country corruption designations indicates that short-term political considerations may still be at work even in the multi-lateral institutions.

It is increasingly being recognized that aid flows can also be counterproductive, not only because they can cause an unwelcome appreciation of the exchange rate and/or enhance aid dependency via a reduction in domestic private savings or tax levels, but also because, in an extended version of the "Dutch Disease," they can lead to a relaxation of the policy reform decision-making process, along with a decline in accountability and an increase in clientelism and corruption. The only reliable way to try to avoid or at least diminish such undesirable side effects of aid is for the recipient to establish its own reform priorities and feel fully in charge of its implementation in both the economic and political dimensions.

4 Suggestions for the future

Aside from this "third way" approach, which we hope both sides will consider, there are additional steps that the United States and Japan can take in the future to improve the effectiveness of their capital flows. In keeping with the 2005 Paris Declaration on Aid Effectiveness, efforts are currently underway in both countries to consolidate the number of aid-dispensing agencies, which historically have been the source of a good deal of confusion, not only in Washington and Tokyo but also, and perhaps more importantly, in the recipient countries. Inefficiencies result not only because of the absence of coordination but also due to highly dysfunctional competition among donor agencies, and the ability of recipients to play the agencies off against each other.

But we also note that, at least in the United States, consolidation has been partly offset by an increased role for the Defense Department associated with the "war on terror." In 2002, the Defense Department managed only 6 percent of aid allocations; in 2005 it managed 22 percent. At the same time, USAID's share has fallen from half of total ODA in 2002 to 39 percent in 2005, undermining some of the benefits of consolidating US aid under the State Department.

The current aid reorganization efforts in both countries, with the US State Department and Japan's Ministry of Foreign Affairs taking increasing control of ODA, seems to imply an enhanced politicization of aid. Inevitably, especially in the United States, we can, therefore, anticipate the increased use of ODA as an instrument in the "war on terror," through the promotion of democracy and other nation-building activities concentrated in presently or potentially friendly countries.

The irony – a serious one in our view – is that the national security argument might resonate even better without the politicization of aid. In poor developing countries, the antidote to terrorists' siren song is aid that works, not aid that rewards corrupt but US-friendly governments. Most terrorists are extra-state actors, while states are mainly enablers; they do not cause terrorism. It is poverty and inequality that breed terrorism, born of a feeling among the disadvantaged that they are perpetual losers in a world system in which countries like the United States and Japan always win. Thus US and Japanese foreign policy goals might be even better served if their activities were perceived as actually relieving global imbalances with the help of aid and private capital flows, rather than using them to encourage a recipient country's elite to support donor foreign policy agendas.

With respect to Japan, which is less invested in the global "war on terror," the apparent increased influence of the Ministry of Foreign Affairs is likely to preference short-term foreign-policy interests. Such a shift probably means more attention will be paid to countries supplying Japan with needed raw materials, supporting Japan in its efforts to gain a seat in the UN Security Council, enhancing its voting power in the IFIs, and the like.

This and the need for donors to coordinate their efforts to avoid wasteful overlap and confusion in recipient countries are indeed at the heart of the aforementioned 2005 Paris Declaration on Aid Effectiveness, to which both Japan and the United States are signatories. That document set out 12 indicators, each with benchmarks to be met by 2010, covering five categories: ownership, alignment, harmonization, managing for results, and mutual accountability. Although these indicators are somewhat less than revolutionary, they represent important steps toward making aid more effective. The World Bank and OECD have been conducting surveys of the 60 signatories – donors and recipients – to the Paris Declaration to determine progress on the indicators. Both Japan and the United States should take the results of these surveys seriously and use them to motivate further reforms in their aid structures.

Yet for all of ODA's importance, when all is said and done, we know that aid is likely to become an even more junior partner to remittance flows from both the United States and Japan in the future. To facilitate the smooth functioning and expansion of this particular, somewhat "under the radar," flow of private foreign capital, a few suggestions are in order. Since both sending and receiving countries stand to benefit from most types of migration and the associated remittance flows, reducing the sometimes quite high transaction costs of remittances should get priority attention. Multilaterally negotiated system encouraging temporary worker migration arrangements would also benefit both parties. To allay the fear that "temporary" would become "permanent," we suggest consideration of a multilateral version of something like the South Korean device of forcing migrants to deposit a portion of their earnings in a special savings account, which would be forfeited if the worker decided not to return home as promised.

Last, we would like to register continued disappointment with the aforementioned timidity with which Japan has promoted its alternative development strategy in the international arena. The end of the Cold War and of burden sharing on aid presented Japan with a unique strategic opportunity to make its development vision a real alternative to the amended Washington Consensus. Yet having pushed for and financed the World Bank's *East Asian Miracle* report in the early 1990s – a step in this direction – Japan has to date not really followed up. Despite initial coolness toward the PRSPs and the Millennium Development Goals, Japan is now supportive. With over a half-century in the aid business, Japan has consistently recognized and bemoaned her second-class status in the realm of development thinking. However, Japan should now be in position to construct a viable alternative development model based on her own historical experience and generally take a more confident leadership role. Japan's role in shaping Vietnam's recent CPRGS may be a sign that Japan is increasingly willing to move in that direction once the current global crisis has ended.

All in all, this remains an exciting time of challenge and opportunity for both Japan and the United States. Inevitably, both countries are currently focusing on their domestic economic problems. But both have shown a willingness to experiment with new mechanisms for delivering official development aid and to recognize the relationships between aid and other capital flows. At no time in recent memory has international development been so clearly linked to the national interest, even as somewhat differently defined by the two countries. It is our hope that this self-interest can increasingly be reflected in the achievement of improved mechanisms and successful development abroad.

Notes

* Gustav Ranis is the Frank Altschul Professor Emeritus of International Economics at Yale University, Stephen Kosack is Assistant Professor at the Kennedy School, Harvard and Ken Togo is Professor of the Economics Department of Musashi University. The research assistance of Shinsuke Tanaka and Atisha Kumar, students in economics at Yale, is gratefully acknowledged, as is the support of the Toyota Foundation.

1 See, e.g., Doss (1996). Ensign (1992) estimates that more than half of Japanese aid from 1966 through the 1980s was for infrastructure, and that the relevant contracts went overwhelmingly to Japanese engineering firms.

2 Yasushi Mieno, then head of the Bank of Japan, added to this line of criticism at the annual meeting of the World Bank and the IMF in 1991: "Experience in Asia has

shown that, although development strategies require a healthy respect for market mechanisms, the role of the government cannot be forgotten" (World Bank 1991).
3 Indeed, there was initially a concern that the grants would be *too* large (see Clemens and Radelet 2003).
4 See Smillie and Helmich (1993) for a good history of the development of US development NGOs.
5 These figures contrast somewhat with official statistics from the OECD/DAC. These list gross outflows from US NGOs as $8.4 billion in 2005, up from $4.4 billion in 2000 and accounting for more than half of the DAC total (2004 dollars). All outflows from US NGOs were in the form of grants.
6 Like the Peace Corps, JOCV sends Japanese abroad to use their skills in helping developing countries in an effort to add what the Japanese call a "human face" to their activities in the developing world. Since it was founded in 1965, JOCV has sent more than 25,000 volunteers abroad.
7 Exact numbers on Japanese NGOs are difficult to obtain. The Japanese NGO Centre for International Cooperation (JANIC) maintains a list of NGOs, but there are inconsistencies and its lists are not regularly updated.
8 Data on remittances from Japan to Latin America are from IADB (2005).
9 For more detail on this third model, see Ranis (2006). Our approach is forward-looking, and therefore differs from the "Payments for Progress" idea recently proposed by Barder and Birdsall (2006) which has a family resemblance to the MCC rationale.

References

Adams, R. and Page, J. (2005), "Do International Migration and Remittances Reduce Poverty in Developing Countries?" *World Development*, 33 (10): 1645–1669.
Barder, O. and Birdsall, N. (2006), "Payments for Progress: A Hands-Off Approach to Foreign Aid," Center for Global Development, Working Paper no. 102.
Clemens, M. and Radelet, S. (2003), "The Millennium Challenge Account: How Much is Too Much, How Long is Long Enough?" Working Paper 23, Washington, DC: Center for Global Development.
DAC (2009), Source OECD International Development Statistics (Electronic Database), Organization for Economic Cooperation and Development, Development Assistance Committee 2009 (cited May 12, 2009).
Doss, V. (1996), "Japan's Development Aid: Self-interest or Economic Partnership?" *International Advances in Economic Research*, 2 (3): 232–243.
Ensign, M.M. (1992), *Doing Good or Doing Well: Japan's Foreign Aid Program*, New York: Columbia University Press.
Hirata, K. (2002), "Whither the Developmental State? The Growing Role of NGOs in Japanese Aid Policymaking," *Journal of Comparative Policy Analysis*, 4 (2): 165–188.
IADB (2005), Remittances to Latin America from Japan, Multilateral Investment Fund, Washington, DC: Inter-American Development Bank.
Iimi, A. and Ojima, Y. (2005), "Complementarities between Grants and Loans,." Working Paper no. 20, Tokyo: Japan Bank for International Cooperation Institute.
Japanese NGO Center for International Cooperation. (1994), *NGO Data Book: Sûji de miru Nihon no NGO*, Tokyo: Japanese NGO Center for International Cooperation.
Kitano, M. and Ishii, N., (2003), "Nihon no Koe wo PRSC he: Betonamu deno Atarasii Kokoromi (Japanese Voice to the Vietnamese PRSC: New Trail in Vietnam)," in *Kokusai Kaihatsu Jyaanaru Sha* (International Development Journal Co. Ltd): 37–39.
Kitano, M., Ishii, N., and Karasawa, M. (2004), "Nihon no Koe wo PRSC he: Betonamu niokeru Ketsujitsu (Japanese Voice to the Vietnamese PRSC: Achievement in

Vietnam)," *Kokusai Kaihatsu Jyaanaru Sha* (International Development Journal Co. Ltd): 86–88.

MOFA (2001), "Japan's Aid Cooperation and Modality," Tokyo: Country Planning Division, Economic Cooperation Bureau, Ministry of Foreign Affairs.

Nanami, A. (2002), "The Role of NGOs in Japan's Aid Policy: Government–NGO Relations," Paper Presented at the Third Biennial Conference of the Aotearoa New Zealand International Development Studies Network (DevNet), Institute of Development Studies, Massey University, Palmerston North, New Zealand.

OECF (1991), "Issues Related to the World Bank's Approach to Structural Adjustment: Proposal from a Major Partner," Occasional Paper no. 1, Tokyo: Overseas Economic Cooperation Fund.

Ranis, G. (2008) "The Right Balance in Aid." *South China Morning Post*, December 27.

Saotome, M. (1999), "Imakoso motomerareru ôru Japan no kokusai kyôryoku." *Gaiko Forum*, 127 (March): 34–40.

Smillie, I. and Helmich, H. (eds.) (1993), *Non-Governmental Organisations and Governments: Stakeholders for Development*, Paris: OECD.

Sunaga, K. (2004), "The Reshaping of Japan's Official Development Assistance (ODA) Charter," Discussion Paper on Development Assistance no. 3, Tokyo: Foundation for Advanced Studies on International Development (FASID).

Tanigaki, S. (2004), Statement by Japan's Minister of Finance, 67th Meeting of the World Bank/IMF Joint Development Committee, Washington, DC.

Tho, T.V. (1999), "Betonamu no Keizai Kaikaku Hatten Senryaku to Nihon no Chiteki Sien (The Vietnamese Economic Development-Development Strategy and Japanese Intellectual Support," in S. Ishikawa and Y. Hara (eds.) *Betonamu no Sijyou Keizaika* (The Vietnamese Transition to Market Economy), Toyo Keizai Sinpousha (in Japanese).

Tocqueville, A. de (1841), *Democracy in America*, fourth edition, New York: J. & H.G. Langley.

USAID (2006), *The Voluntary Foreign Aid Programs: Report of Voluntary Agencies Engaged in Overseas Relief and Development (VolAg Report)*. Washington, DC: USAID.

World Bank (1991), Press Release no. 16, October 15, Washington, DC: World Bank.

World Bank (1993), *The East Asian Miracle: Economic Growth and Public Policy*, Washington, DC: World Bank.

World Bank (1998), *Global Development Finance 1998*, Washington, DC: World Bank.

World Bank (2006), *Global Economic Prospects: Economic Implications of Remittances and Migration*, Washington, DC: World Bank.

World Bank (2008), Global Development Finance, World Bank (cited August 8, 2008), Washington, DC: World Bank. Online, available at: www.worldbank.org/data/onlinedbs/onlinedbases.htm.

11 Lessons from Japan's post-war development experience

Koichi Hamada, Keijiro Otsuka, Gustav Ranis, and Ken Togo

1 From an imitation-based to an innovation-led economy

Chapter 2 by Togo clearly demonstrates that even the Japanese automobile industry, which seems the most competitive globally, managed to survive by receiving the support of the government in the pre-war period. It seems clear that without such government protection this industry might not have developed; at a minimum its development would have been delayed or been much less spectacular. Thus, Togo concludes that a more positive assessment should be given to the idea of infant industry protection than is currently in vogue. The implication is that it makes sense to try to locate genuinely "infant industries" and support them in the years to come. Such a search for future "winners" is admittedly not easy but an increasingly innovative private sector should be able to provide the necessary signals.

Chapter 3 by Otsuka and Sonobe provides evidence based on a large number of case studies conducted in Japan, in other Asian countries and in Sub-Saharan Africa that industrial clusters have made significant contributions to the industrial development in both advanced and less developed countries. As is widely recognized, an advantage of industrial clusters is to reduce transactions costs owing to the geographical proximity of clustered enterprises. What is also emphasized by the authors is the importance of multi-faceted innovations consisting not only of technological innovations but also of simultaneous improvements in management, marketing, and procurement systems, in order to transform industrial clusters from production centers of low-quality to those of high-quality products. While the industrial cluster attracts a variety of human resources useful for multi-faceted innovations, it also facilitates imitations among enterprises in the cluster. Thus, governmental support for the formation of industrial clusters and the stimulation of multi-faceted innovations can be justified.

Chapter 4 by Arikawa explores the changing optimum financial system in the course of economic development based again on the case of post-war Japan. It finds that the indirect financial system led by the main banks contributed to loosening the financial constraints until the end of the 1960s when Japan's rapid catching-up process came to an end. This is partly because the riskiness of investment is generally low when imitation is the engine of growth, so that a handful of main banks can shoulder investment risks, and partly because households at the country's low income stage were highly risk averse and, hence, preferred low-risk, low-return bank savings. Under such conditions, the indirect financial system was effective in mobilizing and allocating limited investment funds by incurring inter-temporal risks. The preservation of such a system in later periods, particularly since the 1990s, led to excessive investment as a consequence of excessive lending. As an economy develops and reaches its technology frontier, it must generate unique new ideas which are inherently risky. Thus, it is much more desirable to share the risk by stock and bond markets, relying on a relatively small number of financial institutions. Yet, the development of stock and bond markets in Japan is still far from adequate for dealing with high investment risks and further reform is needed.

Chapter 5 by Iwai argues that, although the Japanese companies established a highly unique "autonomous" system during the earlier rapid growth period, which was characterized, among other things, by the mutual holding of each others' stocks among a group of related companies, this should not be considered a deviation from the ordinary capitalist system. Instead it is an adjustment to circumstances when firm-specific human capital of workers and engineers must be accumulated in order to benefit from technology imports. In other words, what was needed then was basically the ability to operate factories and machines based on ideas and technologies imported from abroad. What is needed now, however, is the ability to innovate, i.e., to invent new technologies and differentiated new products here at home. Therefore, Japanese companies must now nurture not only firm-specific human resources useful for the operation of machines, but, much more importantly, firm-specific human resources that are conducive to innovation. Iwai forcefully argues that to date such transformation has been incomplete. Although we fully agree with his argument that the Japanese economy needs innovative human resources, we believe that such human resources can also be attracted from the outside. After all, the availability of a variety of human resources belonging to different companies and the effective use of such resources by innovative companies were the key to success in the Silicon Valley of the United States.

Chapter 6 by Kambayashi deals with the legal support provided to the accumulation of firm-specific human capital, particularly through on-the-job training, which was the critical factor underlying the miraculous growth of the Japanese economy in the 1960s. The investment in such human capital will not continue to be forthcoming unless there are established mechanisms that safeguard the return to investors in firm-specific human capital. By reviewing the cases of employee dismissals at the district, high, and supreme court levels, he identifies how the employer's rights to dismiss employees have been increasingly restricted over time. This is likely to be a response to the society's demand for the accumulation of firm-specific human capital. In all likelihood such a system works well during the catch-up period when companies grew fast, based on technology imports, which required a number of firm-specific adaptations. In the post catch-up period, however, the undue restrictions on the dismissal of employees can become obstacles to the better functioning of labor markets which reallocate workers in accordance with the changing comparative advantage of industries.

Chapter 7 by Odaka reports the results of interviews with leading entrepreneurs regarding the success of their management during the high-growth period. He finds that fearing a crisis arising from the fierce competition of other advanced countries, entrepreneurs in post-war Japan quickly introduced quality enhancing practices and implemented them before initiating mass production, which was then followed by strengthened labor management and the quality control of new products. Odaka also points to the importance of cooperation between a company's planning and designing divisions and its production division in raising the efficiency in generating new products and installing new production systems. At present, firm management has become much more complicated due to the increasing importance of advanced scientific knowledge, intellectual property rights, IT technologies, and intensified global competition. The author questions why the current management system of Japanese companies is so slow to adjust to this new business environment.

Chapter 8 by Godo and Hayami attempts to analyze the role of human capital, measured by schooling, in the long-term development of the Japanese economy since the Meiji era. While increased schooling levels of the Japanese undoubtedly contributed to its miraculous growth, Japan has failed to develop the schooling systems needed for the post catch-up period. Particularly problematic is both the low quality and quantity of higher education, including graduate schools. Indeed the proportion of university students who proceed to graduate schools is significantly lower in Japan than in the United States. The authors also believe that Japanese high-school students who are taught to memorize historical data and mathematical formulas without critically questioning the mechanisms and principles which lie behind particular events and relationships will have difficulty becoming creative graduate students.

Chapter 9 by Hamada and Mimaki sheds new light on the effectiveness of Japan's light armament strategy based on a game theoretic framework. Commitment to a light armament strategy ahead of other countries had different implications during the Cold War period when confrontation with the Soviet Union was a critical issue compared to the post-Cold War period when China's presence has increased and North Korea has become a major threat to peace in Northeast Asia. During the Cold War period, armaments by the United States and Japan were substitutes, so that the large military expenditures incurred by the United States increased the temptation for Japan to reduce its own. At the same time the United States requested Japan to increase its budget for non-military purposes, such as ODA going to low-income Asian countries. In contrast, during the post-Cold War period, increased military expenditure by Japan would induce increased armaments on the part of other Asian countries, so that Japan's commitment to a continued light armament policy is likely to mitigate potential political tensions in Asia.

Chapter 10 by Ranis *et al.* argues forcefully that Japan should take a stronger leadership role in the development field and express its views about international development policies much more forcefully. Japan was rightly critical of the Washington Consensus that sometimes seemed to excessively and blindly advocate the absolute rule of free market mechanisms. This view is being criticized by many now, but Japan could have criticized this position much earlier. The authors conclude that continued timidity and adherence to silence by Japan is harmful not only to its own international status but also to the welfare of the developing countries.

Basically each aforementioned study has been conducted independently, even though the authors share the common goal of identifying positive and negative lessons from the post-war Japanese economic development experience. Nonetheless, the studies turned out to be highly complementary, leading to surprisingly coherent and consistent conclusions. These may be summarized as follows:

1   Although the market mechanism must be utilized, there are areas where government intervention helps economic development. One such case is the protection of infant industries which can facilitate the technology imports needed for future development. The protection of the Japanese automobile industry is a good case in point. Although identifying which industries should be protected is not an easy task, it is worth pursuing the selective protection of promising infant industries for a time. Note, however, that the "infant" industries of Japan are now high-tech and science-based advanced industries which may be newly born, unlike in the catch-up phase when targeted industries were already present in the more advanced countries.

2   Industrial clusters reduce transactions costs and create an environment conducive to innovations by attracting human resources useful for generating innovations, but, at the same time, they may reduce the incentive to innovate because imitation is easy within a cluster. Thus, the support by the government of innovations in a high-tech industrial cluster makes sense.

3   In order to support infant industries and cluster-based high-tech industries, Japan also needs major reforms in its education and financial systems so as to strengthen both the quantity and quality of its higher education and so as to generate direct financial systems in place of the currently predominant indirect systems.

4   Japanese companies successfully established "autonomous" organizational systems in which firm-specific human capital investments were actively made, and where the research and development division, the management division, and the production division worked closely together to achieve major efficiency gains. Considering the rapid advancement of science, the current policy of exclusive reliance on one's own employees for the generation of innovations may have to be reconsidered. Also to be reconsidered should be the coordination of the advanced research division, the intellectual property rights division, the IT-based management division, and, once

again, the production division, none of which have been well integrated so
far.

5   As the first non-western advanced country, Japan accumulated valuable knowledge relevant to the development of low-income economies. Hence it should
be able to make a more significant contribution to the development of poor
countries as well as specifically to the goal of poverty reduction. It must also
be recognized that Japan made a large contribution to world peace and security by adhering to the Yoshida Doctrine during the post-Cold War period.

These five points share the same basic recognition, i.e., that *while the Japanese
economy skillfully and admirably built an economic system and institutions
remarkably suitable for imitation-based economic development, it failed to sufficiently change or reform them once the economy had reached its technological
frontier. As a result, its economy has since been stagnant over almost the last
two decades.* This may be termed the "Japanese syndrome" according to which
past success prevents reforms today in key aspects of the economy.

What is needed is the simultaneous reform of several institutions so as to
stimulate innovation. The question arises as to whether it is possible for Japan to
achieve such reforms or is it simply wishful thinking. We believe that the most
fundamental reform required is the reform of higher education, because, after all,
the improvement of human capital is a major determinant of other reforms which
can lead the Japanese economy towards a new sustainable growth path.

2   Potential of the Japanese economy as viewed from its higher education system

There exists a consensus among development economists that it is human capital
in general and education in particular that governs the pace of economic development. Those who are interested in economic growth can confirm statistically
the importance of education as a determinant of the level of income (e.g.,
Glaeser *et al.* 2004).

According to Richard Levin, the president of Yale University, the US government allocated sizeable parts of its budget to university research for the basic
sciences as well as for health, agriculture, defense, and energy, which later led to
the advent of the mainframe computers and integrated circuits in the 1960s and
the development of application software and the internet infrastructure in the
1990s (Levin 2006). Moreover, the National Science Foundation provides
research support for projects but not for universities, thereby favoring competent
young researchers and reducing the influence of universities and established
faculty. In this way universities can become less bureaucratic and more efficient
through increasing the employment of competent younger faculty.

Levin also pointed out that the Chinese Government allocates increasingly
larger amounts to universities to stimulate research, improve the quality of staff,
and strengthen the ability of students with a view to using universities as key
organizations for facilitating economic growth (Levin 2006). In Japan a series of

large-scale centers of excellence programs offered by the Ministry of Education significantly stimulated research at universities, even though they do not really target competent individual researchers. To our surprise and deep regret, the current government run by the Democratic Party of Japan has decided to scale down the valuable center of excellence program because of the allegedly wasteful use of budgetary resources. We cannot overemphasize our fear that such actions can seriously impair the long-term growth of the Japanese economy.

Newsweek (2006) created a ranking of 50 global universities based on the Shanghai Jiaotong Survey and the Times Higher Education Survey. According to this ranking, number one is Harvard University, followed by Stanford University and Yale University. The best university outside of the United States and United Kingdom is the University of Tokyo, which is ranked fourteenth But we should not overlook the fact that only two universities in Japan are included among the top global 50 universities. Detailed examination of the data provided by the Shanghai Jiaotong University indicates the serious shortcomings of the Japanese university, as is shown in Table 11.1. The top 100 universities for each specialized field are selected. The ranking is based on a number of criteria, such as the number of Nobel Prize Laureates among its alumni and the number of citations of journal articles published by the faculty. Although there is always room for doubt on the reliability, objectivity, and accuracy of such rankings, we believe that these data do broadly assess the current state of intellectual and creative ability of Japanese higher education.

Although the performance of Japanese universities is thus generally inferior to that in the United States and the United Kingdom, they perform pretty well in specific fields. For example, in the natural sciences and mathematics five Japanese universities are listed among the top 100, while no other Asian countries appear. In engineering, technology, and computer science, three Japanese universities are listed, along with the Singapore National University and the Hong Kong University of Science and Technology. In life and agricultural sciences, clinical medicine and pharmacy the only Asian entries to appear are Japanese universities. Thus, in these fields, Japanese universities are fairly competitive internationally.

In contrast, only the Hong Kong University of Science and Technology and the Singapore National University are named among the top 100 universities in the social sciences. This is truly disappointing, because knowledge of the social sciences, particularly economics, is undoubtedly valuable in reforming economic systems.

As we have seen in the introductory chapter, per capita GDP is already higher in Singapore and Hong Kong than in Japan and the income gap between the United States and Japan has been widening. Unless Japan successfully catches up with the United States in the natural and social sciences, that gap will continue to widen. Although Singapore and Hong Kong are small in terms of their total GDP so that their total investments in science and technology are relatively small, the intensity of the use of science in these countries may well have surpassed Japan already.

To sum up, Japan can and should improve its research capacity in the natural sciences, which should provide the basis for the development of knowledge-intensive and science-based high-tech industries, whereas inadequate research capacity in the social sciences needs to be addressed if economic reforms and an associated burst of domestic innovations are to take place. Otherwise, the Japanese economy may continue to grow slowly based primarily on technology imports, as in the past.

3 A side glance at the role of monetary policy during the crisis

The chapters in this book are mainly concerned with the real and structural aspects of Japanese development. We have argued that the adherence to techno-logical and human capital development for the sake of importing technology facilitated the miraculous growth at the time. After the peak of the convenience of seeking technology abroad, this strategy encountered a serious drawback.

There is an important factor that brought down the growth trajectory of Japan in the past decade and a half. Because we have dealt principally with the real and structural aspects in this book, so far have we not discussed the serious con-sequences of inappropriate monetary and exchange rate policy. It would take another volume to fully analyze the macroeconomics of deflation, the overvalued yen and recession in Japan. We will be brief and succinct here, however.

During the past 15 years, the macroeconomic fetter was the inappropriate mon-etary policy. Let us illustrate this by explaining the transmission of the recent Lehman crisis. A similar lack of appropriate monetary policy continued over the past 15 years except for the period during the first half of the tenure of the BOJ governor (2003–2006), Toshihiko Fukui, before he changed his flexible monetary policy to the traditional BOJ restrictive policy. The description of the recent global crisis will convey the stance of the BOJ for the whole period under consideration.

The following is our metaphorical account of the Lehman-originated crisis:

> Once upon a time, on the East side of the Pacific, there was a Country A that was inhabited by grasshoppers; on the West side, there was a Country B that was inhabited by ants.
>
> Grasshoppers in Country A lived a high style of life because they had a secret apparatus called "the widow's cruse of Wall Street," which was alleg-edly able to transform, by magic, risky real estate securities into a set of safe securities. They put into the cruse papers that were contaminated by dirt and received gilt-edged securities, called "subprime," in return. In this manner, grasshoppers could afford to enjoy consumption beyond their means by bor-rowing from Country B.
>
> Ants in Country B worked hard to leave estates to their off-spring. They were so pressed to increase their savings that they even bought the securities produced by the financial engineering of Country A.
>
> Suddenly, it was discovered that the magic of the Wall Street cruse was a fake. The processed securities, once seemingly gilt-edged, turned out to be

Table 11.1 Academic ranking top 100 of world universities in 2008 by Shanghai Jiaotong University, China

World rank	Natural science and mathematics (SCI)	World rank	Engineering/ technology and computer science (ENG)	World rank	Life and agricultural science (LIFE)	World rank	Clinical medicine and pharmacy (MED)	World rank	Social science (SOC)
1 (1)	Harvard University	1 (5)	Massachusetts Institute of Technology (MIT)	1 (1)	Harvard University	1 (1)	Harvard University	1 (1)	Harvard University
2 (3)	University of California, Berkeley	2 (2)	Stanford University	2 (5)	Massachusetts Institute of Technology (MIT)	2 (18)	University of California, San Francisco	2 (9)	University of Chicago
3 (8)	Princeton University	3 (26)	University of Illinois, Urbana Champaign	3 (18)	University of California, San Francisco	3 (16)	University of Washington, Seattle	3 (7)	Columbia University
4 (6)	California Institute of Technology	4 (3)	University of California, Berkeley	4 (16)	University of Washington, Seattle	4 (19)	Johns Hopkins University	4 (2)	Stanford University
5 (4)	University of Cambridge	5 (21)	University of Michigan, Ann Arbor	5 (2)	Stanford University	5 (7)	Columbia University	5 (3)	University of California, Berkeley

Asian Countries

8 (20) Tokyo University	19 (76) Tohoku University	28 (22) Kyoto University	38 (22) Kyoto University	51–76 (203–304) Hong Kong University of Science and Technology
16 (22) Kyoto University	23 (22) Kyoto University	30 (20) Tokyo University	48 (20) Tokyo University	77–107 (102–150) National University of Singapore
35 (76) Tohoku University	29 (102–150) National University of Singapore	51–75 (67) Osaka University		
47 (99) Tokyo Institute of Technology	29 (99) Tokyo Institute of Technology			
52–76 (67) Osaka University.	40 (203–304) Hong Kong University of Science and Technology			

Source: Shanghai Jiao Tong University (http://ed.sjtu.edu.cn/ARWU-FIELD2008.htm, April 24, 2009).

Note
The numbers in parentheses are the rankings in 2007.

dirt-edged. Moreover, they were all labeled as AAA securities, and there was no way to distinguish between securities that contained risky elements and those that did not.

What could grasshoppers do under these circumstances? And, furthermore, what could ants do?

In the United States, a country of grasshoppers, the wealth they thought they owned disappeared suddenly. The loss in the value of their assets required a reduction in consumption and investment, an improvement in the current account while the financial system needed restructuring.

Country B, a country of ants, which may represent China or Japan, will also be seriously affected. If US citizens suddenly reduce spending, then exports from China or Japan will substantially decrease. Through this process, China and Japan will share some of the burden that was caused by the United States.

It is important to note that when the subprime lending began in the United States, the Japanese and Chinese systems were functioning normally. The fundamentals in these countries were basically sound when the crisis started, except that they had invested heavily in the financial assets of the United States. In the asset market dimension, the epicenter of the earthquake was in the United States, and its waves were immediately transmitted to foreign asset markets as well as to the currency markets. The sudden disruptions in international asset markets then also caused declines in the flow activities, such as exports, output, and finally in labor markets the world over.

Therefore, the present difficulties were not so much caused by structural problems in the domestic markets of Country B as by triggers from the United States and European financial markets. Price movements in the stock market are abrupt and extremely volatile, while those in the commodity flow markets are slow. Indeed we will argue that the lack of appropriate monetary policies has been a critical factor in keeping Japan in a state of stagnation that has continued for nearly two decades.

Japan's macroeconomic policy stance has exhibited an extreme emphasis on fiscal economic stimuli rather than monetary stimuli. Even scholars in macroeconomics tend to neglect the role of monetary policy that seems to be crucially needed to cope with shocks in asset markets abroad, as in the current crisis. In fact, it is the lack of appropriate monetary policies that should share the blame. It is against the prescription of the policy mix under flexible exchange rates according to the Mundell–Fleming framework.

Let us compare the reaction of some monetary authorities of major countries to illustrate the behavior of the BOJ after the Lehman crisis.

The US Federal Reserve Board (FRB) as well as the Bank of England (BOE) instituted an extremely expansionary monetary policy after the onset of the crisis. The Bank of Japan (BOJ), on the other hand, continued with a rather austere monetary policy. The yen exchange rate soared and Japanese industries had to cope with enhanced export as well as import competition.

The enclosed graphs on global monetary experiences after the sub-prime crisis make a case in point. Measuring the degree of monetary ease by the

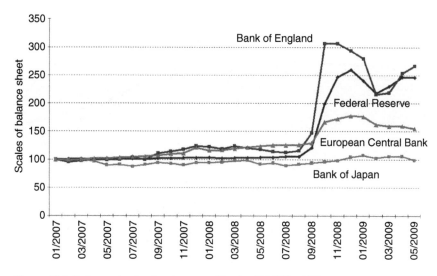

Figure 11.1 Balance sheets of major central banks (1/2007 = 100).

magnitude of the Central Bank's assets, Figure 11.1 contrasts the expansionary monetary policies of the FRB and the BOE with the conservative one of the BOJ. Partly because of these differences, within a half year of Lehman's epic demise, the real exchange rate of the yen appreciated nearly 30 percent (Figure 11.2). Both export and import competing sectors in Japan faced the higher hurdles of an appreciated yen. Industrial production in Japan fell about 30 percent as compared with the 10 percent fall in US industrial production (Figure 11.3).

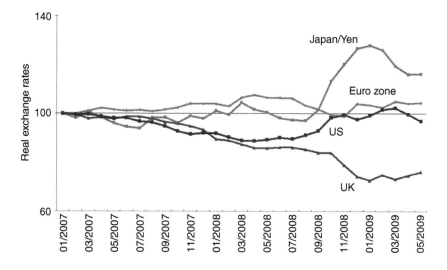

Figure 11.2 Real exchange rates (1–2007 = 100) (source: BIS).

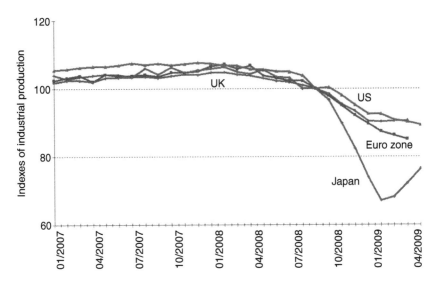

Figure 11.3 Industrial production (2008–2009 = 100) (source: Bloomberg Terminal).

According to standard macroeconomics, a government should expand monetary policy to counteract the reduced external demand caused by the sub-prime
crisis abroad. Expansionary monetary policy would have stimulated not only
domestic demand by lowering interest rates or easing credit conditions, but
would also have supported export demand by forestalling the appreciation of the
home currency. Somehow, the BOJ did not follow this convention. Japan's monetary policy seems indeed to have been conducted in an opposite direction, i.e.,
against the above standard policy prescription (Bernanke 2000; Ito and Mishkin
2005, Hamada and Okada 2009).

There are two points to note in order to understand recent monetary policies
in Japan. First, the open market (purchase) operation is a well known instrument
for monetary expansion. Under the zero or near zero interest situation which prevailed in Japan for a substantial period, this conventional open market operation
partly lost its effect because government short-term securities are almost perfect
substitutes for cash. This is the reason for the fact that unconventional policies
were adopted to rescue the Japanese economy from its lost decade. For example,
the BOJ attempted to buy a certain volume of common stocks and long term
public bonds. Moreover, the Ministry of Finance (MOF) engaged in a huge
exchange intervention, called the "Great Intervention" by John Taylor. The BOJ
sometimes tried to engage in these unconventional operations in the past, but the
continuing deflation clearly demonstrated that the monetary policy of the BOJ
was far short of what was needed.

Second, it is often believed, particularly by the BOJ, that monetary expansion
or interest rate reduction on the part of Japan helps the United States when the
United States is suffering from recession. But this is utterly wrong!

We assume that most readers will agree with the following:

1   A lower rate of interest in the home country normally depreciates the home currency, and appreciates the foreign currency.
2   If inertia exists in wages and prices, then the appreciation of the foreign currency exerts an unfavorable effect on employment and output in the foreign country.

The combination of these two statements clearly implies that the United States will suffer when Japan adopts a policy of lower interest rates or monetary expansion. With respect to fiscal expansion under flexible rates the conventional view is correct: expansion in the home country will help the foreign country in recession.

Monetary expansion, on the other hand, has a negative effect on the income of the other country. Does this process not yield a beggar-thy-neighbor outcome? In the short run, the answer is in the affirmative. It is possible for other countries, however, to counteract this by expanding their monetary policy. As was shown by Hamada and Okada (2009), the end of these reactions and counter reactions will end in a Nash equilibrium of monetary policy that is Pareto optimal for the whole world. The logic is the same as that used by Eichengreen and Sachs (1984), i.e., that competitive devaluations under the gold standard would achieve a Pareto optimum for the world.

In short, a long deflation in Japan clearly indicates that the money supply was insufficient to keep prices stable. Under the zero-interest policy situation, not only conventional open market operations but also unconventional operations with the purchase of long term bonds and other private assets should have been used. Moreover, a foreign currency intervention as done by Zenbei Mizoguchi could have been attempted.

Without appropriate monetary expansion or exchange intervention the real exchange rate appreciated, accompanied by sluggish commodity prices. This yen appreciation created large hurdles for export and import competing industries and lowered Japan's actual growth trajectory even more than its long run real growth potential that has been the main subject of this volume.

4 Legacies and lessons

Japan represents a pioneer in successful economic development based on the importation of technology and managerial knowhow from the more advanced countries. In its modern history it can count on not only a number of successes, but also the experience of some mistakes, particularly the failure of reforms of once successful institutions and systems. This overall experience can be seen as a potential gold mine for those developing economies which attempt to grow following the Japanese model of development. However, the distinction between what should be imitated and what should be avoided cannot be made easily unless the Japanese post-war development experience is carefully reviewed, theoretically analyzed, and properly assessed. This book represents an attempt by Japanese economists and economists interested in the Japanese economy to excavate that gold mine and separate the precious metal from "fools' gold." We believe that the selective time-limited protection of infant industries, the development of industrial clusters, the establishment of systems conducive to investment in firm-specific human capital, the management design of companies to coordinate activities, the timely deployment of the main bank system, and the promotion of education systems, including vocational schools, are useful legacies of the Japanese model of economic development which developing countries may be able to profit from.

Economists must play a role in the reform process in Japan. But unfortunately the usefulness of economics is often underestimated by both political leaders and the general public. It is true that economics has sometimes been subject to political ideology. During the Cold War, studies which advocated government market interventions tended to be underrated, one example being the study of infant industry protection. In the post-Cold War era the research environment for economists for engaging in truly scientific research, free from ideological bias, became much more favorable. Also there has been considerable methodological progress and theoretical advancement in economics, as well as increasing collaboration between natural scientists and economists. Consequently, it is no exaggeration to argue that the time is now ripe for economists to make their contribution to the re-engineering of the economic and social systems in Japan.

The recent long term stagnation of the Japanese economy, alone among the major countries of the world, is prima facie evidence that the growth of the Japanese economy has been constrained by its unique economic system. We believe that the failure to reform a once highly successful system has resulted in Japan becoming only the third most affluent country in Asia, following Singapore and Hong Kong. We also believe that once we identify the sources of that economic stagnation and provide appropriate prescriptions for change, we can help the Japanese economy redirect its future growth trajectory from continued stagnation to sustained growth.

Based on our studies in this volume, we would like to make the following policy recommendations: (*a*) increased governmental support for new high-tech industries, (*b*) promotion of the collaboration between advanced public and private research organizations and private enterprises, (*c*) promotion of direct financial systems to support innovative entrepreneurs, and (*d*) reform of the educational system in the high schools, which should provide training for generating innovative ideas in the universities, including the graduate schools, so as to make them truly competitive internationally. As a result of such reforms Japan as a leading member of a globalizing world should be able to afford to play a leading role in supporting the development of poor economies, the eradication of poverty, and enhanced world security.

What are the most promising new industries that Japan should attempt to develop? Aside from bio, fuel cell engine, nano-technology, and new medical treatment using ES cells, there must surely be other areas of high potential.

Although markets can be expected to sort out the wheat from the chaff in terms of promising and non-promising industries, the government must play a role where important externalities are present. In order to develop appropriate strategies, we need to focus on the development of truly promising industries, and doing so requires the input of scientists, economists, and business leaders. In order to ensure the development of new industries, economists have to devise the proper incentive mechanisms to supplement the function of the private asset market system during this post-subprime loan period.

It must be emphasized that it was relatively easy to identify and nurture the promising industries during the catch-up process precisely because it was a matter of imitating existing industries abroad. Indeed, the Ministry of Trade and Industry played a substantive role in the promotion of a variety of new industries in the course of post-war Japanese economic development. In the current new era of a domestic innovation-oriented economy, the choice set of promising industries is large but relatively unclear. It is therefore a mistake to imply that the government should take a leading role in the development of specific new industries, as it does not possess the relevant information or expertise. Nor should infant industry protection be permanent. It is scientists and business leaders who have better knowledge of what the new promising industries might be. Their ideas must be incorporated into the country's industrial development policies and it is economists who must design appropriate support policies. In other words, in order to transform the Japanese economy from imitation-based to innovation-led systems, the mobilization of a wide range of knowledge and insights possessed by leaders in the scientific and business communities is indispensable. The establishment of institutions facilitating such mobilization would be key. Moreover, by doing so, we would be able to demonstrate to developing countries which endeavor to grow, based on technological and managerial catch-up, how an imitation-based economy can be transformed into an innovation-led economy over time.

It is hard to think of a country in the world that received more benefits from the development of other countries than Japan. The development of Asian countries and the maintenance of a stable political order in Asia confers large benefits on Japan. At the same time, the increasing prosperity of resource-rich Latin American, African, and Central Asian countries yields a variety of benefits for Japan. The Japanese development experience, if carefully assessed by follower countries, can prove instrumental in yielding large benefits to all the parties.

References

Bernanke, Ben (2000) "The Macroeconomics of the Great Depression: A Comparative Approach," *Essays on the Great Depression*, Princeton, NJ: Princeton University Press, pp. 5–37.

Coyle, D. (2007) *The Soulful Science: What Economists Really Do and Why It Matters*, Princeton, NJ: Princeton University Press.

Eichengreen, Barry and Sachs, Jeffrey (1985) "Exchange Rates and Economic Recovery in the 1930s," *Journal of Economic History*, 45, pp. 925–946.

Glaeser, E.L., La Porta, R., Lopez-De-Silanes, F., and Shliefer, A. (2004) "Do Institutions Cause Growth?" *Journal of Economic Growth*, 9, pp. 271–303.

Hamada, Koichi and Okada, Yasushi (2009) "Monetary and International Factors Behind Japan's Lost Decade," *Journal of Japanese and International Economies,* 23, pp. 200–219.

Ito, Takatoshi and Mishkin, Frederic (2005) "Monetary Policy in Japan: Problems and Solutions," in T. Ito, H. Patrick, and D.E. Weinstein (eds.), *Reviving Japan's Economy: Problems and Prescriptions*, Cambridge, MA: MIT Press.

Levin, R. (2006) "World of Knowledge," *Newsweek*, August 21/ 28, 2006.

Newsweek (2006), "The Global Top Ten … And Some Next-Best Picks," *Newsweek*, August 21/ 28, 2006.

Index

9/11 173

Abe, M. & H. 129
abusive dismissal doctrine 77–81, 87–8;
    burden of proof 86; economic dismissal
    doctrine 83; leading cases 81–4; recent
    rulings 84–6
Adams, R. 184
Adult Schools 122–4, 129
Africa, cluster-based industrial
    development 26–9
agriculture 126–7
aid agencies 177–8; consolidation of
    188–9
Akerlof, G.A. 50
Akoten, J. 25, 29
Allen, F. 40, 42, 51
Almeida, H. 44
Alti, A. 44
Aoki, M. 40, 47
Arikawa, Y. 40, 41, 44, 45, 46, 48, 51
arm's-length finance 41–3
Asia: cluster-based industrial development
    26–9; foreign aid 167, 177, 186–7; see
    also East Asia
Asian financial crisis 172–3, 176, 183
Assembly-line production 94–5
Association of Southeast Asian Nations
    (ASEAN) 156–7; Regional Forum
    (ARF) 157
asymmetric information problems 43
automobile design engineers 102–3
automobile industry: dawn of 15–17;
    interaction between policies and
    behavior of manufacturers 17–21;
    matrix-form of organizational
    management 96–8, 101–3;
    organizational complementarity 105–7;
    production management 94; quality
    control 92–3

Automobile Manufacturing Enterprise
    Law (1936) 16, 19, 20, 21, 22

Baigan, Ishida 105
bail-outs 47–50
Bairoch, P. 11
Bangladesh, industrial development 37
Bank of England (BOE) 202, 203
Bank of Japan (BOJ) 199, 202–5
"bank-centered" financial system 40–51
Basel Accord 48
Beason, R. 13
Becker, G. 76
Bernanke, Ben 204
Besanko, D. 97
best practice 104–5
Bingo, industrial clusters 26–7, 32–4
Bognanno, M. 77
Boyer, Mark A. 138–9
burden-sharing 138–9, 142–6, 167, 190
business history see corporate progress

Caballero, R. 49
capital stock analysis, automobile industry
    19–21
capitalism, transition of 67
case law 77, 78–9, 81–6, 87
central banks, balance sheets 202–3
Central Motor Co. 93
Chang, H.-J. 11, 22
Charlton, A. 13
"checkbook diplomacy" 135, 140
chemical industry, mutual co-working
    103
China: defense spending 147, 151;
    development assistance 154; economic
    growth 4–5; industrial development
    26–8, 36; Japanese aid to 154; military
    power 147, 151–4
Civil Code (Article 1) 81; (Article 627) 78

cluster-based industrial development:
economic implications of 35–7;
endogenous model of 29–32; examples
of 32–5; lessons from 193; study sites in
Asia and Africa 26–9
co-working 103–5, 106; historical origins
105
Coase theorem 143
Cold War: aid experiences 166–72;
security strategy 142–6
collaborative working methods 96–103
collective disputes 85–6, 87
Communist bloc, threat from 142–6
comparative advantage 11–12
Comprehensive Poverty Reduction and
Growth Strategy (CPRGS) 186–7, 190
compulsory education 122, 123
Confucian ideology 115
contractual theory of the firm 59, 64
convergence hypothesis 12
corporate nominalism 59–60, 66–7, 68–9;
making of 60–1
corporate progress: "complementarity"
crossing the ocean 105–7; division and
cooperation of labor 103–5; ideas and
application of production management
94–6; ideas and practices of quality
control 92–3; implications of
observations 107–8; interview records
as contemporary economic history
materials 91–2; matrix-form of
organizational management and its
variations 96–103
corporate realism 59–60, 66–7, 68–9, 70
corporate restructuring 48–9
corporate systems: corporate personality
controversy and comparative corporate
system 59–60; definitions of 57–9; future
of 69–70; and human capital 68–9;
lessons from 194; "nominalistic"
corporations 60–1; "realistic"
corporations 61–4; sources of inefficiency
in 66–7; traditions and corporate systems
64–6; transition from industrial capitalism
to post-industrial capitalism 67; varieties
of corporate systems 54–7
costs: abusive dismissal doctrine 77–8;
relationship finance 41, 47–9
credit contraction 49–50
cross-shareholdings 63–5, 70
Cusumano, M.A. 17

DAT Motors: and infant industry policy
17–19; profitability 20–1

Datsun 18–19, 20
De Long, J.B. 12
Deming Prize 92–3, 100
demography, changes in 117
Denso, development philosophy 101–2
developing countries, cluster-based
industrial development: endogenous
development model 29–32; examples of
cluster-based development 32–5;
implications of 35–7; study sites in Asia
and Africa 26–9
Development Bank of Japan 13, 15
development loans/grants 168, 169, 173,
174–5
development philosophy 101–2
direct transactions 33
dismissal regulation: legal systems,
economic growth and human capital
investment 74–5; lessons from 194–5;
role of legal systems in labour market
75–7
distribution awareness 95–6
division of labor 35–6, 103–5
dominant shareholders 60–1, 62
"Dutch disease" 188

East Asia, relevance of "Yoshida
Doctrine" 151–9
East Asian "miracle" 36, 116–18, 120
economic catch-up: Japan v. US 119–24;
Japan's long-term stagnation after
completing 130–1; Korea v. US 124–6;
overview of process of 116–18; Taiwan
v. US 126–9
economic development: comparison of
experiences 2–5; from imitation-based
to innovation-led economy 193–7;
legacies and lessons 205–7; potential
from higher education system 197–9
economic reform, recommendations for
206–7
economic structure, changes in 85
economies of scale 12, 13, 21, 36, 120–1,
128–9
economists, role in reform process 206
economy, implications of cluster-based
industrial development 35–7
education: Dokō Toshio's method of
99–100; enterprise managers 32–3;
implications of time lag between
educational and economic catch-up
129–30; Japan's catch-up with US
119–24; Korea's catch-up with US
124–6; Latin American immigrants 185;

lessons from 195; long-term stagnation after completion of catch-up growth 130–1; measuring average level of 113–16; potential from 197–9; process of economic catch-up 116–18; Taiwan's catch-up with US 126–9

Eichengreen, Barry 205

empirical support, infant industry policy 13–14

"employee-oriented model" 54, 55–7, 64, 69–70

endogenous model, cluster-based industrial development 29–32

engineer-led industries 28–9

engineers, cooperation with production workers 97–8, 100–1, 102–3, 104–5

entrepreneurial ability 32

"eruption phase", clusters 32

Ethiopia, industrial development 34–6

Europe: corporate systems 54–5; wool industry 74–5

evolutionary theory of the firm 59, 64

expansion phase, clusters 29–30, 34, 36–7

expansionary monetary policy 204–5

Export–Import Bank of Japan (JEXIM) 177

externalities 12, 22

Far Eastern Treaty Organization (FETO) 137

Fazzari, S.M. 43, 44

financial constraints 40, 41, 43–7, 50, 193–4

financial crisis and financial systems 49–50

financial disclosure 42

financial systems: arm's-length and relationship finance 41–3; benefits of relationship finance 43–7; cost of relationship finance 47–9; and financial crisis 49–50; lessons from 193–4

Ford 16, 17, 18, 19, 21, 22, 105–7

foreign aid: during Cold War 166–72; as economic diplomacy 154–5; future suggestions 188–90; lessons from 196; and NGOs 178–82; and other associated flows to developing countries 182–5; post-Cold War 172–8; searching for new model of foreign capital flows 185–8

Foreign Assistance Act (1961), US 176

Foreign Assistance Appropriations Act (1986), US 180

foreign capital flows, new model of 185–8

foreign direct investment (FDI) 178, 183–4, 187

free-rider problem 42, 138–42, 143, 145–6, 151, 154, 160

frontier industries 4

Fukami, S. 112, 114, 115, 116, 117, 118, 128

Fukuda, S. 49

Gale, D. 40, 42, 51

game theoretic approach, security strategy 142–50; reaction curves and pay-off matrix 161–3

Gan, J. 49

garment industry 26–9, 32, 36–7

gender and education 113–16, 123, 128

General Survey on Working Conditions 85

genkyoki units, MITI 98

Germany, re-armament 159

Gershenkron, A. 2

Gibson, M. 49

global financial crisis, monetary policy during 199–205

global perspective, economic development 2–5

GM 16, 17, 18, 21, 22, 105–7

Godo, Y. 2, 33, 112, 114, 115, 116, 117, 118, 121, 123, 124, 125, 126, 128

Goto, A. 15

graduate training 4

grass-roots NGOs 181–2

gross domestic product (GDP) 3, 5, 120, 125–7, 198

Grossman, S. 42

growth theory 12

Gulf War (1991) 135, 140, 154

Hamada, K. 142, 204, 205

Hansmann, Henry 56

Hara, M. 85

Hart, O. 42

Hashimoto, M. 77

Hashimoto, Masujiro 17–18

Hatano, S. 135

Hausmann, R. 12

Hayami, Y. 2, 33, 123, 124

Hemmer, C. 156

high-growth period, financial system during 40–51

Hirasawa, J. 80, 82, 83, 84

Hirata, K. 181, 182

Hiroshima Glass Kogyo Co. 83

hold-up problem 66–7, 69

"holding" corporations 61–2

Honda Motor Co. 14–15, 34
Hong Kong University of Science and
    Technology 198
Hong Kong, economic growth 4–5
Hoshi, T. 40, 43, 44, 47–8
Hoshino, T. 157
Hubbard, R.G. 43, 44
human capital 69–70; and higher education
    197–9; inalienability of 68–9;
    investment in 74–7; knowledge-based
    67, 68; organisation-specific 66–7, 68–9
human resource practices 76, 85
humanitarian assistance 180
Hummel, H. 159

Ichikawa v. Nihon Shokuen Seizo Co. 81
"idealist" view, security strategy 135–7,
    159–60
Iimi, A. 174
Ikeda, Hayato 138
Ikeo, K. 42
imitation phase, clusters 29–31
imitation-based economy 193–7
immigrants 184–5, 190
Inada, J. 155
industrial capitalism 68; transition from 67
industrial production 203–4
industrial structure, changes in 117
industrial tribunals 85–6
industrialization 120–2, 127
inefficiency, corporate organizations 66–7
infant industry protection policy:
    automobile industry 14–21; case for
    11–14; lessons from 193
information sharing 99–105
infrastructure investments 186, 187
innovation *see* cluster-based industrial
    development
innovation-led economy 193–7
Inter-American Development Bank 185
interest rates 204–5
International Financial Institutions (IFIs),
    aid from 174–5, 178–9, 182
International Monetary Fund (IMF),
    Structural Adjustment Facility (SAF) 10
International Volunteer Savings Scheme
    182
interventionist aid 170–1, 173
interview records 91–2
investment: and financial systems 43–4,
    46, 47–8, 49, 50–1; in human capital 37,
    74–6, 77, 87–8, 120, 131; infrastructure
    170–1, 174–5, 186–7; in physical capital
    120; return on 55; sectoral preferences

184; *see also* foreign direct investment
    (FDI)
Irwin, D.A. 13, 14
Ishii, N. 186
Ishikawa Gasket Co. Ltd. 95, 108
Ishikawajima Heavy Industries (IHI)
    99–100
Ito, T. 49, 50, 204
Itoh, M. 15
Ivashina, V. 49
Iwama, Y. 159

Jacoby, S. 56
Japan Bank for International Cooperation
    (JBIC) 177
Japan International Cooperation Agency
    (JICA) 25, 175, 182, 186–7; Research
    Institute 177–8; "Study on the Economic
    Development Policy in the Transition
    towards a Market-Oriented Economy in
    the Socialist Republic of Vietnam" 186
Japan of Cooperation Volunteers (JOCV)
    181
Japan–Vietnam Joint Initiative 187
Japanese NGO Center for International
    Cooperation (JANIC) 181
Jensen, M. 59
Jitsuyo Motors 18
Johnson, C. 9–10
joint ventures 105–7
"just in time" 94

Kadokawa Bunka Shinko Zaidan 84
Kambayashi, R. 77, 80, 82, 83, 84, 86, 87
Kang, J. 40, 48
Kaplan, S. 43–4
Kashyap, A. 44
Katada, S.N. 155
Kato, T. 77
Katzenstein, P.J. 156
Kazuo, Koike 106
Keiretsu firms 43
Kimura, M. 129
Kitano, M. 186
knowledge spillovers 13
knowledge-based human capital 67, 68–9
Kochi Hoso Co. 81–2
Kohama, H. 121
Koike, K. 77
Komiya, R. 10
Korea: economic catch-up process 116–18;
    economic growth 4–5; economic and
    educational catch-up with US 124–6;
    education level 113–16

Kosaka. M. 137
Kraakman, Reinier 56
Krugman, P.R. 9, 14, 25
Kwaishinsha Automobile Factory: and
    infant industry policy 17–19;
    profitability 20–1

Labor Lawyers Association of Japan 84
labor market, role of legal systems 75–7
labor productivity 116–17
Labor Standards Act 87: (Article 32) 77;
    (Article 19) 78; (Article 20) 78; (Article
    18–2) 84–6
Labor Union Act: (Article 7) 78, 83
labor–management relations 83–4
large firms 41, 44
Latin American immigrants 184–5
Lau, L.J. 120
Law Review Committee, MITI 98–9
Lawrence, R.Z. 13
legal systems *see* dismissal regulation
"Lego method" 104–5, 106
Levin, Richard 197
limited arming, pre-emptive strategy of
    142–50
List, Friedrich 11
loan contracts 75–6
local ownership, aid projects 187–8
long-term employment 77
low-quality products 31
low-voltage electric machinery industry 29

McGinn, N.F. 129
Machine Industry Law (1956) 15
machine tool industry 28–9
macroeconomic efficiency 116–17
"main bank" system *see* "bank-centered"
    financial system
Majluf, N. 43
manufacturers' behavior, automobile
    industry 17–21
market failure 6, 12, 14
market-based financial system 40
market-oriented development 10, 22,
    171–2, 187
Marshall Aid 180
Marshall, A. 25–6
Matrix-form of organizational
    management 96–103
Meckling, W. 59
merchant-led industries 28–31
Merton, R.C. 41–2
Military Automobile Subsidizing Law
    (1918) 16, 18, 20

military education 122, 123–4
military expenditure 136, 139, 143, 145,
    147, 150, 151–4, 156
"military style heavy industrialization"
    120–2
Millennium Challenge Corporation (MCC)
    173–4, 176, 187
Millennium Development Goals (MDGs)
    175, 190
Ministry of Economy, Trade, and Industry
    (METI) 177–8
Ministry of Education 198
Ministry of Finance 14, 177–8, 204
Ministry of Foreign Affairs (MOFA) 157,
    175, 177, 178, 182, 189
Ministry of International Trade and
    Industry (MITI) 9–10, 14–15;
    management style 98–9
Mishkin, Frederic 204
Miwa, Y. 10
Miyajima, H. 41, 48, 50
Mizoguchi, T. 126
monetary policy 199–205
Moon, D. 117
moral hazard problem 48, 66–7, 69
Morishima, M. 77
motorcycle industry 28, 34
Mottaleb, K.A. 26, 29, 37
multilateral security framework 56–8
Muramatsu, K. 86, 87
Mutoh, H. 15
mutually holding corporations 63–4
Myers, S. 43

Nadvi, K. 25
Nagai, Y. 140
Nakajima, S. 138
Nakamura, S. 15, 16
Nam, V.H. 25
Nanami, A. 181
Nash equilibrium 145, 146, 148, 161–3, 205
National Defense Program Outline
    (NDPO) (2004) 158–9
National Science Foundation 197
National Security Strategy (NSS), US 151,
    173
National Westminster Bank 84
natural sciences 198–9
neoclassical growth theory 12
New United Motor Manufacturing Inc.
    (NUMMI) 105–7
Nippon Shokubai Co. Ltd. 103
Nissan Motors 16, 22; and infant industry
    policy 17–19; profitability 20–1

no-fault layoffs 79–81, 82
non-governmental organizations (NGOs) and aid 178–82
North Atlantic Treaty Organisation (NATO) 137, 143, 144, 156, 159
North, D. 74–5, 86

Obstfeld, M. 9, 14
Odagiri, H. 15
Official Development Assistance (ODA): Charter 155, 175, 177; *see also* foreign aid
Ogawa, K. 42
Ogawa, S. 96
Ohashi, H. 13
Ohkawa, K. 2, 20
Ojima, Y. 174
Okada, Yasushi 204, 205
Okuda, K. 105
Okuno, H. 85
Olson, M. 143
on-the-job training (OJT) 76, 85, 99
"one investment produces another investment" 120
Ono, A. 43
open market (purchase) operations 204
open-ended labor contracts 78, 85
oral history (OH) records 91–2
Organisation for Economic Co-operation and Development (OECD) 172, 189; Development Assistance Committee 169
Organization for Security and Cooperation in Europe (OSCE) 157
organizational complementarity 105–7
organizational management: automobile design engineers 102–3; clashes of vertical and horizontal axes 96–8; development philosophy 101–2; education methods 99–100; matrix-form, MITI style 98–9; mutual co-working 103–5; technical information sharing 100–1
organizational tension/friction 103–5
organization-specific human capital 66–7; importance of 68–9
Otsuka, K. 1–2, 12, 25–6, 28–9, 33, 37
Overseas Economic Cooperation Fund (OECF) 171, 177
ownership structure, corporations 57–64

Page, J. 184
Pareto efficiency 145, 148
Pareto optimality 205
Paris Declaration on Aid Effectiveness 179, 188, 189

Park Chong-hui 125, 129
partnership firms 57, 58
Peace Constitution 136, 137, 138, 142, 145, 154, 158, 159, 160
peace dividend 135, 136, 154, 156
peacekeeping interventions 158–9
Peek, J. 40, 48
per capita GDP 116–17, 119–29
per capita income 3–5
Petersen, B.C. 43, 44
Petersen, M.A. 48
physical capital 68–9, 120
physical capital–labor ratio 116–17, 119–29
"picking winners" problem 14
Pinkowitz, L. 44, 45
Piore, M.J. 25
political influence, and infant industry policy 14
Population Census 85
Porter, M.E. 25
Post-Cold War period: aid experiences 172–8; security strategy 147–59
post–industrial capitalism 68–70; transition to 67
Poverty Reduction Strategy Credits (PRSCs) 175
Poverty Reduction Strategy Papers (PRSPs) 173, 175, 186–8, 190
pre-emptive light arms announcement 147–50
pre-emptive security strategy 142–50
Presidential Advisory Committee on Voluntary Foreign Aid, US 180
primary education 121, 125, 130–1
principal-agent model 14
printed circuit-board (PCB) industry 28, 29
private capital flows 182–5, 189–90
private charitable giving 178–80, 181–2
production management, ideas and application 94–6
productivity-enhancing information 76–7
profitability, automobile industry 19–21
project aid 168–9, 174–5, 186–7
property rights 58
protectionism 22
public–private partnerships, aid 179–80
"pull system" 94
Pyo, H. 117
pyramidal ownership system 61–2

quality control (QC), circles 76; ideas and practices 92–3, 100, 107 quality improvement phase, clusters 29–30, 32–4, 36–7

Raisian, J. 77
Rajan, R.G. 48
Ramseyer, M.J. 10
Ranis, G. 14
re-armament, fears of 158–9
real exchange rates 203
"realist" view security strategy 135–7, 151, 159–60
regional conflicts 158–9
relationship finance 41–3; benefits of 43–7; cost of 47–9; and financial crises 49–50
remittances 183, 184–5, 189–90
reparations program 167
"request-based" aid 170–1
research and development (R&D) 51, 103, 100–1, 108, 181
research, universities 197–8
retail trade 95–6
Ricardo, David 12
Rix, A. 154
Rodrik, D. 10, 12, 14, 22
Rosengren, E. 40, 48
Rosovsky, H. 2
Ruan, J. 25
rural industrialisation 28, 33

Sabel, C.F. 25
Sachs, Jeffrey 205
Samuelson, Paul 22
Saotome, M. 182
Sasaki, Y. 49, 50
Sato, S. 135
Saxenian, A. 25
Scharfstein, D. 49
Schmitz, H. 25
Schumpeter, Joseph A. 31, 36, 67
scientist-led industries 37
"screening effect", education 129–30
secondary education 121, 122, 123–4, 125, 128, 130–1
sectoral allocation, aid 174–5
security dependence 135, 137–9
security policy *see* "Yoshida doctrine"
security regionalism 156–9
Self-Defense Forces (SDF) 158–9, 161
"self-help" aid 170–2
self-owning corporations 62
Seven-Eleven Japan 95–6
Shafiqul, I. 140
Shanghai Jiaotong University 198

share repurchases 62
"shareholder-oriented model" 54, 55–7, 64–6
Shiller, R. 50
Shimazaki v. Toyo Sanso 79, 82–3
Shivdasani, A. 48
Shleifer, A. 6
shoe industry 32, 34, 36
Singapore National University 198
Singapore: economic growth 4–5; education 131
single proprietorship firms 57, 58
"single-product flow with workload equalization" 94–5
small and medium sized enterprises (SMEs) 43, 49, 92, 128
Smith, Adam 103–5
social sciences 198–9
Sonobe, T. 12, 25, 26, 28, 29, 32, 35, 36, 37
Sontoku, Ninomiya 105
Southeast Asia Treaty Organization (SEATO) 137
spin-offs 30–3
stagnation, following completion of catch-up growth 130–1
"standardized tasks" 94
Stiglitz, J.E. 13, 22
"stoppable lines" 95
strategic complements 147–50
strategic rationale, foreign aid 167, 173, 174, 176–7, 178, 189
strategic substitutes, world of 142–6
structural adjustment programs 10, 14, 166, 168, 173, 175, 186
Stulz, R. 40
subprime lending crisis 199–205
subsidies, automobile industry 15, 16, 18, 20–1
Sumitomo Electric Industries 108; quality control 93; technical information sharing 100–1
Sumitomo group 64
Summit 96
Sunaga, K. 174
"supermarket method" 94
Supreme Court 79, 82
Survey on Labor Disputes 85

Taiwan: economic catch-up process 116–18; economic growth 4–5; educational and economic catch-up with US 126–9; education level 112–32; industrial development 28–9, 37

Tanaka, K. 56, 57
Tanigaki, S. 175
Tax Act (1936), US 179–80
tax code 181
Taylor, C.F. 34
technical information sharing 100–1
technology development, Denso 101–2
technology transfer 2, 37
technology-borrowing 128–9, 130–1
terrorism and foreign aid 189
tertiary education 121–2, 125, 126, 128,
  130–1
theoretical framework of aid 170–2
theoretical support infant industry policy
  11–12
"thirds payment system" 105
Tho, T.V. 187
Thomas, R. 74–5, 86
tied aid 168, 169, 173–4, 177, 186, 187–8
Tobata Casting 18
Tocqueville, Alexis de 179
Toshio, Dokō 99–100
Tokyo Automobile Industries Co. 16
Tokyo District Court 84–6, 87
Tokyo High Court 79, 82
Tokyo Stock Exchange (TSE) 44–5
Toyoda Automatic Loom Works 19
Toyoda, Eiji 92–3, 94
Toyota Motor Corporation 16, 22, 57;
  clashes of vertical and horizontal
  management axes 96–8; co-working
  104; design engineers 102–3; and infant
  industry policy 19; quality control 92–3
Toyota Production System (TPS) 94–5,
  106–8
traditions and corporate systems 64–6
training, industry 99–100
transaction costs 35, 59, 185, 190, 193,
  196

Uchida, H. 42
UK: economic growth 3; legal system
  74–5; monetary policy 202–3; working
  practices 104
Umemura, M. 126
union shop agreements 81, 82
United Autoworkers Union (UAW) 106
University of Tokyo 198
University Order (1915) 121
university rankings 198
university research 197–8
US Agency for International Development
  (USAID) 176, 178, 180–1, 189
US Department of Defense 188–9; "Report

on Allied Contribution to Common
  Defense" reports 139, 140–1
US Federal Reserve Board (FRB) 202, 203
US Peace Corps 180, 181
US: aid experiences 166–85; automobile
  industry 16, 105–7; Cold War security
  142–6; corporate system 54–6, 59–60,
  61, 64–6; defense spending 151;
  economic catch-up process 116–18;
  economic crises 69; economic growth
  3–4; economic and educational catch-up
  with Japan 119–24; economic and
  educational catch-up with Korea 124–6;
  economic and educational catch-up with
  Taiwan 126–9; education 113–16,
  121–2; employment legislation 77;
  foreign aid 177–90; industrial policy 10,
  11; Japan's security dependence on 135,
  137–9; monetary policy 202–3;
  peacekeeping interventions 158; post-
  Cold War security 147–50, 156–8;
  relationship finance 43; subprime
  lending crisis 199–205; universities 198;
  working practices 104, 107–8
US–Japan Mutual Security Assistance
  (MSA) Act (1951) 140

Vernon, R. 34
Vietnam, foreign aid 186–7
"Visible Japanese Aid" 181–2
"visual control" 95
vocational education 122–4, 129
Vocational Education Order (1897) 122
Vocational Supplementary Schools (VSSs)
  122, 129
Vogel, Ezra 55
voluntary retirement 80

Wade, R. 14
Wang, Q.K. 154
Wang, S. 163
"war on terror" 151, 189
"Washington Consensus" 10, 22, 171–2,
  187
Watanabe, M. 121
Weinstein, D.E. 13
Whittaker, D.H. 25
Williamson, R. 44, 45
Winter, S. 59
World Bank 188, 189; *East Asian Miracle*
  report 14, 166, 171, 190; Structural
  Adjustment Loans (SALs) 10, 14, 168,
  173, 186
World War II 137, 138, 170

Xinbo, W. 159

Yamakage, S. 157
Yamamura, E. 25, 32
Yasumoto, D.T. 139
Yoda, T. 139
"Yoshida doctrine": Cold War period
142–6; historical development 137–42;
lessons from 195; modifying 158–9;
negative legacy of 156–8; positive
legacies of 154–5; pre-emptive light

arms announcement and strategic
structure of post-Cold War period
147–50; relevance in East Asia today
151–4
Yoshida, S. 137–8
Yutaka Seimitsu Kōgyō 93

Zeckhauser, R. 143
Zhang, X. 25
Zingales, L. 42, 43–4
zombie firms 49–50